The Mises Reader

Published 2016 by the Mises Institute. This work is licensed under a Creative Commons Attribution-NonCommercial-NoDerivs 4.0 International License. http://creativecommons.org/licenses/by-nc-nd/4.0/

Mises Institute
518 West Magnolia Ave.
Auburn, Ala. 36832
mises.org

paperback edition: 978-1-61016-665-2
large print edition: 978-1-61016-666-9
epub: 978-1-61016-669-0

The Mises Reader

SHAWN RITENOUR
EDITOR

MISESINSTITUTE
AUBURN, ALABAMA

Contents

CHAPTER 15: PRICE CONTROLS
Economic Policy

CHAPTER 16: KEYNES AND KEYNESIANISM
Planning for Freedom

Human Action

CHAPTER 17: ECONOMIC PROGRESS
Economic Policy

Human Action

CHAPTER 18: THE IMPORTANCE OF LIBERTY

CHAPTER 19: ECONOMIC METHOD
Money, Methods, and the Market Process

CHAPTER 20: APPRECIATIONS

Introduction

Knowledge of the principles of the free society is not something that everyone is born with or something that we just catch like the common cold. The principles of liberty must be carefully passed on from one generation to the next if they are to survive, let alone flourish. Each generation must learn anew from their predecessors the virtues of private property and the consequences of statism. It is even more crucial today, in our contemporary intellectual environment, to have something to offer besides empty platitudes about how we can all "just get along." Today's citizen who is interested in things economic, can do no better than to turn to Ludwig von Mises. In his life and work Mises provides the intelligent person a vision for the importance of truth, economics, liberty, and scholarship that continually inspires to greatness.[1]

The reason Mises is so important can be understood by looking at our halls of learning. It is no secret that state-run elementary and secondary schools are failing their charges. Year after year we hear the all-too-familiar

---

[1]For a good and accessible overview of Mises's thought see *The Essential von Mises* and *Ludwig von Mises: Scholar, Creator, Hero* (Auburn, Ala.: Mises Institute, 2009), both by Murray N. Rothbard. They are combined in one volume in Rothbard (2009). A more extensive biography of Mises can be found in Israel Kirzner's *Ludwig von Mises: The Man and His Economics* (Wilmington, Del.: ISI Book, 2001). Jörg Guido Hülsmann's massive *Mises: The Last Knight of Liberalism* (Auburn, Ala.: Mises Institute, 2007) is the most extensive biography and the standard-bearer on Mises's life and work.

reports telling us again and again how test scores are falling. Such dismal performance sows the seeds for a meager harvest reaped by these same students as they enter college. Fewer and fewer of them graduate high school with a basic knowledge about history, literature, science, and math. It should not surprise us that 20 percent of all college freshmen in the United States need remedial classes.[2] It is particularly disheartening to observe the decayed condition of modern American higher education. Not so very long ago, the college was seen as a most important institution charged with transmitting Western civilization from one generation to the next. It was here that students had the luxury of critically examining what different voices throughout time have answered when considering the big questions regarding man, life, death, and God. The goal was not an endless pursuit for pursuit's sake, but was indeed pursuit for true answers to these questions.

Most people, I am sure, recognize that this is no longer the case. Most college faculties are now dominated, especially in the humanities, by one manifestation or another of deconstructionism. Everything is up for grabs and, at worst, the intellectual sees his chief end as the destruction of the foundations of Western civilization so that we can all dance on its ruins.

On the economic front, things are not much better. Several years ago a college near mine was having a political debate of sorts and evidently could not find anyone on their campus to defend the free market position, so they asked some of my students if they would participate. The report back from my students was by turns outrageous and depressing. From their opponents, there were numerous serious calls for stronger anti-trust regulation, energy regulation, increased state funding of education, subsidization of business, increased welfare, socialized health care, state urban planning, increased environmental regulation, an $11/hour living wage, regulations forcing insurance companies to cover abortions, and increased gun ownership restrictions.

This is what happens when intellectuals, teachers, and college professors see themselves as destroyers instead of cultivators. If we want to preserve our noble cultural inheritance, we cannot think that it will happen automatically. It is always easier to destroy than to maintain and build up. If civilization is not to descend into barbarism, we must teach each generation the importance of truth, liberty, and private property. It is not called

---

[2] A. Lu, *States Reform Remedial College Education* (2013). Available at: http://www.pewstates.org/projects/stateline/headlines/states-reform-college-remedial-education-85899492704

culture for nothing. We must cultivate civilization. A former colleague of mine reminds me from time to time that as professors we are indeed the thin tweed line separating civilization from barbarism. Recently, however, the barbarians have been winning because the troops charged with manning the thin tweed line have been either absent without leave or actually fighting for the enemy.

What makes the fight more difficult is that to preserve society, it is not enough merely to oppose destructive philosophies, although oppose them we must. We also must offer a positive and real alternative. As Mises warns us at the end of his book, *The Anti-capitalist Mentality*,

> An "anti-something" movement displays a purely negative attitude. It has no chance whatever to succeed. Its passionate diatribes virtually advertise the program they attack. People must fight for something they want to achieve, not simply reject an evil, no matter how bad it may be. They must, without any reservations, endorse the program of the market economy.[3]

In this, Mises was, perhaps unwittingly, in agreement with the Apostle Paul who told us many years ago to hate indeed that which is evil, but also to cling to that which is good. In order to maintain our cultural inheritance, we must not only oppose statism but also teach our students to cultivate and nurture the roots of civilization: the free society of voluntary exchange built on private property.

In today's intellectual vacuum, students need someone to whom they can look for an example of sound scholarship that provides true answers to the important economic and political questions of the day. They could do no better than to turn to the writings of Ludwig von Mises. The life and work of Mises provides students with a magnificent example of what an economist, a scholar, and, in many ways, what a person should be.

This is certainly true in my own experience. As a freshman at a Christian liberal arts college in Northwest Iowa, I was instinctively conservative. I thought, for instance, that low taxes were better than high taxes, low inflation was better than high inflation, and communism was a bad economic and political system. However, I could not satisfactorily explain why.

---

[3]Ludwig von Mises, *The Anti-capitalist Mentality* (New York: D. Van Nostrand, 1956), p. 112.

That same year I joined the Conservative Book Club. As a member I agreed to buy four books from the Club over the course of three years. One month the Club was offering this book *Human Action* by some Austrian economist I had never heard of as its featured alternative. Because of its price, it was allowed to count for two of my required purchases. I thought, "hey, pretty economical," and upon encouragement from my economics professor, I went ahead and bought it. The book changed my life. In Mises's own memoirs, he recounts how near Christmas in 1903 he read Carl Menger's *Principles of Economics* and that book made him an economist.[4] Well, *Human Action* did the same for me.

I found the book at once inspiring and intimidating. I plowed into it with an eager mind and immediately was impressed with Mises's intellect and his rigorous logic. What also impressed me was the density of Mises's arguments. He did not waste words that did not advance his theories. As such, *Human Action* can be rather daunting for readers relatively new to economics. On the one hand, I had several *eureka!* moments as Mises unpacked the logic demonstrating another economic truth. A number of times I also found some of it rather slow-going. Many times I read and re-read pages to gain a sense of understanding. I would start at the top of a page and by the time I had worked my way down to the bottom, I forgot what the main point was, so I had to start again. Some of it is quite technical, so I had to slow way down to grasp material. I would read passages, sections, and chapters and need to set the book aside for a bit while I thought about, puzzled over, evaluated, and, finally, achieved understanding. It took me five years of off-and-on reading in the midst of my other studies and then work to complete reading it the first time through. Now all of this work was definitely worth it. The benefit from reading and re-reading *Human Action* is incalculable. Still, I began to look for a less taxing way of becoming acquainted with Mises's ideas.

During my time in college, while I was still working through *Human Action*, I sought out other more accessible books by Mises. This was years before the advent of the internet and mises.org. I had to turn to that ancient institution called the library and I discovered that our college library had a collection of shorter essays by Mises published by Libertarian Press in a collection entitled *Planning for Freedom and Sixteen Other Essays*. This book proved to be a more accessible introduction to Mises's thought. I

---

[4]Ludwig von Mises, *Memoirs* (Auburn, Ala.: Mises Institute, 2009), p. 25.

began reading it during my free time and did not stop until I had come to the end. *Planning for Freedom* turned out to be the first book by Mises that I read completely. As I read, I began to put together an economic and political philosophy that revolved around private property. It was the writings of Mises that provided me the intellectual foundation to evaluate and integrate what I was being taught in school. Looking back on those years, I have grown to appreciate the wisdom expressed in the sentiment by Mark Thornton that one of the best ways to become introduced to the work of Ludwig von Mises is through some of his shorter, more popular works.[5] While sacrificing nothing in the way of sound economic theory, they are more accessible and in any event are not as intimidating as Mises's 881-page *magnum opus*.

In this anthology, I have sought to bring you the best of both worlds. An attempt has been made to acquaint the reader with the broad spectrum of Mises's ideas and analyses in a way that is more accessible and less daunting. The selections include, therefore, several shorter, more popular works side-by-side with excerpts from longer, more scholarly and technically difficult works. A special feature of this collection is the inclusion of an appreciation of Eugen von Böhm-Bawerk, available for the first time in English, translated from the French by Karl-Friederich Israel. It is my hope that this book will provide a user-friendly gateway into the brilliance of Mises, because we desperately need his wisdom as much now as in any other time in our history.

The work of Ludwig von Mises is an important guide for thoughtful citizens because he strongly, yet matter-of-factly sets forth economics as the pursuit of truth. Not the truth of the passing fancy, nor the so-called "small t-truth" that is always in danger of being refuted by the latest bit of empirical data; but economic truth that will stand for all ages. Misesian economic theory is a triumphant response to the epistemological relativism of today because it is economics developed in light of reality.

Upon reading the works of Mises, one is immediately set forth on the right road, because Mises begins where economics must begin — human action. All of his economic theorems and corollaries are deduced from the non-controversial axiom that people engage in purposeful behavior. This immediately sets his theories on intellectual bedrock.

---

[5]Mark Thornton, from a Mises Wire post "How to Read Mises," October 8, 2013. https://mises.org/blog/how-read-mises

As I read the opening chapters of *Human Action* during my sophomore year, I had a sort of epiphany as all of the conclusions I had learned in my economics classes began to fall into logical place. The law of demand was not merely a plausible sounding notion that is true only in an unrealizable ideal world. It was not the necessary implication of arbitrary assumptions that must be tested again and again. Mises showed that economics is logically whole and that demand is rooted in the law of marginal utility which itself is deduced from the premise that human beings act purposefully. Readers of Mises are not left walking on the shifting sand of empiricism, but on the solid ground of true axioms and sound logic.

A former student of mine who received his J.D. at Harvard Law School had a similar reaction. He once told me that while he appreciated the insights that economics in general gives him in the field of law and economics, what sets Mises above all others in his mind is Mises's focus on individual human action. The modern focus on bell curves and treating people as rats in mazes, he said, makes it difficult to imagine the practical implication of economic theory relating to a contract case between Joe and Bob. Mises's framework starts with people like Joe and Bob.

In arguing for economic truth, Mises explicitly rejects relativism. A much-too-large segment of our intellectual culture is under the spell of postmodernism. One root of such thinking is what Mises termed polylogism, the idea that different groups of people have different mental categories and systems of logic. Marxists, for instance, argue that there is an inseparable gulf between the proletariat mind and the bourgeois mind. Not that they have different opinions on things, but that they have entirely different laws of logic and ways of thinking. The same notions are found in feminist academic circles and in all brands of multiculturalism. These theories attempt to shield their subscribers from criticism made by those outside of their particular cults. Mises refutes such illogic by stressing that truth is truth no matter who says it. He writes,

> A theory is either correct or incorrect. ... But a theory can never be valid for a bourgeois or an American if it is invalid for a proletarian or a Chinese.[6]

Mises's demolition of polylogism provides students a basis from which they can reply to the Marxist, feminist, and racist theories of criticism that have been running amok within the humanities for some time.

---

[6]Ludwig von Mises, *Human Action* (Auburn, Ala.:Mises Institute [1949] 1998), p. 91.

The work of Mises is also important for today because Mises provides a clear understanding of why economics is important by asking the right and important questions and providing correct answers. His books and essays are not consumed with inquiries regarding what the stock market will do in the next six months, or will a federal funds rate of 0.25 percent achieve full employment or should it be 0.5 percent.

While Mises does help us speak to such questions, he focuses on the larger, more fundamental issues. A key theme that runs throughout the work of Mises, for instance, is the consideration of the survival of civilization. Mises warns that social progress is not automatic. In *Human Action* he explains that our

> civilization was able to spring into existence because the peoples were dominated by ideas which were the application of the teachings of economics to the problems of economic policy. It will and must perish if the nations continue to pursue the course which they entered upon under the spell of doctrines rejecting economic thinking.[7]

The work of Mises is important to the survival of civilization because it helps pass along knowledge to a new generation of students. And this knowledge helps answer one of the most pressing dilemmas of our human existence — a dilemma that has been with us since the beginning of time. How do we deal with the fundamental condition of scarcity? As we are reminded by that eminent modern philosopher and former student of the London School of Economics Mick Jagger, "You can't always get what you want." We are presented with the question: How do we go about our business in this world of scarcity without descending into a barbaric struggle for survival?

Because of the relative material comfort we possess in the West, it is natural for this question to never have occurred to most people. The brilliance of Mises, however, lies in the fact that he invites us to ponder this very real question and then sets out the right answer. He explains that in order to escape starvation and a barbaric struggle for survival, it is crucial that we take advantage of social cooperation through the division of labor. Without the division of labor, everyone would have to produce all that he or she consumes. Each person would have to produce his own food, plus his own house, plus his own clothes, plus all the other goods that make his

---

[7] Mises, *Human Action*, p. 10.

life better. Without the division of labor, no one would be able to specialize in that thing he does relatively better than everyone else. Our total wealth would be greatly reduced and we would be left living largely from hand to mouth.

By reading Mises, however, students clearly see that as the result of our ability to exchange goods with one another, we can specialize in producing only those things at which we are most efficient and then trade the surplus we don't need for other things we want. As we specialize, our productivity goes up individually and the total wealth of our community increases. The division of labor through voluntary exchange allows us to rise above a barbaric struggle for existence in which we hope that we are one of the fittest that will survive. The division of labor allows us to build civilization.

However the expansion of the division of labor has challenges of its own. And it is here that Mises is really in his element. An economy that has taken advantage of an extensive division of labor is very complex and yet, decentralized. Such an economy features a multitude of different markets in which the participants must coordinate their activities if we want to avoid recessions and depressions. The biggest problem for this decentralized economy to work is that all of the various producers have to know what to produce, how much to produce, and how to produce it.

This can only be done if some method of calculation exists. No other economist of his day stressed this point more than Mises. Indeed in the 1920s Mises demonstrated that the lack of economic calculation is the Achilles heel of socialism. Alternatives must be compared to one another if producers are to know how best to fulfill the desires of consumers for goods and services. Even if they know what consumers want they must be able to compare alternative ways to produce it. Should we build this house with wooden studs or metal? Blown or rolled insulation? Air or coil heating? This can be known only if there is a common denominator we can use to assess the relative value of each alternative. We cannot simply use physical units of goods for the comparison. Saying that ten two-by-fours are worth less than fifty nails because ten is less than fifty is like saying I'm taller than you because I'm 5 foot 8 and you are 98.6 degrees Fahrenheit.

Mises recognizes that what makes such comparisons even harder is that we all value goods subjectively, according to our personal preferences. We cannot, therefore, measure value because there are no objective units of value measurement.

Again it was Mises who demonstrated that voluntary exchange in a monetary economy opens the door to a solution. In a monetary economy, every good is exchanged against money, so every price is expressed in terms of the monetary unit — in our case dollars and cents. Even though value is subjective, in a free market, people manifest their values by voluntarily deciding what they will pay for particular products and services. These objective prices, therefore, are reflections of subjective values. Entrepreneurs are able to use these objective prices to calculate expected profit and loss and act accordingly. In a free market, Mises shows, entrepreneurs are able to plan for the future and consumers will receive what they most want.

Socialism, on the other hand, is doomed because there is no way for the central planner to efficiently allocate factors of production because there is no way to calculate profit and loss. In a completely socialistic economy all of the means of production are owned by the state. There is, therefore, no actual exchange of goods, and hence no actual prices that reflect the actual subjective values of human beings. Producers, then, have no way to calculate whether their actions are productive or wasteful from the point of view of society. What is called a planned economy is, instead, as Mises so eloquently put it, "groping about in the dark."

I once had a student from China who cited *Human Action* as the book that finally turned him away from socialism. He had read all of *Human Action*, praising it for its readability. He told me that reading *Human Action* helped him realize that Communism was an impossible utopia. Mises's explanation of the devastating economic consequences of war also attracted this student to read further works by Mises.

The moral of the story is that voluntary exchange in a monetary economy allows us to have the civilization we enjoy. In order to engage in voluntary exchange using money, however, Mises stresses that it is necessary for people to own private property. You cannot exchange what you do not own. If there is no ownership of private property, there is no actual exchange. If there is no exchange, there is no division of labor and there is no money so there are neither money prices, nor economic calculation. We would be left with chaos, not civilization. For civilization to survive, consequently, Mises teaches us that society must be a private property order. If people are able to own and trade their property as they see fit, wealth increases and civilization prospers.

The insights of Mises do not stop with his critique of socialism, however. From his 1929 collection of essays *A Critique of Interventionism* through the rest of his career, he continually explained to whomever would listen that even if the state does not fully socialize the economy, but intervenes only here and there, this too hinders the workings of the price system. To the extent that the state intervenes and curbs the free actions of individuals through price controls, monetary inflation, product restrictions, taxation, and subsidization, to that extent will prices for goods not accurately reflect the values of the people in that society. Such intervention will make it that much harder for entrepreneurs to do their job and one should expect to see shortages in some industries and surpluses in another.

You can see, then, that Mises builds his economic theory into a massive, logically integrated edifice of truth. More than any other economist of his day, Mises demonstrates that laws of economics are indeed laws every bit as universal and irrevocable as the laws of chemistry and physics, and we violate them at our peril. It is this fact that enables the study of economics to be a noble endeavor for everyone. In *Human Action*, Mises comments on the role of the economist by likening him to a chemist warning people against poisoning themselves. He writes,

> A man who chooses between drinking a glass of milk and a glass of a solution of potassium cyanide does not choose between two beverages; he chooses between life and death. A society that chooses between capitalism and socialism does not choose between two social systems; it chooses between social cooperation and the disintegration of society. Socialism is not an alternative to capitalism; it is an alternative to any system under which men can live as *human* beings. To stress this point is the task of economics as it is the task of biology and chemistry to teach that potassium cyanide is not a nutriment but a deadly poison.[8]

Indeed, one of the most important benefits received from reading Mises is the ability to critically evaluate public policy.

When assigned in a college class long ago to research the viability of the social security system, the first place I turned to was *Human Action*. The passage I read then I have never forgotten. It is a passage that is as timely as today's headlines. Mises writes,

> One may try to justify [social security] by declaring that the wage earners lack the insight and the moral strength

---

[8]Mises, *Human Action*, p. 676.

to provide spontaneously for their own future. But then it is not easy to silence the voices of those who ask whether it is not paradoxical to entrust the nation's welfare to the decisions of voters whom the law itself considers incapable of managing their own affairs.[9]

This is dynamite for the intelligent person who wants to truly understand the nature of hydra-headed interventionism that pushes a myriad of statist policies including inflationism, the welfare-warfare state, Keynesian fiscal management, socialized medicine, and countless business regulations that serve only to hamper mutually beneficial exchange.

Today people are increasingly urged to support this or that political program advertised as solving a vexing social problem with no understanding of economics and hence no frame of reference from which to evaluate different policies. All that is mustered in justification for interventionism are feelings that make people want to "do something." The economics of Mises is the crucial antidote for the current interventionist ideology supporting the progressive march to economic fascism. Citizens acquainted with Mises quickly understand that any sort of middle-of-the-road economic policy does indeed lead to socialism.

Ludwig von Mises does not only provide us a vision of economic truth, however. He also inspires us to greatness by presenting the student an example of what an outstanding scholar should be. It does not take the reader of Mises's work very long to see what a breadth of knowledge Mises had. Murray Rothbard once recounted how, when someone first recommended *Human Action* to him, he asked, "What is it about?" The response to Rothbard was "Everything." A student in one of my managerial economics courses was impressed with the same observation. I had assigned from *Human Action* a brief section about the distinction between the manager and the entrepreneur. He liked what was assigned, so he began to read through the first part of the book. He was greatly impressed and told me, "He doesn't write just about economics. It's all there, of course, but he also writes about everything else." This student now has a standard for real scholarship.

Throughout Mises's works are insightful discussions about history, philosophy, political science, sociology, and even aesthetics. He makes not only references to, but thoughtful comments on the likes of Aristotle,

---

[9]Ibid., p. 613.

Bentham, Bismark, Comte, Locke, Kant, Marx, Mill, Napoleon, Tacitus, Saint Francis of Assisi, and Spinoza. As he once explained in his New York University Seminar,

> One of the indispensable prerequisites of a master of economics is a perfect knowledge of history, the history of ideas and of civilization, and of social, economic, and political history. To know one field well, one must also know other fields.[10]

In another instance Mises cited a number of authors in French and German. One student spoke up, asking, "Why are you giving these citations, Professor? I can't read French and German." Mises replied simply, "Learn it. You are engaged in scholarly activities."[11] He also encouraged his students not only to read authors with which they agreed, but to read about an issue from all sides. A student who reads Mises is inspired to be such a scholar.

Looking at Mises the scholar, the contemporary student learns a valuable lesson in integrity. His life was a never-ending fight for economic truth, liberty, scholarly excellence, and the principles of the free market. As he notes in his autobiography, at a particularly depressing time in his life when it appeared that he had become merely "an historian of decline," he remembered his personal motto adopted from a line out of Virgil: "Do not give in to the evil, but proceed ever the more against it." Throughout his life, he did just that.

His research and logical analysis convinced him of the negative consequences of socialism and interventionism. He never wavered from those convictions and his steadfastness cost him plenty. He did without a salaried academic appointment because he was not willing to be a court intellectual. However, he never grew bitter about this. In his autobiography he writes,

> I was sometimes accused of representing my viewpoint in a manner too abrupt and intransigent. It was also claimed that I could have accomplished more had I displayed a greater willingness to compromise. ... When I look back at

---

[10]John Chamberlain, "My Years with Ludwig von Mises," *The Freeman* 27, no. 2 (February 1977): 126–27.

[11]Margit von Mises, *My Years with Ludwig von Mises* (New Rochelle, New York: Arlington Press, 1976), pp. 135–36.

my work ... my only regret is my willingness to compromise, and not my intransigence.[12]

The reason for his uncompromising attitude is that he took his work as
a scholar seriously. Mises thought, "In science, compromise is a betrayal of
truth."[13] Would that more contemporary economists had the same convictions.

Ludwig von Mises truly was an intellectual giant among men and, as
Murray Rothbard[14] saw, his thought and causal-realist framework is the
best alternative to the economic paradigm of our age. In the contemporary fog of the modern academy, Mises serves as a lighthouse, warning
unsuspecting students of the perils of bad economics and statist economic
policies, while illuminating students to the principles of the free society.

The book in your hands is intended to give a taste of the many facets
of Mises's thought in a way that accessibly communicates most of his key
contributions to the social sciences. It therefore includes excerpts from his
larger and more technically demanding works side-by-side with shorter,
more introductory articles and lectures. The finished product is sort of an
intelligent person's guide to the work of Ludwig von Mises. It is especially
suitable for those with an interest in Mises, but find jumping right into
Human Action, *Socialism*, or *The Theory of Money and Credit* rather daunting. The hope is to give the reader a survey of Mises's insights in a format
that nourishes his intellectual soul, while also whetting the appetite for his
larger corpus of work. Those ready to dive into deeper Misesian waters are
encouraged to pick up *The Mises Reader Unabridged* which contains all of
the material in *The Mises Reader* plus over 125 pages of additional material, primarily from his more scholarly works. It is hoped that together
these two volumes will foster a rising generation of citizens more thoroughly acquainted with sound economics and the principles of the free
society.

If we want to preserve our civilization from the cultural destroyers,
post-modern relativists, and enemies of freedom, we must provide our
generation of inquisitive minds with a sound alternative. We must direct
our fellow sojourners to a literature that defends truth and property and

---

[12]Mises, *Memoirs*, p. 60.

[13]Ibid., p. 61.

[14]Murray N. Rothbard, "Ludwig von Mises and the Paradigm for our Age," *Modern Age* (Fall 1971): 370–79.

inspires us to greatness. Fortunately we have such a literature to turn to — a literature of freedom. Those desiring to beat back the barbarians at the gate, would do well to begin with the works of Ludwig von Mises. In him, the reader will find, as Murray Rothbard found, a scholar, creator, and hero.

Shawn Ritenour
Grove City College

CHAPTER 1

Human Action

EPISTEMOLOGICAL PROBLEMS OF ECONOMICS[1]

1. The Basic Concept of Action and its Categorial Conditions

The starting point of our reasoning is not behavior, but action, or, as it is redundantly designated, rational action. Human action is conscious behavior on the part of a human being. Conceptually it can be sharply and clearly distinguished from unconscious activity, even though in some cases it is perhaps not easy to determine whether given behavior is to be assigned to one or the other category.

As thinking and acting men, we grasp the concept of action. In grasping this concept we simultaneously grasp the closely correlated concepts of value, wealth, exchange, price, and cost. They are all necessarily implied in the concept of action, and together with them the concepts of valuing, scale of value and importance, scarcity and abundance, advantage and disadvantage, success, profit, and loss. The logical unfolding of all these concepts and

---

[1][Ludwig von Mises, *Epistemological Problems of Economics*, 3d ed. (1933; Auburn, Ala.: Mises Institute, 2003), chap. 1, sec. 2: "The Scope and Meaning of the System of *A Priori* Theorems," pp. 24–27, 33–37.]

categories in systematic derivation from the fundamental category of action and the demonstration of the necessary relations among them constitutes the first task of our science. The part that deals with the elementary theory of value and price serves as the starting point in its exposition. There can be no doubt whatever concerning the aprioristic character of these disciplines.

The most general prerequisite of action is a state of dissatisfaction, on the one hand, and, on the other, the possibility of removing or alleviating it by taking action. (Perfect satisfaction and its concomitant, the absence of any stimulus to change and action, belong properly to the concept of a perfect being. This, however, is beyond the power of the human mind to conceive. A perfect being would not act.) Only this most general condition is necessarily implied in the concept of action. The other categorial conditions of action are independent of the basic concept; they are not necessary prerequisites of concrete action. Whether or not they are present in a particular case can be shown by experience only. But where they are present, the action necessarily falls under definite laws that flow from the categorial determinacy of these further conditions.

It is an empirical fact that man grows old and dies and that therefore he cannot be indifferent to the passage of time. That this has been man's experience thus far without exception, that we do not have the slightest evidence to the contrary, and that scarcely any other experience points more obviously to its foundation in a law of nature — all this in no way changes its empirical character. The fact that the passage of time is one of the conditions under which action takes place is established empirically and not a priori. We can without contradiction conceive of action on the part of immortal beings who would never age. But in so far as we take into consideration the action of men who are not indifferent to the passage of time and who therefore economize time because it is important to them whether they attain a desired end sooner or later, we must attribute to their action everything that necessarily follows from the categorial nature of time. The empirical character of our knowledge that the passage of time is a condition of any given action in no way affects the aprioristic character of the conclusions that necessarily follow from the introduction of the category of time. Whatever follows necessarily from empirical knowledge — e.g., the propositions of the agio theory of interest — lies outside the scope of empiricism.

Whether the exchange of economic goods (in the broadest sense, which also includes services) occurs directly, as in barter, or indirectly, through a medium of exchange, can be established only empirically. However, where and in so far as media of exchange are employed, all the propositions that are essentially valid with regard to indirect exchange must hold true. Everything asserted by the quantity theory of money, the theory of the relation between the quantity of money and interest, the theory of fiduciary media, and the circulation-credit theory of the business cycle, then becomes inseparably connected with action. All these theorems would still be meaningful even if there had never been any indirect exchange; only their practical significance for our action and for the science that explains it would then have to be appraised differently. However, the heuristic importance of experience for the analysis of action is not to be disregarded. Perhaps if there had never been indirect exchange, we would not have been able to conceive of it as a possible form of action and to study it in all its ramifications. But this in no way alters the aprioristic character of our science.

These considerations enable us to assess critically the thesis that all or most of the doctrines of economics hold only for a limited period of history and that, consequently, theorems whose validity is thus limited historically or geographically should replace, or at least supplement, those of the universally valid theory. All the propositions established by the universally valid theory hold to the extent that the conditions that they presuppose and precisely delimit are given. Where these conditions are present, the propositions hold without exception. This means that these propositions concern action as such; that is, that they presuppose only the existence of a state of dissatisfaction, on the one hand, and the recognized possibility, on the other, of relieving this dissatisfaction by conscious behavior, and that, therefore, the elementary laws of value are valid without exception for all human action. When an isolated person acts, his action occurs in accordance with the laws of value. Where, in addition, goods of higher order are introduced into action, all the laws of the theory of imputation are valid. Where indirect exchange takes place, all the laws of monetary theory are valid. Where fiduciary media are created, all the laws of the theory of fiduciary media (the theory of credit) are valid. There would be no point in expressing this fact by saying that the doctrines of the theory of money are true only in those periods of history in which indirect exchange takes place. ...

4. The Distinction Between Means and Ends: The "Irrational"

Most of the objections raised against the science of action stem from a misconception of the distinction between means and ends. In the strict sense, the end is always the removal of a dissatisfaction. However, we can doubtless also designate as an end the attainment of that condition of the external world which brings about our state of satisfaction either directly or indirectly, or which enables us to perform, without further difficulties, the act through which satisfaction is to be obtained. If the removal of the feeling of hunger is the end sought, the procuring of food and its preparation for eating can also be considered as ends; if one seeks the removal of the feeling of cold as an end, the heating of one's quarters can just as well be called an end. If additional measures are needed for the removal of dissatisfaction, then the attainment of any particular step along the way toward the desired final condition is also designated as an end. In this sense the acquisition of money in the market economy and, proximately, the division of labor are designated as ends of action; in this sense too the attainment of all things that indirectly promote the end of want-satisfaction appear as proximate or intermediate ends.

In the course of attaining the primary end, secondary ends are attained. A man walks from A to B. He would choose the shortest route if other, secondary ends did not demand satisfaction. He makes a detour if he can walk in the shade a little longer; if he can include in his walk another place, C, which he wants to look for; if, by doing so, he can avoid dangers that may be lying in wait for him on the shortest route; or if he just happens to like the longer route. If he decides on a detour, we must infer that at the moment of decision the attainment of such secondary ends was of greater importance in his judgment than the saving of distance. Consequently, for him the "detour" was no detour at all, since his walk brought him greater satisfaction or — at least from the point of view that he took of his situation at the moment of decision — was expected to bring greater satisfaction than the attainment of his destination by the shorter route. Only one who does not have these secondary ends in mind can call the longer way a detour. As far as our stroller was concerned, it was the correct route, that is, the route that promised the greatest satisfactions.[2]

Since satisfaction and dissatisfaction depend only on the subjective view of the individual, there is no room for argument on this question in a science that does not presume to establish a scale of values or to make judgments of value. Its conception of an end, in the strict sense, is more deductive than empirical: ends are determined by the wishes and the desires of the individual. Whenever reference is made to the greater or

---

[2]Cf. Lionel Robbins, *An Essay on the Nature and Significance of Economic Science* (London, 1932), p. 23.

lesser appropriateness of means, this can only be from the point of view of the acting individual.

We must next deal with the objection of those who never weary of asserting that man does not act rationally at all. It has never been disputed that man does not always act correctly from the objective point of view; that is, that either from ignorance of causal relations or because of an erroneous judgment of the given situation, in order to realize his ends he acts differently from the way in which he would act if he had correct information. In 1833 the method of healing wounds was different from that used in 1933, and in 2033 still another way will presumably be thought suitable. Statesmen, field marshals, and stock-market speculators act differently at present from the way in which they would act if they knew exactly all the data needed for an accurate judgment of conditions. Only a perfect being, whose omniscience and omnipresence would enable him to survey all the data and every causal relationship, could know how each erring human being would have to act at every moment if he wanted to possess the divine attribute of omniscience. If we were to attempt to distinguish rational action from irrational action, we should not only be setting ourselves up as a judge over the scales of value of our fellow men, but we should also be declaring our own knowledge to be the only correct, objective standard of knowledge. We should be arrogating to ourselves the position that only an all-knowing being has the power to occupy.

The assertion that there is irrational action is always rooted in an evaluation of a scale of values different from our own. Whoever says that irrationality plays a role in human action is merely saying, that his fellow men behave in a way that he does not consider correct. If we do not wish to pass judgment on the ends and the scales of value of other people and to claim omniscience for ourselves, the statement, "He acts irrationally," is meaningless, because it is not compatible with the concept of action. The "seeking to attain an end" and the "striving after a goal" cannot be eliminated from the concept of action. Whatever does not strive after goals or seek the attainment of ends reacts with absolute passivity to an external stimulus and is without a will of its own, like an automaton or a stone. To be sure, man too is as far outside the effective range of his action as a reed in the wind. But in so far as he is able to do anything, he always acts: even negligence and passivity are action if another course of conduct could have been chosen. And the conduct that is determined by the unconscious, in the Freudian sense, or by the subconscious, is also action in so far as conscious behavior could prevent it but neglects to do so. Even in the unconscious and apparently senseless behavior of the neurotic and the psychopath there is meaning, i.e., there is striving after ends and goals.[3]

Everything that we say about action is independent of the motives that cause it and of the goals toward which it strives in the individual case. It makes no difference whether action springs from altruistic or from egoistic motives, from a noble or from a base disposition; whether it is directed toward the attainment of materialistic or idealistic ends; whether it arises from exhaustive and painstaking deliberation or follows fleeting impulses and passions. The laws of catallactics that economics expounds are valid for every exchange regardless of whether those involved in it have acted wisely or unwisely or whether they were actuated by economic or non-economic motives.[4] The causes of action and the goals toward which it strives are data for the theory of action: upon their concrete configuration depends the course of action taken in the individual case, but the nature of action as such is not thereby affected.

These considerations have an evident bearing on the widespread tendency of the present age to appeal to the irrational. The concepts rational and irrational are not applicable to ends at all. Whoever wishes to pass judgment on ends may praise or condemn them as good or evil, fine or vulgar, etc. When the expressions "rational" and "irrational" are applied to the means employed for the attainment of an end, such a usage has significance only from the standpoint of a definite technology. However, the use of means other than those prescribed as "rational" by this technology can be accounted for in only two possible ways: either the "rational" means were not known to the actor, or he did not employ them because he wished to attain still other ends — perhaps very foolish ones from the point of view of the observer. In neither of these two cases is one justified in speaking of "irrational" action.

Action is, by definition, always rational. One is unwarranted in calling goals of action irrational simply because they are not worth striving for from the point of view of one's own valuations. Such a mode of expressions leads to gross misunderstandings. Instead of saying that irrationality plays a role in action, one should accustom oneself to saying merely: There are

---

[3]Cf. Sigmund Freud, *Lectures on the Introduction to Psychoanalysis*, 17th lecture.

[4]Cf. Philip Wicksteed, *The Common Sense of Political Economy*, ed. Robbins (London, 1933), vol. 1, p. 28.

people who aim at different ends from those that I aim at, and people who employ different means from those I would employ in their situation. ❧

HUMAN ACTION[5]

1. Purposeful Action and Animal Reaction

Human action is purposeful behavior. Or we may say: Action is will put into operation and transformed into an agency, is aiming at ends and goals, is the ego's meaningful response to stimuli and to the conditions of its environment, is a person's conscious adjustment to the state of the universe that determines his life. Such paraphrases may clarify the definition given and prevent possible misinterpretations. But the definition itself is adequate and does not need complement or commentary.

Conscious or purposeful behavior is in sharp contrast to unconscious behavior, i.e., the reflexes and the involuntary responses of the body's cells and nerves to stimuli. People are sometimes prepared to believe that the boundaries between conscious behavior and the involuntary reaction of the forces operating within man's body are more or less indefinite. This is correct only as far as it is sometimes not easy to establish whether concrete behavior is to be considered voluntary or involuntary. But the distinction between consciousness and unconsciousness is nonetheless sharp and can be clearly determined.

The unconscious behavior of the bodily organs and cells is for the acting *ego* no less a datum than any other fact of the external world. Acting man must take into account all that goes on within his own body as well as other data, e.g., the weather or the attitudes of his neighbors. There is, of course, a margin within which purposeful behavior has the power to neutralize the working of bodily factors. It is feasible within certain limits to get the body under control. Man can sometimes succeed through the power of his will in overcoming sickness, in compensating for the innate or acquired insufficiency of his physical constitution, or in suppressing reflexes. As far as this is possible, the field of purposeful action is extended.

---

[5][Ludwig von Mises, *Human Action* (1949; Auburn, Ala.: Mises Institute, 1998), chap. 1: "Acting Man," pp. 11–16.]

If a man abstains from controlling the involuntary reaction of cells and nerve centers, although he would be in a position to do so, his behavior is from our point of view purposeful.

The field of our science is human action, not the psychological events which result in an action. It is precisely this which distinguishes the general theory of human action, praxeology, from psychology. The theme of psychology is the internal events that result or can result in a definite action. The theme of praxeology is action as such. This also settles the relation of praxeology to the psychoanalytical concept of the subconscious. Psychoanalysis too is psychology and does not investigate action but the forces and factors that impel a man toward a definite action. The psychoanalytical subconscious is a psychological and not a praxeological category. Whether an action stems from clear deliberation, or from forgotten memories and suppressed desires which from submerged regions, as it were, direct the will, does not influence the nature of the action. The murderer whom a subconscious urge (the *Id*) drives toward his crime and the neurotic whose aberrant behavior seems to be simply meaningless to an untrained observer both act; they like anybody else are aiming at certain ends. It is the merit of psychoanalysis that it has demonstrated that even the behavior of neurotics and psychopaths is meaningful, that they too act and aim at ends, although we who consider ourselves normal and sane call the reasoning determining their choice of ends nonsensical and the means they choose for the attainment of these ends contrary to purpose.

The term "unconscious" as used by praxeology and the term "subconscious" as applied by psychoanalysis belong to two different systems of thought and research. Praxeology no less than other branches of knowledge owes much to psychoanalysis. The more necessary is it then to become aware of the line which separates praxeology from psychoanalysis.

Action is not simply giving preference. Man also shows preference in situations in which things and events are unavoidable or are believed to be so. Thus a man may prefer sunshine to rain and may wish that the sun would dispel the clouds. He who only wishes and hopes does not interfere actively with the course of events and with the shaping of his own destiny. But acting man chooses, determines, and tries to reach an end. Of two things both of which he cannot have together he selects one and gives up the other. Action therefore always involves both taking and renunciation.

To express wishes and hopes and to announce planned action may be forms of action in so far as they aim in themselves at the realization of a certain purpose. But they must not be confused with the actions to which they refer. They are not identical with the actions they announce, recommend, or reject. Action is a real thing. What counts is a man's total behavior, and not his talk about planned but not realized acts. On the other hand action must be clearly distinguished from the application of labor. Action means the employment of means for the attainment of ends. As a rule one of the means employed is the acting man's labor. But this is not always the case. Under special conditions a word is all that is needed. He who gives orders or interdictions may act without any expenditure of labor. To talk or not to talk, to smile or to remain serious, may be action. To consume and to enjoy are no less action than to abstain from accessible consumption and enjoyment.

Praxeology consequently does not distinguish between "active" or energetic and "passive" or indolent man. The vigorous man industriously striving for the improvement of his condition acts neither more nor less than the lethargic man who sluggishly takes things as they come. For to do nothing and to be idle are also action, they too determine the course of events. Wherever the conditions for human interference are present, man acts no matter whether he interferes or refrains from interfering. He who endures what he could change acts no less than he who interferes in order to attain another result. A man who abstains from influencing the operation of physiological and instinctive factors which he could influence also acts. Action is not only doing but no less omitting to do what possibly could be done.

We may say that action is the manifestation of a man's will. But this would not add anything to our knowledge. For the term *will* means nothing else than man's faculty to choose between different states of affairs, to prefer one, to set aside the other, and to behave according to the decision made in aiming at the chosen state and forsaking the other. ▶

CHAPTER 2

Action and Value

HUMAN ACTION[1]

1. Ends and Means

The result sought by an action is called its end, goal, or aim. One uses these terms in ordinary speech also to signify intermediate ends, goals, or aims; these are points which acting man wants to attain only because he believes that he will reach his ultimate end, goal, or aim in passing beyond them. Strictly speaking the end, goal, or aim of any action is always the relief from a felt uneasiness.

A means is what serves to the attainment of any end, goal, or aim. Means are not in the given universe; in this universe there exist only things. A thing becomes a means when human reason plans to employ it for the attainment of some end and human action really employs it for this purpose. Thinking man sees the serviceableness of things, i.e., their ability to minister to his ends, and acting man makes them means. It is of primary importance to realize that parts of the external world become means only through the operation of the human mind and its offshoot,

---

[1][Ludwig von Mises, *Human Action* (1949; Auburn, Ala.: Mises Institute, 1998), chap. 4: "A First Analysis of the Category of Analysis," pp. 92–98.]

human action. External objects are as such only phenomena of the physical universe and the subject matter of the natural sciences. It is human meaning and action which transform them into means. Praxeology does not deal with the external world, but with man's conduct with regard to it. Praxeological reality is not the physical universe, but man's conscious reaction to the given state of this universe. Economics is not about things and tangible material objects; it is about men, their meanings and actions. Goods, commodities, and wealth and all the other notions of conduct are not elements of nature; they are elements of human meaning and conduct. He who wants to deal with them must not look at the external world; he must search for them in the meaning of acting men.

Praxeology and economics do not deal with human meaning and action as they should be or would be if all men were inspired by an absolutely valid philosophy and equipped with a perfect knowledge of technology. For such notions as absolute validity and omniscience there is no room in the frame of a science whose subject matter is erring man. An end is everything which men aim at. A means is everything which acting men consider as such.

It is the task of scientific technology and therapeutics to explode errors in their respective fields. It is the task of economics to expose erroneous doctrines in the field of social action. But if men do not follow the advice of science, but cling to their fallacious prejudices, these errors are reality and must be dealt with as such. Economists consider foreign exchange control as inappropriate to attain the ends aimed at by those who take recourse to it. However, if public opinion does not abandon its delusions and governments consequently resort to foreign exchange control, the course of events is determined by this attitude. Present-day medicine considers the doctrine of the therapeutic effects of mandrake as a fable. But as long as people took this fable as truth, mandrake was an economic good and prices were paid for its acquisition. In dealing with prices economics does not ask what things are in the eyes of other people, but only what they are in the meaning of those intent upon getting them. For it deals with real prices, paid and received in real transactions, not with prices as they would be if men were different from what they really are.

Means are necessarily always limited, i.e., scarce with regard to the services for which man wants to use them. If this were not the case, there would not be any action with regard to them. Where man is not restrained by the insufficient quantity of things available, there is no need for any action.

It is customary to call the end the ultimate good and the means goods. In applying this terminology economists mainly used to think as technologists and not as praxeologists. They differentiated between *free goods* and *economic goods*. They called free goods things available in superfluous abundance which man does not need to economize. Such goods are, however, not the object of any action. They are general conditions of human welfare; they are parts of the natural environment in which man lives and acts. Only the economic goods are the substratum of action. They alone are dealt with in economics.

Economic goods which in themselves are fitted to satisfy human wants directly and whose serviceableness does not depend on the cooperation of other economic goods, are called consumers' goods or goods of the first order. Means which can satisfy wants only indirectly when complemented by cooperation of other goods are called producers' goods or factors of production or goods of a remoter or higher order. The services rendered by a producers' good consist in bringing about, by the cooperation of complementary producers' goods, a product. This product may be a consumers' good; it may be a producers' good which when combined with other producers' goods will finally bring about a consumers' good. It is possible to think of the producers' goods as arranged in orders according to their proximity to the consumers' good for whose production they can be used. Those producers' goods which are nearest to the production of a consumers' good are ranged in the second order, and accordingly those which are used for the production of goods of the second order in the third order and so on.

The purpose of such an arrangement of goods in orders is to provide a basis for the theory of value and prices of the factors of production. It will be shown later how the valuation and the prices of the goods of higher orders are dependent on the valuation and the prices of the goods of lower orders produced by their expenditure. The first and ultimate valuation of external things refers only to consumers' goods. All other things are valued according to the part they play in the production of consumers' goods.

It is therefore not necessary actually to arrange producers' goods in various orders from the second to the nth. It is no less superfluous to enter into pedantic discussions of whether a concrete good has to be called a good of the lowest order or should rather be attributed to one of the higher orders. Whether raw coffee beans or roast coffee beans or ground coffee or coffee prepared for drinking or only coffee prepared and mixed with cream and sugar are to be called a consumers' good ready for consumption is of no importance. It is immaterial which manner of speech we adopt. For with regard to the problem of valuation, all that we say about a consumers' good can be applied to any good of a higher order (except those of the highest order) if we consider it as a product.

An economic good does not necessarily have to be embodied in a tangible thing. Nonmaterial economic goods are called services.

2. The Scale of Value

Acting man chooses between various opportunities offered for choice. He prefers one alternative to others.

It is customary to say that acting man has a scale of wants or values in his mind when he arranges his actions. On the basis of such a scale he satisfies what is of higher value, i.e., his more urgent wants, and leaves unsatisfied what is of lower value, i.e., what is a less urgent want. There is no objection to such a presentation of the state of affairs. However, one must not forget that the scale of values or wants manifests itself only in the reality of action. These scales have no independent existence apart from the actual behavior of individuals. The only source from which our knowledge concerning these scales is derived is the observation of a man's actions. Every action is always in perfect agreement with the scale of values or wants because these scales are nothing but an instrument for the interpretation of a man's acting.

Ethical doctrines are intent upon establishing scales of value according to which man should act but does not necessarily always act. They claim for themselves the vocation of telling right from wrong and of advising man concerning what he should aim at as the supreme good. They are normative disciplines aiming at the cognition of what ought to be. They are not neutral with regard to facts; they judge them from the point of view of freely adopted standards.

This is not the attitude of praxeology and economics. They are fully aware of the fact that the ultimate ends of human action are not open to examination from any absolute standard. Ultimate ends are ultimately given, they are purely subjective, they differ with various people and with the same people at various moments in their lives. Praxeology and economics deal with the means for the attainment of ends chosen by the acting individuals. They do not express any opinion with regard to such problems as whether or not sybaritism is better than asceticism. They apply to the means only one yardstick, viz., whether or not they are suitable to attain the ends at which the acting individuals aim.

The notions of abnormality and perversity therefore have no place in economics. It does not say that a man is perverse because he prefers the disagreeable, the detrimental, and the painful to the agreeable, the beneficial, and the pleasant. It says only that he is different from other people; that he likes what others detest; that he considers useful what others want to avoid; that he takes pleasure in enduring pain which others avoid because it hurts them. The polar notions normal and perverse can be used anthropologically for the distinction between those who behave as most people do and outsiders and atypical exceptions; they can be applied biologically for the distinction between those whose behavior preserves the vital forces and those whose behavior is self-destructive; they can be applied in an ethical sense for the distinction between those who behave correctly and those who act otherwise than they should. However, in the frame of a theoretical science of human action, there is no room for such a distinction. Any examination of ultimate ends turns out to be purely subjective and therefore arbitrary.

Value is the importance that acting man attaches to ultimate ends. Only to ultimate ends is primary and original value assigned. Means are valued derivatively according to their serviceableness in contributing to the attainment of ultimate ends. Their valuation is derived from the valuation of the respective ends. They are important for man only as far as they make it possible for him to attain some ends.

Value is not intrinsic, it is not in things. It is within us; it is the way in which man reacts to the conditions of his environment.

Neither is value in words and in doctrines. It is reflected in human conduct. It is not what a man or groups of men say about value that counts, but how they act. The bombastic oratory of moralists and the inflated pompousness of party programs are significant as such. But they influence the course of human events only as far as they really determine the actions of men.

3. The Scale of Needs

Notwithstanding all declarations to the contrary, the immense majority of men aim first of all at an improvement of the material conditions of well-being. They want more and better food, better homes and clothes, and a thousand other amenities. They strive after abundance and health. Taking these goals as given, applied physiology tries to determine what means are best suited to provide as much satisfaction as possible. It distinguishes, from this point of view, between man's "real" needs and imaginary and spurious appetites. It teaches people how they should act and what they should aim at as a means.

The importance of such doctrines is obvious. From his point of view the physiologist is right in distinguishing between sensible action and action contrary to purpose. He is right in contrasting judicious methods of nourishment from unwise methods. He may condemn certain modes of behavior as absurd and opposed to "real" needs. However, such judgments are beside the point for a science dealing with the reality of human action. Not what a man should do, but what he does, counts for praxeology and economics. Hygiene may be right or wrong in calling alcohol and nicotine poisons. But economics must explain the prices of tobacco and liquor as they are, not as they would be under different conditions.

There is no room left in the field of economics for a scale of needs different from the scale of values as reflected in man's actual behavior. Economics deals with real man, weak and subject to error as he is, not with ideal beings, omniscient and perfect as only gods could be. ▶

THEORY AND HISTORY[2]

1. Judgments of Value and Propositions of Existence

Propositions asserting existence (affirmative existential propositions) or nonexistence (negative existential propositions) are descriptive. They assert something about the state of the whole universe or of parts of the universe. With regard to them questions of truth and falsity are significant. They must not be confounded with judgments of value.

Judgments of value are voluntaristic. They express feelings, tastes, or preferences of the individual who utters them. With regard to them there cannot be any question of truth and falsity. They are ultimate and not subject to any proof or evidence.

Judgments of value are mental acts of the individual concerned. As such they must be sharply distinguished from the sentences by means of

---

[2][Ludwig von Mises, *Theory and History* (1957; Auburn, Ala.: Mises Institute, 1985), chap. 1: "Judgments of Value," pp. 19–25.]

which an individual tries to inform other people about the content of his judgments of value. A man may have some reason to lie about his valuations. We may describe this state of affairs in the following way: Every judgment of value is in itself also a fact of the actual state of the universe and as such may be the topic of existential propositions. The sentence "I prefer Beethoven to Lehar" refers to a judgment of value. If looked upon as an existential proposition, it is true if I really prefer Beethoven and act accordingly and false if I in fact prefer Lehar and for some reasons lie about my real feelings, taste, or preferences. In an analogous way the existential proposition "Paul prefers Beethoven to Lehar" may be true or false. In declaring that with regard to a judgment of value there cannot be any question of truth or falsity, we refer to the judgment as such and not to the sentences communicating the content of such a judgment of value to other people.

2. Valuation and Action

A judgment of value is purely academic if it does not impel the man who utters it to any action. There are judgments which must remain academic because it is beyond the power of the individual to embark upon any action directed by them. A man may prefer a starry sky to the starless sky, but he cannot attempt to substitute the former state which he likes better for the latter he likes less.

The significance of value judgments consists precisely in the fact that they are the springs of human action. Guided by his valuations, man is intent upon substituting conditions that please him better for conditions which he deems less satisfactory. He employs means in order to attain ends sought.

Hence the history of human affairs has to deal with the judgments of value that impelled men to act and directed their conduct. What happened in history cannot be discovered and narrated without referring to the various valuations of the acting individuals. It is not the task of the historian qua historian to pass judgments of value on the individuals whose conduct is the theme of his inquiries. As a branch of knowledge history utters existential propositions only. But these existential propositions often refer to the presence or absence of definite judgments of value in the minds of the acting individuals. It is one of the tasks of the specific understanding of the historical sciences to establish what content the value judgments of the acting individuals had.

It is a task of history, for example, to trace back the origin of India's caste system to the values which prompted the conduct of the generations who developed, perfected, and preserved it. It is its further task to discover what the consequences of this system were and how these effects influenced the value judgments of later generations. But it is not the business of the historian to pass judgments of value on the system as such, to praise or to condemn it. He has to deal with its relevance for the course of affairs, he has to compare it with the designs and intentions of its authors and supporters and to depict its effects and consequences. He has to ask whether or not the means employed were fit to attain the ends the acting individuals sought.

It is a fact that hardly any historian has fully avoided passing judgments of value. But such judgments are always merely incidental to the genuine tasks of history. In uttering them the author speaks as an individual judging from the point of view of his personal valuations, not as a historian.

3. The Subjectivity of Valuation

All judgments of value are personal and subjective. There are no judgments of value other than those asserting *I* prefer, *I* like better, *I* wish.

It cannot be denied by anybody that various individuals disagree widely with regard to their feelings, tastes, and preferences and that even the same individuals at various instants of their lives value the same things in a different way. In view of this fact it is useless to talk about absolute and eternal values.

This does not mean that every individual draws his valuations from his own mind. The immense majority of people take their valuations from the social environment into which they were born, in which they grew up, that moulded their personality and educated them. Few men have the power to deviate from the traditional set of values and to establish their own scale of what appears to be better and what appears to be worse.

What the theorem of the subjectivity of valuation means is that there is no standard available which would enable us to reject any ultimate judgment of value as wrong, false, or erroneous in the way we can reject an existential proposition as manifestly false. It is vain to argue about ultimate judgments of value as we argue about the truth or falsity of an existential proposition. As soon as we start to refute by arguments an ultimate judgment of value, we look upon it as a means to attain definite ends. But then we merely shift the discussion to another plane. We no longer view the principle concerned as an ultimate value but as a means to attain an ultimate value, and we are again faced with the same problem. We may, for instance, try to show a Buddhist that to act in conformity with the teachings of his creed results in effects which we consider disastrous. But we are silenced if he replies that these effects are in his opinion lesser evils or no evils at all compared to what would result from nonobservance of his rules of conduct. His ideas about the supreme good, happiness, and eternal bliss are different from ours. He does not care for those values his critics are concerned with, and seeks for satisfaction in other things than they do.

4. The Logical and Syntactical Structure of Judgments of Value

A judgment of value looks upon things from the point of view of the man who utters it. It does not assert anything about things as they are. It manifests a man's affective response to definite conditions of the universe as compared with other definite conditions.

Value is not intrinsic. It is not in things and conditions but in the valuing subject. It is impossible to ascribe value to one thing or state of affairs only. Valuation invariably compares one thing or condition with another thing or condition. It grades various states of the external world. It contrasts one thing or state, whether real or imagined, with another thing or state, whether real or imagined, and arranges both in a scale of what the author of the judgment likes better and what less.

It may happen that the judging individual considers both things or conditions envisaged as equal. He is not concerned whether there is *A* or *B*. Then his judgment of value expresses indifference. No action can result from such a neutral disposition.

Sometimes the utterance of a judgment of value is elliptical and makes sense only if appropriately completed by the hearer. "I don't like measles" means "I prefer the absence of measles to its presence." Such incompleteness is the mark of all references to freedom. Freedom invariably means freedom from (absence of) something referred to expressly or implicitly. The grammatical form of such judgments may be qualified as negative. But it is vain to deduce from this idiomatic attire of a class of judgments of value any statements about their content and to blame them for an alleged negativism. Every judgment of value allows of a formulation in which the more highly valued thing or state is logically expressed in both a positive and a negative way, although sometimes a language may not have developed the appropriate term. Freedom of the press implies the rejection or negation of censorship. But, stated explicitly, it means a state of affairs in which the author alone determines the content of his publication as distinct from a state in which the police has a right to interfere in the matter.

Action necessarily involves the renunciation of something to which a lower value is assigned in order to attain or to preserve something to which a higher value is assigned. Thus, for instance, a definite amount of leisure is renounced in order to reap the product of a definite amount of labor. The renunciation of leisure is the means to attain a more highly valued thing or state.

There are men whose nerves are so sensitive that they cannot endure an unvarnished account of many facts about the physiological nature of the human body and the praxeological character of human action. Such people take offense at the statement that man must choose between the most sublime things, the loftiest human ideals, on the one hand, and the wants of his body on the other. They feel that such statements detract from the nobility of the higher things. They refuse to notice the fact that there arise in the life of man situations in which he is forced to choose between fidelity to lofty ideals and such animal urges as feeding.

Whenever man is faced with the necessity of choosing between two things or states, his decision is a judgment of value no matter whether or not it is uttered in the grammatical form commonly employed in expressing such judgments. ▶

CHAPTER 3

Action in Time

HUMAN ACTION[1]

1. The Temporal Character of Praxeology

The notion of change implies the notion of temporal sequence. A rigid, eternally immutable universe would be out of time, but it would be dead. The concepts of change and of time are inseparably linked together. Action aims at change and is therefore in the temporal order. Human reason is even incapable of conceiving the ideas of timeless existence and of timeless action.

He who acts distinguishes between the time before the action, the time absorbed by the action, and the time after the action has been finished. He cannot be neutral with regard to the lapse of time.

Logic and mathematics deal with an ideal system of thought. The relations and implications of their system are coexistent and interdependent. We may say as well that they are synchronous or that they are out of time. A perfect mind could grasp them all in one thought. Man's inability to accomplish this makes thinking itself an action, proceeding step by step

---

[1][Ludwig von Mises, *Human Action* (1949; Auburn, Ala.: Mises Institute, 1998), chap. 5: "Time," pp. 99–104.]

from the less satisfactory state of insufficient cognition to the more sat-isfactory state of better insight. But the temporal order in which knowl-edge is acquired must not be confused with the logical simultaneity of all parts of this aprioristic deductive system. Within this system the notions of anteriority and consequence are metaphorical only. They do not refer to the system, but to our action in grasping it. The system itself implies neither the category of time nor that of causality. There is functional cor-respondence between elements, but there is neither cause nor effect.

What distinguishes the praxeological system from the logical system epistemologically is precisely that it implies the categories both of time and of causality. The praxeological system too is aprioristic and deductive. As a system it is out of time. But change is one of its elements. The notions of sooner and later and of cause and effect are among its constituents. Anteriority and consequence are essential concepts of praxeological rea-soning. So is the irreversibility of events. In the frame of the praxeological system any reference to functional correspondence is no less metaphorical and misleading than is the reference to anteriority and consequence in the frame of the logical system.[2]

2. Past, Present, and Future

It is acting that provides man with the notion of time and makes him aware of the flux of time. The idea of time is a praxeological category.

Action is always directed toward the future; it is essentially and neces-sarily always a planning and acting for a better future. Its aim is always to render future conditions more satisfactory than they would be without the interference of action. The uneasiness that impels a man to act is caused by a dissatisfaction with expected future conditions as they would prob-ably develop if nothing were done to alter them. In any case action can influence only the future, never the present that with every infinitesimal fraction of a second sinks down into the past. Man becomes conscious of time when he plans to convert a less satisfactory present state into a more satisfactory future state.

---

[2]In a treatise on economics there is no need to enter into a discussion of the endeavors to construct mechanics as an axiomatic system in which the concept of function is substituted for that of cause and effect. It will be shown later that axiomatic mechanics cannot serve as a model for the treatment of the economic system.

For contemplative meditation time is merely duration, "la durée pure, dont l'écoulement est continu, et où l'on passe, par gradations insensibles, d'un état à l'autre: Continuité réellement vécue."[3] The "now" of the present is continually shifted to the past and is retained in the memory only. Reflecting about the past, say the philosophers, man becomes aware of time.[4] However, it is not recollection that conveys to man the categories of change and of time, but the will to improve the conditions of his life.

Time as we measure it by various mechanical devices is always past, and time as the philosophers use this concept is always either past or future. The present is, from these aspects, nothing but an ideal boundary line separating the past from the future. But from the praxeological aspect there is between the past and the future a real extended present. Action is as such in the real present because it utilizes the instant and thus embodies its reality.[5] Later retrospective reflection discerns in the instant passed away first of all the action and the conditions which it offered to action. That which can no longer be done or consumed because the opportunity for it has passed away, contrasts the past with the present. That which cannot yet be done or consumed, because the conditions for undertaking it or the time for its ripening have not yet come, contrasts the future with the past. The present offers to acting opportunities and tasks for which it was hitherto too early and for which it will be hereafter too late.

The present qua duration is the continuation of the conditions and opportunities given for acting. Every kind of action requires special conditions to which it must be adjusted with regard to the aims sought. The concept of the present is therefore different for various fields of action. It has no reference whatever to the various methods of measuring the passing of time by spatial movements. The present encloses as much of the time passed away as still is actual, i.e., of importance for acting. The present contrasts itself, according to the various actions one has in view, with the Middle Ages, with the nineteenth century, with the past year, month, or day, but no less with the hour, minute, or second just passed away. If a man says: Nowadays Zeus is no longer worshiped, he has a present in

---

[3]Henri Bergson, *Matière et mémoire* (7th ed. Paris, 1911), p. 205.

[4]Edmund Husserl, "Vorlesungen zur Phänomenologie des inneren Zeitbewusstseins," *Jahrbuch für Philosophie und Phänomenologische Forschung* (1928), vol. 9, pp. 391ff.; Alfred Schütz, *Der sinnhafte Aufbau der sozialen Welt* (Vienna, 1932), pp. 45ff.

[5]"Ce que j'appelle mon présent, c'est mon attitude vis-à-vis de l'avenir immédiat, c'est nom action imminente." Bergson, *Matière et mémoire*, p. 152.

mind other than that the motorcar driver who thinks: *Now* it is still too early to turn.

As the future is uncertain it always remains undecided and vague how much of it we can consider as *now* and present. If a man had said in 1913: At present — now — in Europe freedom of thought is undisputed, he would have not foreseen that this present would very soon be a past.

3. *The Economization of Time*

Man is subject to the passing of time. He comes into existence, grows, becomes old, and passes away. His time is scarce. He must economize it as he does other scarce factors.

The economization of time has a peculiar character because of the uniqueness and irreversibility of the temporal order. The importance of these facts manifests itself in every part of the theory of action.

Only one fact must be stressed at this point. The economization of time is independent of the economization of economic goods and services. Even in the land of Cockaigne man would be forced to economize time, provided he were not immortal and not endowed with eternal youth and indestructible health and vigor. Although all his appetites could be satisfied immediately without any expenditure of labor, he would have to arrange his time schedule, as there are states of satisfaction which are incompatible and cannot be consummated at the same time. For this man, too, time would be scarce and subject to the aspect of *sooner* and *later*.

4. *The Temporal Relation Between Actions*

Two actions of an individual are never synchronous; their temporal relation is that of sooner and later. Actions of various individuals can be considered as synchronous only in the light of the physical methods for the measurement of time. Synchronism is a praxeological notion only with regard to the concerted efforts of various acting men.[6]

A man's individual actions succeed one another. They can never be effected at the same instant; they can only follow one another in more or less rapid succession. There are actions which serve several purposes at

---

[6]In order to avoid any possible misunderstanding it may well be expedient to emphasize that this theorem has nothing at all to do with Einstein's theorem concerning the temporal relation of spatially distant events.

one blow. It would be misleading to refer to them as a coincidence of various actions.

People have often failed to recognize the meaning of the term "scale of value" and have disregarded the obstacles preventing the assumption of synchronism in the various actions of an individual. They have interpreted a man's various acts as the outcome of a scale of value, independent of these acts and preceding them, and of a previously devised plan whose realization they aim at. The scale of value and the plan to which duration and immutability for a certain period of time were attributed, were hypostasized into the cause and motive of the various individual actions. Synchronism which could not be asserted with regard to various acts was then easily discovered in the scale of value and in the plan. But this overlooks the fact that the scale of value is nothing but a constructed tool of thought. The scale of value manifests itself only in real acting; it can be discerned only from the observation of real acting. It is therefore impermissible to contrast it with real acting and to use it as a yardstick for the appraisal of real actions.

It is no less impermissible to differentiate between rational and allegedly irrational acting on the basis of a comparison of real acting with earlier drafts and plans for future actions. It may be very interesting that yesterday goals were set for today's acting other than those really aimed at today. But yesterday's plans do not provide us with any more objective and nonarbitrary standard for the appraisal of today's real acting than any other ideas and norms.

The attempt has been made to attain the notion of a nonrational action by this reasoning: If a is preferred to b and b to c, logically a should be preferred to c. But if actually c is preferred to a, we are faced with a mode of acting to which we cannot ascribe consistency and rationality.[7] This reasoning disregards the fact that two acts of an individual can never be synchronous. If in one action a is preferred to b and in another action b to c, it is, however short the interval between the two actions may be, not permissible to construct a uniform scale of value in which a precedes b and b precedes c. Nor is it permissible to consider a later third action as coincident with the two previous actions. All that the example proves is that value judgments are not immutable and that therefore a scale of value,

---

[7]Cf. Felix Kaufmann, "On the Subject-Matter of Economic Science," *Economica* 13: 390.

which is abstracted from various, necessarily nonsynchronous actions of an individual, may be self-contradictory.[8]

One must not confuse the logical concept of consistency (viz., absence of contradiction) and the praxeological concept of consistency (viz., constancy or clinging to the same principles). Logical consistency has its place only in thinking, constancy has its place only in acting.

Constancy and rationality are entirely different notions. If one's valuations have changed, unremitting faithfulness to the once espoused principles of action merely for the sake of constancy would not be rational but simply stubborn. Only in one respect can acting be constant: in preferring the more valuable to the less valuable. If the valuations change, acting must change also. Faithfulness, under changed conditions, to an old plan would be nonsensical. A logical system must be consistent and free of contradictions because it implies the coexistence of all its parts and theorems. In acting, which is necessarily in the temporal order, there cannot be any question of such consistency. Acting must be suited to purpose, and purposefulness requires adjustment to changing conditions.

Presence of mind is considered a virtue in acting man. A man has presence of mind if he has the ability to think and to adjust his acting so quickly that the interval between the emergence of new conditions and the adaptation of his actions to them becomes as short as possible. If constancy is viewed as faithfulness to a plan once designed without regard to changes in conditions, then presence of mind and quick reaction are the very opposite of constancy.

When the speculator goes to the stock exchange, he may sketch a definite plan for his operations. Whether or not he clings to this plan, his actions are rational also in the sense which those eager to distinguish rational acting from irrational attribute to the term "rational." This speculator in the course of the day may embark upon transactions which an observer, not taking into account the changes occurring in market conditions, will not be able to interpret as the outcome of constant behavior. But the speculator is firm in his intention to make profits and to avoid losses. Accordingly he must adjust his conduct to the change in market

---

[8]Cf. [Philip H.] Wicksteed, *The Common Sense of Political Economy*, ed. Robbins (London, 1933), vol. 1, pp. 32ff.; [Lionel] Robbins, *An Essay on the Nature and Significance of Economic Science,* 2d ed. (London, 1935), pp. 91ff.

conditions and in his own judgment concerning the future development of prices.[9]

However one twists things, one will never succeed in formulating the notion of "irrational" action whose "irrationality" is not founded upon an arbitrary judgment of value. Let us suppose that somebody has chosen to act inconstantly for no other purpose than for the sake of refuting the praxeological assertion that there is no irrational action. What happens here is that a man aims at a peculiar goal, viz., the refutation of a praxeological theorem, and that he accordingly acts differently from what he would have done otherwise. He has chosen an unsuitable means for the refutation of praxeology, that is all. ...

1. Uncertainty and Acting[10]

The uncertainty of the future is already implied in the very notion of action. That man acts and that the future is uncertain are by no means two independent matters. They are only two different modes of establishing one thing.

We may assume that the outcome of all events and changes is uniquely determined by eternal unchangeable laws governing becoming and development in the whole universe. We may consider the necessary connection and interdependence of all phenomena, i.e., their causal concatenation, as the fundamental and ultimate fact. We may entirely discard the notion of undetermined chance. But however that may be, or appear to the mind of a perfect intelligence, the fact remains that to acting man the future is hidden. If man knew the future, he would not have to choose and would not act. He would be like an automaton, reacting to stimuli without any will of his own.

---

[9]Plans too, of course, may be self-contradictory. Sometimes their contradictions may be the effect of mistaken judgment. But sometimes such contradictions may be intentional and serve a definite purpose. If, for instance, a publicized program of a government or a political party promises high prices to the producers and at the same time low prices to the consumers, the purpose of such an espousal of incompatible goals may be demagogic. Then the program, the publicized plan, is self-contradictory; but the plan of its authors who wanted to attain a definite end through the endorsement of incompatible aims and their public announcement, is free of any contradiction.

[10][Mises, *Human Action*, chap. 6: "Uncertainty," pp. 105–15.]

Some philosophers are prepared to explode the notion of man's will as an illusion and self-deception because man must unwittingly behave according to the inevitable laws of causality. They may be right or wrong from the point of view of the prime mover or the cause of itself. However, from the human point of view action is the ultimate thing. We do not assert that man is "free" in choosing and acting. We merely establish the fact that he chooses and acts and that we are at a loss to use the methods of the natural sciences for answering the question why he acts this way and not otherwise.

Natural science does not render the future predictable. It makes it possible to foretell the results to be obtained by definite actions. But it leaves impredictable two spheres: that of insufficiently known natural phenomena and that of human acts of choice. Our ignorance with regard to these two spheres taints all human actions with uncertainty. Apodictic certainty is only within the orbit of the deductive system of aprioristic theory. The most that can be attained with regard to reality is probability.

It is not the task of praxeology to investigate whether or not it is permissible to consider as certain some of the theorems of the empirical natural sciences. This problem is without practical importance for praxeological considerations. At any rate, the theorems of physics and chemistry have such a high degree of probability that we are entitled to call them certain for all practical purposes. We can practically forecast the working of a machine constructed according to the rules of scientific technology. But the construction of a machine is only a part in a broader program that aims at supplying the consumers with the machine's products. Whether this was or was not the most appropriate plan depends on the development of future conditions which at the time of the plan's execution cannot be forecast with certainty. Thus the degree of certainty with regard to the technological outcome of the machine's construction, whatever it may be, does not remove the uncertainty inherent in the whole action. Future needs and valuations, the reaction of men to changes in conditions, future scientific and technological knowledge, future ideologies and policies can never be foretold with more than a greater or smaller degree of probability. Every action refers to an unknown future. It is in this sense always a risky speculation.

The problems of truth and certainty concern the general theory of human knowledge. The problem of probability, on the other hand, is a primary concern of praxeology.

2. *The Meaning of Probability*

The treatment of probability has been confused by the mathematicians. From the beginning there was an ambiguity in dealing with the calculus of probability. When the Chevalier de Méré consulted Pascal on the problems involved in the games of dice, the great mathematician should have frankly told his friend the truth, namely, that mathematics cannot be of any use to the gambler in a game of pure chance. Instead he wrapped his answer in the symbolic language of mathematics. What could easily be explained in a few sentences of mundane speech was expressed in a terminology which is unfamiliar to the immense majority and therefore regarded with reverential awe. People suspected that the puzzling formulas contain some important revelations, hidden to the uninitiated; they got the impression that a scientific method of gambling exists and that the esoteric teachings of mathematics provide a key for winning. The heavenly mystic Pascal unintentionally became the patron saint of gambling. The textbooks of the calculus of probability gratuitously propagandize for the gambling casinos precisely because they are sealed books to the layman.

No less havoc was spread by the equivocations of the calculus of probability in the field of scientific research. The history of every branch of knowledge records instances of the misapplication of the calculus of probability which, as John Stuart Mill observed, made it "the real opprobrium of mathematics."[11] Some of the worst errors have arisen in our day in the interpretation of the methods of physics.

The problem of probable inference is much bigger than those problems which constitute the field of the calculus of probability. Only preoccupation with the mathematical treatment could result in the prejudice that probability always means frequency.

A further error confused the problem of probability with the problem of inductive reasoning as applied by the natural sciences. The attempt to substitute a universal theory of probability for the category of causality characterizes an abortive mode of philosophizing, very fashionable only a few years ago.

A statement is probable if our knowledge concerning its content is deficient. We do not know everything which would be required for a definite decision between true and not true. But, on the other hand, we do

---

[11]John Stuart Mill, *A System of Logic Ratiocinative and Inductive* (new impression; London, 1936), p. 353.

know something about it; we are in a position to say more than simply *non liquet* or *ignoramus*.

There are two entirely different instances of probability; we may call them class probability (or frequency probability) and case probability (or the specific understanding of the sciences of human action). The field for the application of the former is the field of the natural sciences, entirely ruled by causality; the field for the application of the latter is the field of the sciences of human action, entirely ruled by teleology.

3. Class Probability

Class probability means: We know or assume to know, with regard to the problem concerned, everything about the behavior of a whole class of events or phenomena; but about the actual singular events or phenomena we know nothing but that they are elements of this class.

We know, for instance, that there are ninety tickets in a lottery and that five of them will be drawn. Thus we know all about the behavior of the whole class of tickets. But with regard to the singular tickets we do not know anything but that they are elements of this class of tickets.

We have a complete table of mortality for a definite period of the past in a definite area. If we assume that with regard to mortality no changes will occur, we may say that we know everything about the mortality of the whole population in question. But with regard to the life expectancy of the individuals we do not know anything but that they are members of this class of people.

For this defective knowledge the calculus of probability provides a presentation in symbols of the mathematical terminology. It neither expands nor deepens nor complements our knowledge. It translates it into mathematical language. Its calculations repeat in algebraic formulas what we knew beforehand. They do not lead to results that would tell us anything about the actual singular events. And, of course, they do not add anything to our knowledge concerning the behavior of the whole class, as this knowledge was already perfect — or was considered perfect — at the very outset of our consideration of the matter.

It is a serious mistake to believe that the calculus of probability provides the gambler with any information which could remove or lessen the risk of gambling. It is, contrary to popular fallacies, quite useless for the gambler, as is any other mode of logical or mathematical reasoning. It is the characteristic mark of gambling that it deals with the unknown, with pure chance. The gambler's hopes for success are not based on substantial considerations. The nonsuperstitious gambler thinks: "There is a slight chance [or, in other words: 'it is not impossible'] that I may win; I am ready to put up the stake required. I know very well that in putting it up I am behaving like a fool. But the biggest fools have the most luck. Anyway!"

Cool reasoning must show the gambler that he does not improve his chances by buying two tickets instead of one of a lottery in which the total amount of the winnings is smaller than the proceeds from the sale of all tickets. If he were to buy all the tickets, he would certainly lose a part of his outlay. Yet every lottery customer is firmly convinced that it is better to buy more tickets than less. The habitués of the casinos and slot machines never stop. They do not give a thought to the fact that, because the ruling odds favor the banker over the player, the outcome will the more certainly result in a loss for them the longer they continue to play. The lure of gambling consists precisely in its unpredictability and its adventurous vicissitudes.

Let us assume that ten tickets, each bearing the name of a different man, are put into a box. One ticket will be drawn, and the man whose name it bears will be liable to pay 100 dollars. Then an insurer can promise to the loser full indemnification if he is in a position to insure each of the ten for a premium of ten dollars. He will collect 100 dollars and will have to pay the same amount to one of the ten. But if he were to insure one only of them at a rate fixed by the calculus, he would embark not upon an insurance business, but upon gambling. He would substitute himself for the insured. He would collect ten dollars and would get the chance either of keeping it or of losing that ten dollars and ninety dollars more.

If a man promises to pay at the death of another man a definite sum and charges for this promise the amount adequate to the life expectancy as determined by the calculus of probability, he is not an insurer but a gambler. Insurance, whether conducted according to business principles or according to the principle of mutuality, requires the insurance of a whole class or what can reasonably be considered as such. Its basic idea is pooling and distribution of risks, not the calculus of probability. The mathematical operations that it requires are the four elementary operations of arithmetic. The calculus of probability is mere byplay.

This is clearly evidenced by the fact that the elimination of hazardous risk by pooling can also be effected without any recourse to actuarial methods. Everybody practices it in his daily life. Every businessman includes in his normal cost accounting the compensation for losses which regularly occur in the conduct of affairs. "Regularly" means in this context: The amount of these losses is known as far as the whole class of the various items is concerned. The fruit dealer may know, for instance, that one of every fifty apples will rot in this stock; but he does not know to which individual apple this will happen. He deals with such losses as with any other item in the bill of costs.

The definition of the essence of class probability as given above is the only logically satisfactory one. It avoids the crude circularity implied in all definitions referring to the equiprobability of possible events. In stating that we know nothing about actual singular events except that they are elements of a class the behavior of which is fully known, this vicious circle is disposed of. Moreover, it is superfluous to add a further condition called the absence of any regularity in the sequence of the singular events.

The characteristic mark of insurance is that it deals with the whole class of events. As we pretend to know everything about the behavior of the whole class, there seems to be no specific risk involved in the conduct of the business.

Neither is there any specific risk in the business of the keeper of a gambling bank or in the enterprise of a lottery. From the point of view of the lottery enterprise the outcome is predictable, provided that all tickets have been sold. If some tickets remain unsold, the enterpriser is in the same position with regard to them as every buyer of a ticket is with regard to the tickets he bought.

4. Case Probability

Case probability means: We know, with regard to a particular event, some of the factors which determine its outcome; but there are other determining factors about which we know nothing.

Case probability has nothing in common with class probability but the incompleteness of our knowledge. In every other regard the two are entirely different.

There are, of course, many instances in which men try to forecast a particular future event on the basis of their knowledge about the behavior of the class. A doctor may determine the chances for the full recovery of his patient if he knows that 70 per cent of those afflicted with the same disease recover. If he expresses his judgment correctly, he will not say more than that the probability of recovery is 0.7, that is, that out of ten patients not more than three on the average die. All such predictions about external events, i.e., events in the field of the natural sciences, are of this character. They are in fact not forecasts about the issue of the case in question, but statements about the frequency of the various possible outcomes. They are based either on statistical information or simply on the rough estimate of the frequency derived from nonstatistical experience.

So far as such types of probable statements are concerned, we are not faced with case probability. In fact we do not know anything about the case in question except that it is an instance of a class the behavior of which we know or think we know.

A surgeon tells a patient who considers submitting himself to an operation that thirty out of every hundred undergoing such an operation die. If the patient asks whether this number of deaths is already full, he has misunderstood the sense of the doctor's statement. He has fallen prey to the error known as the "gambler's fallacy." Like the roulette player who concludes from a run of ten red in succession that the probability of the next turn being black is now greater than it was before the run, he confuses case probability with class probability.

All medical prognoses, when based only on physiological knowledge, deal with class probability. A doctor who hears that a man he does not know has been seized by a definite illness will, on the basis of his general medical experience, say: His chances for recovery are 7 to 3. If the doctor himself treats the patient, he may have a different opinion. The patient is a young, vigorous man; he was in good health before he was taken with the illness. In such cases, the doctor may think, the mortality figures are lower; the chances for this patient are not 7:3, but 9:1. The logical approach remains the same, although it may be based not on a collection of statistical data, but simply on a more or less exact résumé of the doctor's own experience with previous cases. What the doctor knows is always only the behavior of classes. In our instance the class is the class of young, vigorous men seized by the illness in question.

Case probability is a particular feature of our dealing with problems of human action. Here any reference to frequency is inappropriate, as our statements always deal with unique events which as such — i.e., with regard to the problem in question — are not members of any class. We can form a class "American presidential elections." This class concept may prove useful or even necessary for various kinds of reasoning, as, for instance, for a treatment of the matter from the viewpoint of constitutional law. But if we are dealing with the election of 1944 — either, before the election, with its future outcome or, after the election, with an analysis of the factors which determined the outcome — we are grappling with an individual, unique, and nonrepeatable case. The case is characterized by its unique merits, it is a class by itself. All the marks which make it permissible to subsume it under any class are irrelevant for the problem in question.

Two football teams, the Blues and the Yellows, will play tomorrow. In the past the Blues have always defeated the Yellows. This knowledge is not knowledge about a class of events. If we were to consider it as such, we would have to conclude that the Blues are always victorious and that the Yellows are always defeated. We would not be uncertain with regard to the outcome of the game. We would know for certain that the Blues will win again. The mere fact that we consider our forecast about tomorrow's game as only probable shows that we do not argue this way.

On the other hand, we believe that the fact that the Blues were victorious in the past is not immaterial with regard to the outcome of tomorrow's game. We consider it as a favorable prognosis for the repeated success of the Blues. If we were to argue correctly according to the reasoning appropriate to class probability, we would not attach any importance to this fact. If we were not to resist the erroneous conclusion of the "gambler's fallacy," we would, on the contrary, argue that tomorrow's game will result in the success of the Yellows.

If we risk some money on the chance of one team's victory, the lawyers would qualify our action as a bet. They would call it gambling if class probability were involved.

Everything that outside the field of class probability is commonly implied in the term probability refers to the peculiar mode of reasoning involved in dealing with historical uniqueness or individuality, the specific understanding of the historical sciences.

Understanding is always based on incomplete knowledge. We may know the motives of the acting men, the ends they are aiming at, and the means they plan to apply for the attainment of these ends. We have a definite opinion with regard to the effects to be expected from the operation of these factors. But this knowledge is defective. We cannot exclude beforehand the possibility that we have erred in the appraisal of their influence or have failed to take into consideration some factors whose interference we did not foresee at all, or not in a correct way.

Gambling, engineering, and speculating are three different modes of dealing with the future.

The gambler knows nothing about the event on which the outcome of his gambling depends. All that he knows is the frequency of a favorable outcome of a series of such events, knowledge which is useless for his undertaking. He trusts to good luck, that is his only plan.

Life itself is exposed to many risks. At any moment it is endangered by disastrous accidents which cannot be controlled, or at least not sufficiently. Every man banks on good luck. He counts upon not being struck by lightning and not being bitten by a viper. There is an element of gambling in human life. Man can remove some of the chrematistic consequences of such disasters and accidents by taking out insurance policies. In doing so he banks upon the opposite chances. On the part of the insured the insurance is gambling. His premiums were spent in vain if the disaster does not occur.[12] With regard to noncontrollable natural events man is always in the position of a gambler.

The engineer, on the other hand, knows everything that is needed for a technologically satisfactory solution of his problem, the construction of a machine. As far as some fringes of uncertainty are left in his power to control, he tries to eliminate them by taking safety margins. The engineer knows only soluble problems and problems which cannot be solved under the present state of knowledge. He may sometimes discover from adverse experience that his knowledge was less complete than he had assumed and that he failed to recognize the indeterminateness of some issues which he thought he was able to control. Then he will try to render his knowledge more complete. Of course he can never eliminate altogether the element of gambling present in human life. But it is his principle to operate only within an orbit of certainty. He aims at full control of the elements of his action.

It is customary nowadays to speak of "social engineering." Like planning, this term is a synonym for dictatorship and totalitarian tyranny. The idea is to treat human beings in the same way in which the engineer treats the stuff out of which he builds his bridges, roads, and machines. The social engineer's will is to be substituted for the will of the various people he plans to use for the construction of his utopia. Mankind is to be divided into two classes: the almighty dictator, on the one hand, and the underlings who are to be reduced to the status of mere pawns in his plans and cogs in his machinery, on the other. If this were feasible, then of course the social engineer would not have to bother about understanding

---

[12]In life insurance the insured's stake spent in vain consists only in the difference between the amount collected and the amount he could have accumulated by saving.

other people's actions. He would be free to deal with them as technology deals with lumber and iron.

In the real world acting man is faced with the fact that there are fellow men acting on their own behalf as he himself acts. The necessity to adjust his actions to other people's actions makes him a speculator for whom success and failure depend on his greater or lesser ability to understand the future. Every investment is a form of speculation. There is in the course of human events no stability and consequently no safety. ❿

CHAPTER 4

Society, Exchange, and the Division of Labor

HUMAN ACTION[1]

1. Autistic Exchange and Interpersonal Exchange

Action always is essentially the exchange of one state of affairs for another state of affairs. If the action is performed by an individual without any reference to cooperation with other individuals, we may call it autistic exchange. An instance: the isolated hunter who kills an animal for his own consumption; he exchanges leisure and a cartridge for food.

Within society cooperation substitutes interpersonal or social exchange for autistic exchanges. Man gives to other men in order to receive from them. Mutuality emerges. Man serves in order to be served.

The exchange relation is the fundamental social relation. Interpersonal exchange of goods and services weaves the bond which unites men into society. The societal formula is: *do ut des*. Where there is no intentional mutuality, where an action is performed without any design of being benefited by a concomitant action of other men, there is no interpersonal

---

[1][Ludwig von Mises, *Human Action* (1949; Auburn, Ala.: Mises Institute, 1998), chap. 10: "Exchange within Society," pp. 195–98.]

exchange, but autistic exchange. It does not matter whether the autistic action is beneficial or detrimental to other people or whether it does not concern them at all. A genius may perform his task for himself, not for the crowd; however, he is an outstanding benefactor of mankind. The robber kills the victim for his own advantage; the murdered man is by no means a partner in this crime, he is merely its object; what is done, is done against him.

Hostile aggression was a practice common to man's nonhuman forebears. Conscious and purposeful cooperation is the outcome of a long evolutionary process. Ethnology and history have provided us with interesting information concerning the beginning and the primitive patterns of interpersonal exchange. Some consider the custom of mutual giving and returning of presents and stipulating a certain return present in advance as a precursory pattern of interpersonal exchange.[2] Others consider dumb barter as the primitive mode of trade. However, to make presents in the expectation of being rewarded by the receiver's return present or in order to acquire the favor of a man whose animosity could be disastrous, is already tantamount to interpersonal exchange. The same applies to dumb barter which is distinguished from other modes of bartering and trading only through the absence of oral discussion.

It is the essential characteristic of the categories of human action that they are apodictic and absolute and do not admit of any gradation. There is action or nonaction, there is exchange or nonexchange; everything which applies to action and exchange as such is given or not given in every individual instance according to whether there is or there is not action and exchange. In the same way the boundaries between autistic exchange and interpersonal exchange are sharply distinct. Making one-sided presents without the aim of being rewarded by any conduct on the part of the receiver or of third persons is autistic exchange. The donor acquires the satisfaction which the better condition of the receiver gives to him. The receiver gets the present as a God-sent gift. But if presents are given in order to influence some people's conduct, they are no longer one-sided, but a variety of interpersonal exchange between the donor and the man whose conduct they are designed to influence. Although the emergence of interpersonal exchange was the result of a long evolution, no gradual transition is conceivable between autistic and interpersonal exchange.

---

[2] Gustav Cassel, *The Theory of Social Economy*, trans. S.L. Banon (new ed; London, 1932), p. 371.

There were no intermediary modes of exchange between them. The step which leads from autistic to interpersonal exchange was no less a jump into something entirely new and essentially different than was the step from automatic reaction of the cells and nerves to conscious and purposeful behavior, to action.

2. Contractual Bonds and Hegemonic Bonds

There are two different kinds of social cooperation: cooperation by virtue of contract and coordination, and cooperation by virtue of command and subordination or hegemony.

Where and as far as cooperation is based on contract, the logical relation between the cooperating individuals is symmetrical. They are all parties to interpersonal exchange contracts. John has the same relation to Tom as Tom has to John. Where and as far as cooperation is based on command and subordination, there is the man who commands and there are those who obey his orders. The logical relation between these two classes of men is asymmetrical. There is a director and there are people under his care. The director alone chooses and directs; the others — the wards — are mere pawns in his actions.

The power that calls into life and animates any social body is always ideological might, and the fact that makes an individual a member of any social compound is always his own conduct. This is no less valid with regard to a hegemonic societal bond. It is true, people are as a rule born into the most important hegemonic bonds, into the family and into the state, and this was also the case with the hegemonic bonds of older days, slavery and serfdom, which disappeared in the realm of Western civilization. But no physical violence and compulsion can possibly force a man against his will to remain in the status of the ward of a hegemonic order. What violence or the threat of violence brings about is a state of affairs in which subjection as a rule is considered more desirable than rebellion. Faced with the choice between the consequences of obedience and of disobedience, the ward prefers the former and thus integrates himself into the hegemonic bond. Every new command places this choice before him again. In yielding again and again he himself contributes his share to the continuous existence of the hegemonic societal body. Even as a ward in such a system he is an acting human being, i.e., a being not simply yielding to blind impulses, but using his reason in choosing between alternatives.

What differentiates the hegemonic bond from the contractual bond is the scope in which the choices of the individuals determine the course of events. As soon as a man has decided in favor of his subjection to a hegemonic system, he becomes, within the margin of this system's activities and for the time of his subjection, a pawn of the director's actions. Within the hegemonic societal body and as far as it directs its subordinates' conduct, only the director acts. The wards act only in choosing subordination; having once chosen subordination they no longer act for themselves, they are taken care of.

In the frame of a contractual society the individual members exchange definite quantities of goods and services of a definite quality. In choosing subjection in a hegemonic body a man neither gives nor receives anything that is definite. He integrates himself into a system in which he has to render indefinite services and will receive what the director is willing to assign to him. He is at the mercy of the director. The director alone is free to choose. Whether the director is an individual or an organized group of individuals, a directorate, and whether the director is a selfish maniacal tyrant or a benevolent paternal despot is of no relevance for the structure of the whole system.

The distinction between these two kinds of social cooperation is common to all theories of society. Ferguson described it as the contrast between warlike nations and commercial nation;[3] Saint Simon as the contrast between pugnacious nations and peaceful or industrial nations; Herbert Spencer as the contrast between societies of individual freedom and those of a militant structure;[4] Sombart as the contrast between heroes and peddlers.[5] The Marxians distinguish between the "gentile organization" of a fabulous state of primitive society and the eternal bliss of socialism on the one hand and the unspeakable degradation of capitalism on the other hand.[6] The Nazi philosophers distinguish the counterfeit system of bourgeois security from the heroic system of authoritarian *Führertum*. The valuation of both systems is different with the various sociologists. But they

---

[3]Cf. Adam Ferguson, *An Essay on the History of Civil Society* (new ed; Basel, 1789), p. 208.

[4]Cf. Herbert Spencer, *The Principles of Sociology* (New York, 1914), vol. 3, pp. 575–611.

[5]Cf. Werner Sombart, *Haendler und Helden* (Munich, 1915).

[6]Cf. Frederick Engels, *The Origin of the Family, Private Property and the State* (New York, 1942), p. 144.

fully agree in the establishment of the contrast and no less in recognizing that no third principle is thinkable and feasible.

Western civilization as well as the civilization of the more advanced Eastern peoples are achievements of men who have cooperated according to the pattern of contractual coordination. These civilizations, it is true, have adopted in some respects bonds of hegemonic structure. The state as an apparatus of compulsion and coercion is by necessity a hegemonic organization. So is the family and its household community. However, the characteristic feature of these civilizations is the contractual structure proper to the cooperation of the individual families. There once prevailed almost complete autarky and economic isolation of the individual household units. When interfamilial exchange of goods and services was substituted for each family's economic self-sufficiency, it was, in all nations commonly considered civilized, a cooperation based on contract. Human civilization as it has been hitherto known to historical experience is preponderantly a product of contractual relations.

Any kind of human cooperation and social mutuality is essentially an order of peace and conciliatory settlement of disputes. In the domestic relations of any societal unit, be it a contractual or a hegemonic bond, there must be peace. Where there are violent conflicts and as far as there are such conflicts, there is neither cooperation nor societal bonds. Those political parties which in their eagerness to substitute the hegemonic system for the contractual system point at the rottenness of peace and of bourgeois security, extol the moral nobility of violence and bloodshed and praise war and revolution as the eminently natural methods of interhuman relations, contradict themselves. For their own utopias are designed as realms of peace. The Reich of the Nazis and the commonwealth of the Marxians are planned as societies of undisturbed peace. They are to be created by pacification, i.e., the violent subjection of all those not ready to yield without resistance. In a contractual world various states can quietly coexist. In a hegemonic world there can only be one Reich or commonwealth and only one dictator. Socialism must choose between a renunciation of the advantages of division of labor encompassing the whole earth and all peoples and the establishment of a world-embracing hegemonic order. It is this fact that made Russian Bolshevism, German Nazism, and Italian Fascism "dynamic," i.e., aggressive. Under contractual conditions empires are dissolved into a loose league of autonomous member nations. The hegemonic system is bound to strive after the annexation of all independent states.

The contractual order of society is an order of right and law. It is a government under the rule of law (*Rechtsstaat*) as differentiated from the welfare state (*Wohlfahrtsstaat*) or paternal state. Right or law is the complex of rules determining the orbit in which individuals are free to act. No such orbit is left to wards of a hegemonic society. In the hegemonic state there is neither right nor law; there are only directives and regulations which the director may change daily and apply with what discrimination he pleases and which the wards must obey. The wards have one freedom only: to obey without asking questions. ❱

SOCIALISM[7]

1. The Nature of Society

The idea of human destiny dominates all the more ancient views of social existence. Society progresses towards a goal fore-ordained by the deity. Whoever thinks in this way is logically correct if, in speaking of progress and retrogression, of revolution and counterrevolution, of action and reaction he lays on these concepts the emphasis adopted by so many historians and politicians. History is judged according as it brings mankind nearer to the goal or carries it farther away.

Social science, however, begins at the point where one frees oneself from such habits, and indeed from all valuation. Social science is indeed teleological in the sense in which every causal study of the will must be. But its concept of purpose is wholly comprised in the causal explanation. For social science causality remains the fundamental principle of cognition, the maintenance of which must not be impaired even by teleology.[8] Since it does not evaluate purposes, it cannot speak of evolution to a higher plane, in the sense let us say, of Hegel and Marx. For it is by no means proved that all evolution leads upwards, or that every later stage is a higher one. No more, of course, can it agree with the pessimistic philosophers of history, who see in the historical process a decline, a progressive approach to a bad end. To ask what are the driving forces of historical evolution is to ask what is the nature of society and the origin and causes of the changes

---

[7][Ludwig von Mises, *Socialism* (1922; Indianapolis, Ind.: Liberty Classics, 1981), chap. 18: "Society," pp. 256–78.]

[8][Hermann] Cohen, *Logik der reinen Erkenntnis*, 2nd ed. (Berlin, 1914), p. 359.

in social conditions. What society is, how it originates, how it changes — these alone can be the problems which scientific sociology sets itself.

That the social life of men resembles the biological process is an observation of ancient date. It lies at the basis of the famous legend of Menenius Agrippa, handed down to us by Livy. Social science did itself little good when, inspired by the triumph of Biology in the nineteenth century, voluminous works developed this analogy to the point of absurdity. What is the use of calling the products of human activity "social intercellular substance"?[9] Who was enlightened when scholars disputed which organ of the social body corresponded to the central nervous system? The best comment on this form of sociological study was the remark of an economist, to the effect that anyone who compared money with blood and the circulation of money with the circulation of blood would be making the same contribution to economics as would be made to biology by a man who compared blood with money and the blood-circulation with the circulation of money. Modern biology has borrowed from social science some of its most important concepts — that of evolution, of the division of labour, and of the struggle for existence. But it has not stopped short at metaphorical phrases and conclusions by analogy; rather has it proceeded to make profitable use of what it had gained. On the other hand biological-sociology did nothing but play a futile word-spinning game with the ideas it borrowed back. The romantic movement, with its "organic" theory of the state has done even less to clear up our knowledge of social interrelations. Because it deliberately cold-shouldered the most important achievement of social science up to that date — the system of classical Political Economy — it was unable to utilize the doctrine of the division of labour,

---

[9]As is done by [Paul von] Lilienfeld, *La pathologie sociale* (Paris, 1896), p. 95. When a government takes a loan from the House of Rothschild organic sociology conceives the process as follows: "*La maison Rothschild agit, dans cette occasion, parfaitement en analogie avec l'action d'un groupe de cellules qui, dans le corps humain, coopèrent à la production du sang nécessaire à l'alimentation du cerveau dans l'espoir d'en être indemnisées par une réaction des cellules de la substance grise dont ils ont besoin pour s'activer de nouveau et accumuler de nouvelles énergies.*" ("The House of Rothschild's operation, on such an occasion, is precisely similar to the action of a group of human body cells which cooperate in the production of the blood necessary for nourishing the brain, in the hope of being compensated by a reaction of the gray matter cells which they need to reactivate and to accumulate new energies.") (Ibid., p. 104.) This is the method which claims that it stands on "firm ground" and explores "the Becoming of Phenomena step by step, proceeding from the simpler to the more complex." See Lilienfeld, *Zur Verteidigung der organischen Methode in der Soziologie* (Berlin, 1898), p. 75.

that part of the classical system which must be the starting point of all sociology, as it is of modern biology.[10]

Comparison with the biological organism should have taught sociology one thing: that the organism can only be conceived as a system of organs. This, however, merely means that the essence of the organism is the division of labour. Only division of labour makes the parts become members; it is in the collaboration of the members that we recognize the unity of the system, the organism.[11] This is true of the life of plants and animals as well as of society. As far as the principle of the division of labour is concerned, the social body may be compared with the biological. The division of labour is the *tertium comparationis* (basis for comparison) of the old simile.

The division of labour is a fundamental principle of all forms of life.[12] It was first detected in the sphere of social life when political economists emphasized the meaning of the division of labour in the social economy. Biology then adopted it, at the instigation in the first place of Milne Edwards in 1827. The fact that we can regard the division of labour as a general law must not, however, prevent us from recognizing the fundamental differences between division of labour in the animal and vegetable organism on the one hand and division of labour in the social life of human beings on the other. Whatever we imagine to be the origin, evolution, and meaning of the physiological division of labour, it clearly does not shed any light on the nature of the sociological division of labour. The process that differentiates and integrates homogeneous cells is completely different from that which led to the growth of human society out of self-sufficient individuals. In the second process, reason and will play their part in the coalescence, by which the previously independent units form a larger unit and become parts of a whole, whereas the intervention of such forces in the first process is inconceivable.

Even where creatures such as ants and bees come together in "animal communities," all movements and changes take place instinctively and unconsciously. Instinct may very well have operated at the beginning and

---

[10]It is characteristic that just the romantics stress excessively society's organic character, whereas liberal social philosophy has never done so. Quite understandably. A social theory which was genuinely organic did not need to stress obtrusively this attribute of its system.

[11]Cohen, *Logik der reinen Erkenntnis*, p. 349.

[12][Oscar] Hertwig, *Allgemeine Biologie*, 4th ed. (Jena, 1912), pp. 500ff; Hertwig, *Zur Abwehr des ethischen, des sozialen und des politischen Darwinismus* (Jena, 1918), pp. 69ff.

in the earliest stages of social formation also. Man is already a member of a social body when he appears as a thinking, willing creature, for the thinking man is inconceivable as a solitary individual. "Only amongst men does man become a man" (Fichte). The development of human reason and the development of human society are one and the same process. All further growth of social relations is entirely a matter of will. Society is the product of thought and will. It does not exist outside thought and will. Its being lies within man, not in the outer world. It is projected from within outwards.

Society is co-operation; it is community in action.

To say that Society is an organism, means that society is division of labour.[13] To do justice to this idea we must take into account all the aims which men set themselves and the means by which these are to be attained. It includes every inter-relation of thinking and willing man. Modern man is a social being, not only as one whose material needs could not be supplied in isolation, but also as one who has achieved a development of reason and of the perceptive faculty that would have been impossible except within society. Man is inconceivable as an isolated being, for humanity exists only as a social phenomenon and mankind transcended the stage of animality only in so far as co-operation evolved the social relationships between the individuals. Evolution from the human animal to the human being was made possible by and achieved by means of social cooperation and by that alone. And therein lies the interpretation of Aristotle's dictum that man is the ζῶονπολιτιχον (the living body politic).

2. The Division of Labour as the Principle of Social Development

We are still far from understanding the ultimate and most profound secret of life, the principle of the origin of organisms. Who knows whether we shall ever discover it? All we know today is that when organisms are formed, something which did not exist before is created out of individuals. Vegetable and animal organisms are more than conglomerations of single cells, and society is more than the sum of the individuals of which it is composed. We have not yet grasped the whole significance of this fact. Our thoughts are still limited by the mechanical theory of the conservation of energy and of matter, which is never able to tell us how one can become two. Here again, if we are to extend our knowledge of the nature

---

13[Jean] Izoulet, *La cité moderne* (Paris, 1894), pp. 35ff.

of life, understanding of the social organization will have to precede that of the biological.

Historically division of labour originates in two facts of nature: the inequality of human abilities and the variety of the external conditions of human life on the earth. These two facts are really one: the diversity of Nature, which does not repeat itself but creates the universe in infinite, inexhaustible variety. The special nature of our inquiry, however, which is directed towards sociological knowledge, justifies us in treating these two aspects separately.

It is obvious that as soon as human action becomes conscious and logical it must be influenced by these two conditions. They are indeed such as almost to force the division of labour on mankind.[14] Old and young, men and women co-operate by making appropriate use of their various abilities. Here also is the germ of the geographical division of labour; man goes to the hunt and woman to the spring to fetch water. Had the strength and abilities of all individuals and the external conditions of production been everywhere equal the idea of division of labour could never have arisen. Man would never of himself have hit upon the idea of making the struggle for existence easier by co-operation in the division of labour. No social life could have arisen among men of equal natural capacity in a world which was geographically uniform.[15] Perhaps men would have joined together to cope with tasks which were beyond the strength of individuals, but such alliances do not make a society. The relations they create are transient, and endure only for the occasion that brings them about. Their only importance in the origin of social life is that they create a *rapprochement* between men

---

[14][Émile] Durkheim, *De la division du travail social* (Paris, 1893), pp. 294ff. endeavours (following Comte and against Spencer) to prove that the division of labour prevails not because, as the economists think, it increases output but as a result of the struggle for existence. The denser the social mass the sharper the struggle for existence. This forces individuals to specialize in their work, as otherwise they would not be able to maintain themselves. But Durkheim overlooks the fact that the division of labour makes this possible only because it makes labour more productive. Durkheim comes to reject the theory of the importance of the greater productivity in the division of labour through a false conception of the fundamental idea of utilitarianism and of the law of the satiation of wants (ibid., 218ff., 257ff.). His view that civilization is called forth by changes in the volume and density of society is untenable. Population grows because labour becomes more productive and is able to nourish more people, not vice versa.

[15]On the important part played by the local variety of productive conditions in the origin of the division of labour see [Karl] von den Steinen, *Unter den Naturvölkern Zentralbrasiliens*, 2nd ed. (Berlin, 1897), pp. 196ff.

which brings with it mutual recognition of the difference in the natural capacities of individuals and thus in turn gives rise to the division of labour.

Once labour has been divided, the division itself exercises a differentiating influence. The fact that labour is divided makes possible further cultivation of individual talent and thus co-operation becomes more and more productive. Through co-operation men are able to achieve what would have been beyond them as individuals, and even the work which individuals are capable of doing alone is made more productive. But all this can only be grasped fully when the conditions which govern increase of productivity under co-operation are set out with analytical precision.

The theory of the international division of labour is one of the most important contributions of Classical Political Economy. It shows that as long as — for any reasons — movements of capital and labour between countries are prevented, it is the comparative, not the absolute, costs of production which govern the geographical division of labour.[16] When the same principle is applied to the personal division of labour it is found that the individual enjoys an advantage in co-operating not only with people superior to himself in this or that capacity but also with those who are inferior to himself in every relevant way. If, through his superiority to B, A needs three hours' labour for the production of one unit of commodity p compared with B's five, and for the production of commodity q two hours against B's four, then A will gain if he confines his labour to producing q and leaves B to produce p. If each gives sixty hours to producing both p and q, the result of A's labour is $20p + 30q$, of B's $12p + 15q$, and for both together $32p + 45q$. If however, A confines himself to producing q alone he produces sixty units in 120 hours, whilst B, if he confines himself to producing p, produces in the same time twenty-four units. The result of the activity is then $24p + 60q$, which, as p has for A a substitution value of $3:2q$ and for B one of $5:4q$, signifies a larger production than $32p + 45q$. Therefore it is obvious that every expansion of the personal division of labour brings advantages to all who take part in it. He who collaborates with the less talented, less able, and less industrious individuals gains an advantage equally as the man who associated with the more talented, more able, and more industrious. The advantage of the division of labour is mutual; it is

---

16[David] Ricardo, *Principles of Political Economy and Taxation*, in *Works*, ed. John Ramsay MacCulloch, 2nd. (London, 1852), pp. 76ff.; [John Stuart] Mill, *Principles of Political Economy* (People's ed.; London, 1867), pp. 348ff.; [C.F.] Bastable, *The Theory of International Trade*, 3rd ed. (London, 1900), pp. 16ff.

not limited to the case where work is done which the solitary individual could never have carried out.

The greater productivity of work under the division of labour is a unifying influence. It leads men to regard each other as comrades in a joint struggle for welfare, rather than as competitors in a struggle for existence. It makes friends out of enemies, peace out of war, society out of individuals.[17]

3. Organism and Organization

Organism and organization are as different from each other as life is from a machine, as a flower which is natural from one which is artificial. In the natural plant each cell lives its own life for itself while functioning reciprocally with the others. What we call living is just this self-existence and self-maintenance. In the artificial plant the separate parts are members of the whole only as far as the will of him, who united them, has been effective. Only to the extent to which this will is effective are the parts within the organization inter-related. Each part occupies only the place given to it, and leaves that place, so to speak, only on instructions. Within this framework the parts can live, that is, exist for themselves, only in so far as the creator has put them alive into his creation. The horse which the driver has harnessed to the cart lives as a horse. In the organization, the "team," the horse is just as foreign to the vehicle as is an engine to the car it drives. The parts may use their life in opposition to the organization, as, for instance, when the horse runs away with the carriage or the tissue out of which the artificial flower is made disintegrates under chemical action. Human organization is no different. Like society it is a result of will. But in this case the will no more produces a living social organism than the flower-maker produces a living rose. The organization holds together as long as the creating will is effective, no longer. The parts which compose the organization merge into the whole only so far as the will of the creator can impose itself upon them and their life can be fixed in the organization. In the battalion on parade there is one will, the will of the commander. Everything else so far as it functions within the organization is lifeless machinery. In this

---

[17]"Trade makes the human race, which originally has only the unity of the species, into a really unitary society." See Heymann Steinthal, *Allgemeine Ethik* (Berlin, 1885), p. 208. Trade, however, is nothing more than a technical aid of the division of labour. On the division of labour in the sociology of Thomas Aquinas see Edmund Schreiber, *Die volkswirtschaftlichen Anschauungen der Scholastik seit Thomas von Aquin* (Jena, 1913), pp. 19ff.

destruction of the will, or that portion of it which does not serve the purpose of the body of troops, lies the essence of military drill. The soldier in the phalangial order, fighting in line, in which the body of troops must be nothing more than an organization — is drilled. Within the mass there is no life. Whatever life the individual lives is by the side of, or outside the body of troops — against it perhaps, but never in it. Modern warfare, based on the skirmisher's personal enterprise, has to make use of the individual soldier, of his thought and his will. So the army no longer simply drills the soldier. It seeks to educate him.

Organization is an association based on authority, organism is mutuality. The primitive thinker always sees things as having been organized from outside, never as having grown themselves, organically. He sees the arrow which he has carved, he knows how it came into existence and how it was set in motion. So he asks of everything he sees, who made it and who sets it in motion. He inquires after the creation of every form of life, the authors of every change in nature, and discovers an animistic explanation. Thus the Gods are born. Man sees the organized community with its contrast of rulers and ruled, and, accordingly, he tries to understand life as an organization, not as an organism. Hence the ancient conception of the head as the master of the body, and the use of the same term "head" for the chief of the organization.

In recognizing the nature of the organism and sweeping away the exclusiveness of the concept of organization, science made one of its great steps forward. With all deference to earlier thinkers one may say that in the domain of Social Science this was achieved mainly in the eighteenth century, and that Classical Political Economy and its immediate precursors played the chief part. Biology took up the good work, flinging off all animistic and vitalistic beliefs. For modern biology the head is no longer the crown, the ruler of the body. In the living body there is no longer leader and followers, a contrast of sovereign and subjects, of means and purpose. There are only members, organs.

To seek to organize society is just as crazy as it would be to tear a living plant to bits in order to make a new one out of the dead parts. An organization of mankind can only be conceived after the living social organism has been killed. The collectivist movements are therefore fore-doomed to failure. It may be possible to create an organization embracing all mankind. But this would always be merely an organization, side by side with which social life would continue. It could be altered and destroyed by the forces of social life, and it certainly would be destroyed from the moment it tried to rebel against these forces. To make Collectivism a fact one must first kill all social life, then build up the collectivist state. The Bolshevists are thus quite logical in wishing to dissolve all traditional social ties, to destroy the social edifice built up through countless centuries, in order to erect a new structure on the ruins. Only they overlook the fact that isolated individuals, between whom no kind of social relations exist, can no longer be organized.

Organizations are possible only as long as they are not directed against the organic or do it any injury. All attempts to coerce the living will of human beings into the service of something they do not want must fail. An organization cannot flourish unless it is founded on the will of those organized and serves their purposes.

4. The Individual and Society

Society is not mere reciprocity. There is reciprocity amongst animals, for example when the wolf eats the lamb or when the wolf and she-wolf mate. Yet we do not speak of animal societies or of a society of wolves. Wolf and lamb, wolf and she-wolf, are indeed members of an organism — the organism of Nature. But this organism lacks the specific characteristic of the social organism: it is beyond the reach of will and action. For the same reason, the relation between the sexes is not, as such, a social relation. When a man and a woman come together they follow the law which assigns to them their place in Nature. Thus far they are ruled by instinct. Society exists only where willing becomes a co-willing and action co-action. To strive jointly towards aims which alone individuals could not reach at all, or not with equal effectiveness — that is society.[18]

Therefore, Society is not an end but a means, the means by which each individual member seeks to attain his own ends. That society is possible at all is due to the fact that the will of one person and the will of another find themselves linked in a joint endeavour. Community of work springs from community of will. Because I can get what I want only if my fellow citizen gets what he wants, his will and action become the means by which I can attain my own end. Because my willing necessarily includes his willing,

---

[18]Therefore, too, one must reject the idea of Guyau, which derives the social bond directly from bi-sexuality. See [Jean-Marie] Guyau, *Sittlichkeit ohne Pflicht*, trans. [Elisabeth] Schwarz (Leipzig, 1909), pp. 113ff.

my intention cannot be to frustrate his will. On this fundamental fact all social life is built up.[19]

The principle of the division of labour revealed the nature of the growth of society. Once the significance of the division of labour had been grasped, social knowledge developed at an extraordinary pace, as we see from a comparison between Kant and those who came after him. The doctrine of the division of labour as put forward by eighteenth-century economists, was far from fully developed when Kant wrote. It had yet to be made precise by the Ricardian Theory of International Trade. But the Doctrine of the Harmony of Interests had already anticipated its far-reaching application to social theory. Kant was untouched by these ideas. His only explanation of society, therefore, is that there is an impulse in human beings to form a society, and a second contrary impulse that seeks to split up society.

---

[19]Fouillée argues as follows against the utilitarian theory of society, which calls society a "moyen universal" ("universal means") (Belot): "*Tout moyen n'a qu'une valeur provisoire; le jour où un instrument dont je me servais me devient inutile ou nuisible, je le mets de côté. Si la société n' est qu'un moyen, le jour où, exceptionnellement, elle se trouvera contraire à mes fins, je me delivrerai des lois sociales et moyens. sociaux. ... Aucune considération sociale ne pourra empêcher la révolte de l'individu tant qu'on ne lui aura pas montré que la société est établie pour des fins qui sont d'abord et avant tout ses vraies fins à lui-même et qui, de plus, ne sont pas simplement des fins de plaisir ou d'intérêt, l'intérêt n'étant que le plaisir différé et attendu pour l'avenir ... L'idée d'intérêt est précisément ce qui divise les hommes, malgré les rapprochements qu'elle peut produire lorsqu'il y a convergence d'intérêts sur certains points.*" ("Every means has only a temporary value; the day when a means ceases to serve me or becomes harmful to me, I cast it aside. If society is only a means, the day when, by some special circumstances, it is found to act contrary to my ends, I will free myself from its social laws and social means. ... No social consideration can prevent an individual from rebelling when it has not been demonstrated to him that society exists for ends which are primarily and above all his own true ends and, further, which are not simply for the ends of pleasure or self-interest, self-interest being only pleasure postponed and expected in the future. ... The idea of self-interest is precisely what divides men, in spite of the cooperation it can produce when self-interests coincide in certain instances.") [Alfred] Fouillée, *Humanitaires et libertaires au point de vue Sociologique et moral* (Paris, 1914), pp. 146 ff.; see also [Jean-Marie] Guyau, *Die englische Ethik der Gegenwart*, trans. Peusner (Leipzig, 1914), pp. 372 ff. Fouillée does not see that the provisional value which society gets as a means, lasts as long as the conditions of human life, given by nature, continue unchanged and as long as man continues to recognize the advantages of human co-operation. The "eternal," not merely provisional, existence of society follows from the eternity of the conditions on which it is built up. Those in power may demand of social theory that it should serve them by preventing the individual from revolting against society, but this is by no means a scientific demand. Besides no social theory could, as easily as the utilitarian, induce the social individual to enrol himself voluntarily in the social union. But when an individual shows that he is an enemy of society there is nothing left for society to do but make him harmless.

The antagonism of these two tendencies is used by Nature to lead men towards the ultimate goal to which it wishes to lead them.[20] It is difficult to imagine a more threadbare idea than such an attempt to explain society by the interplay of two impulses, the impulse "to socialize oneself" and the impulse "to isolate oneself." Obviously it goes no farther than the attempt to explain the effects of opium from the *virtus dormitiva, cuius est natura sensus assupire* (the sleep-inducing property whose nature is to dull the senses).

Once it has been perceived that the division of labour is the essence of society, nothing remains of the antithesis between individual and society. The contradiction between individual principle and social principle disappears.

5. *The Development of the Division of Labour*

In so far as the individual becomes a social being under the influence of blind instinct, before thought and will are fully conscious, the formation of society cannot be the subject of sociological inquiry. But this does not mean that Sociology must shift the task of explaining the origins of society on to another science, accepting the social web of mankind as a given fact. For if we decide — and this is the immediate consequence of equating society and division of labour — that the structure of society was incomplete at the appearance of the thinking and willing human being and that the constructive process is continuous throughout history, then we must seek a principle which makes this evolution intelligible to us. The economic theory of the division of labour gives us this principle. It has been said that the happy accident which made possible the birth of civilization was the fact that divided labour is more productive than labour without division. The division of labour extends by the spread of the realization that the more labour is divided the more productive it is. In this sense the extension of the division of labour is economic progress: it brings production nearer to its goal — the greatest possible satisfaction of wants, and this progress is sociological progress also, for it involves the intensification of the social relation.

It is only in this sense, and if all teleological or ethical valuation is excluded, that it is legitimate to use the expression "progress" sociologically

---

[20][Immanuel] Kant, "Idee zu einer allgemeinen Geschichte in weltbürgerlicher Absicht" (*Collected Works*), vol. 1, pp. 227ff.

in historical inquiry. We believe that we can observe a certain tendency in the changes of social conditions and we examine each single change separately, to see whether and how far this assumption is compatible with it. It may be that we make various assumptions of this kind, each of which corresponds in like measure to experience. The problem next arises of the relations between these assumptions, whether they are independent of each other or whether they are connected internally. We should then have to go further, and define the nature of the connection. But all that this amounts to is a study, free from valuation and based on a hypothesis, of the course of successive changes.

If we disregard those theories of evolution that are naively built up on value judgments, we shall find, in the majority of the theories claiming to interpret social evolution, two outstanding defects which render them unsatisfactory. The first is that their evolutionary principle is not connected with society as such. Neither Comte's law of the three stages of the human mind nor Lamprecht's five stages of social-psychical development gives any clue to the inner and necessary connection between evolution of the mind and evolution of society. We are shown how society behaves when it has entered a new stage, but we want to know more, namely by what law society originates and transforms itself. The changes which we see as social changes are treated by such theories as facts acting on society from outside; but we need to understand them as the workings of a constant law. The second defeat is that all these theories are "stage" theories (*Stufentheorien*). For the stage-theories there is really no such thing as evolution, that is, no continuous change in which we can recognize a definite trend. The statements of these theories do not go beyond establishing a definite sequence of events; they give no proof of the causal connection between the stages constituting the sequence. At best they succeed in establishing parallels between the sequence of events in different nations. But it is one thing to divide human life into childhood, youth, maturity, and old age, it is another to reveal the law which governs the growth and decay of the organism. A certain arbitrariness attaches to every theory of stages. The delimitation of the stages always fluctuates.

Modern German economic history has undoubtedly done right in making the division of labour the basis of its theory of evolution. But it has not been able to free itself from the old traditional scheme of development by stages. Its theory is still a stage-theory. Thus Bücher distinguishes the stage of the closed domestic economy (pure production for one's own use, barterless economy), the stage of town economy (production for clients, the stage of direct exchange), and the stage of national economy (production for markets, the stage of the circulation of goods).[21] Schmoller differentiates the periods of village economy, town economy, territorial economy, and state economy.[22] Philippovich distinguishes closed domestic economy and trade economy, and within trade economy he finds the period of the locally limited trade, the period of trade controlled by the state and limited to the state area, and the period of free trade (developed national economy, Capitalism).[23] Against these attempts to force evolution into a general scheme many grave objections have been raised. We need not discuss what value such classification may have in revealing the characteristics of clearly defined historical epochs and how far they may be admitted as aids to description. At any rate they should be used with great discretion. The barren dispute over the economic life of the nations of antiquity shows how easily such classifying may lead to our mistaking the shadow of scholastic word-splitting for the substance of historical reality. For sociological study the stage theories are useless.[24] They mislead us in regard to one of the most important problems of history — that of deciding how far historical evolution is continuous. The solution of this problem usually takes the form either of an assumption, that social evolution — which it should be remembered is the development of the division of labour — has moved in an uninterrupted line, or by the assumption that each nation has progressed step-by-step over the same ground. Both assumptions are beside the point. It is absurd to say that evolution is uninterrupted when we can clearly discern periods of decay in history, periods when the division of labour has retrogressed. On the other hand, the progress achieved by individual nations by reaching a higher stage of the division of labour is never completely lost. It spreads to other nations and hastens their evolution. The fall of the ancient world undoubtedly put back economic evolution for centuries. But more recent historical research has shown that the ties connecting the economic civilization of antiquity with

---

[21][Karl] Bücher, *Die Entstehung der Volkswirtschaft*, First collection, 10th ed. (Tübingen, 1917), p. 91.

[22][Gustav] Schmoller, *Grundriss der allgemeinen Volkswirtschaftslehre* (Munich, 1920), vol. 2, pp. 760 ff.

[23][Eugen von] Philippovich, *Grundriss der politischen Ökonomie*, 11th ed. (Tübingen, 1916), vol. 1, pp. 11 ff.

[24]On the stages theory see also my *Grundprobleme der Nationalökonomie* (Jena, 1933), pp. 106 ff.

that of the Middle Ages were much stronger than people used to assume. The Exchange Economy certainly suffered badly under the storm of the great migration of peoples, but it survived them. The towns on which it depended, were not entirely ruined, and a link was soon made between the remnants of town-life and the new development of traffic by barter.[25] In the civilization of the towns a fragment of the social achievements of antiquity was preserved and carried over into the life of the Middle Ages.

Progress in the division of labour depends entirely on a realization of its advantages, that is, of its higher productivity. The truth of this first became fully evident through the free-trade doctrines of the physiocrats and the classical eighteenth-century political economy. But in rudiments it is found in all arguments favouring peace, wherever peace is praised, or war condemned. History is a struggle between two principles, the peaceful principle, which advances the development of trade, and the militarist-imperialist principle, which interprets human society not as a friendly division of labour but as the forcible repression of some of its members by others. The imperialistic principle continually regains the upper hand. The liberal principle cannot maintain itself against it until the inclination for peaceful labour inherent in the masses shall have struggled through to full recognition of its own importance as a principle of social evolution. Wherever the imperialistic principle is in force peace can only be local and temporary: it never lasts longer than the facts which created it. The mental atmosphere with which Imperialism surrounds itself is little suited to the promotion of the growth of the division of labour within state frontiers; it practically prohibits the extension of the division of labour beyond the political-military barriers which separate the states. The division of labour needs liberty and peace. Only when the modern liberal thought of the eighteenth century had supplied a philosophy of peace and social collaboration was the basis laid for the astonishing development of the economic civilization of that age — an age branded by the latest imperialistic and socialistic doctrines as the age of crass materialism, egotism and capitalism.

Nothing could be more perverted than the conclusions drawn in this connection by the materialistic conception of history, which represents the development of social ideology as dependent on the stage of technical evolution which has been attained. Nothing is more erroneous than Marx's well-known saying: "The handmill produces a society with feudal

---

25[Alphons] Dopsch, *Wirtschaftliche und soziale Grundlagen der europäischen Kulturentwicklung* (Vienna, 1918), vol. 1, pp. 91ff.

lords, the steam-mill a society with industrial capitalists."[26] It is not even formally correct. To try and explain social evolution through the evolution of technique is merely to side-track the problem without in any way solving it. For on such a conception, how are we to explain technical evolution itself?

Ferguson showed that the development of technique depends on social conditions, and that each age gets as far in technique as is permitted by the stages it has reached in the social division of labour.[27] Technical advances are possible only where the division of labour has prepared the way for their application. The mass manufacturing of shoes presupposes a society in which the production of shoes for hundreds of thousands or millions of human beings can be united in a few enterprises. In a society of self-sufficing peasants there is no possible use for the steam mill. Only the division of labour could inspire the idea of placing mechanical forces at the service of manufacture.[28]

To trace the origin of everything concerned with society in the development of the division of labour has nothing in common with the gross and naive materialism of the technological and other materialistic theories of history. Nor does it by any means signify, as disciples of the idealistic philosophy are apt to maintain, an inadmissible limitation of the concept of social relations. Neither does it restrict society to the specifically material. That part of social life which lies beyond the economic is indeed the ultimate aim, but the ways which lead to it are governed by the law of all rational action; wherever they come into question there is economic action.

---

[26][Karl] Marx, *Das Elend der Philosophie*, p. 92. In the formulations which Marx later on gave to his conception of history he avoided the rigidity of this earliest version. Behind such indefinite expressions as "productive forces" and "conditions of production" are hidden the critical doubts which Marx may meanwhile have experienced. But obscurity, opening the way to multitudinous interpretations, does not make an untenable theory tenable.

[27][Adam] Ferguson, *Abhandlung über die Geschichte der bürgerlichen Gesellschaft*, trans. Dorn (Jena, 1904), pp. 237 ff.; also [Paul] Barth, *Die Philosophie der Geschichte als Soziologie*, 2nd ed. (Leipzig, 1915), Part 1, pp. 578 ff.

[28]All that remains of the materialist conception of history, which appeared with the widest possible claims, is the discovery that all human and social action is decisively influenced by the scarcity of goods and the disutility of labour. But the Marxists can least admit just this, for all they say about the future socialist order of society disregards these two economic conditions.

6. Changes in the Individual in Society

The most important effect of the division of labour is that it turns the independent individual into a dependent social being. Under the division of labour social man changes, like the cell which adapts itself to be part of an organism. He adapts himself to new ways of life, permits some energies and organs to atrophy and develops others. He becomes one-sided. The whole tribe of romantics, the unbending *laudatores temporis acti* (praisers of time past), have deplored this fact. For them the man of the past who developed his powers "harmoniously" is the ideal: an ideal which alas no longer inspires our degenerate age. They recommend retrogression in the division of labour, hence their praise of agricultural labour, by which they always mean the almost self-sufficing peasant.[29]

Here, again the modern socialist outdoes the rest. Marx promises that in the higher phase of the communist society "the enslaving subjection of individuals under the division of labour, and with this also the contrast between mental and bodily labour, shall have disappeared."[30] Account will be taken of the human "need for change." "Alternation of mental and bodily labour" will "safeguard man's harmonious development."[31]

We have already dealt with this illusion. Were it possible to achieve all human aims with only that amount of labour which does not itself cause any discomfort but at the same time relieves the sensation of displeasure that arises from doing nothing, then labour would not be an economic

---

[29]Adam Müller says about "the vicious tendency to divide labour in all branches of private industry and in government business too," that man needs "an all round, I might say a sphere-round field of activity." If the "division of labour in large cities or industrial or mining provinces cuts up man, the completely free man, into wheels, rollers, spokes, shafts, etc., forces on him an utterly one-sided scope in the already one-sided field of the provisioning of one single want, how can one then demand that this fragment should accord with the whole complete life and with its law, or with legality; how should the rhombuses, triangles, and figures of all kinds accord separately with the great sphere of political life and its law?" See Adam Müller, *Ausgewählte Abhandlungen*, ed. Baxa (Jena, 1921), p. 46.

[30][Karl] Marx, *Zur Kritik des sozialdemokratischen Parteiprogramms von Gotha* (New York, 1920), p. 17. Innumerable passages in his writings show how falsely Marx conceived the nature of labour in industry. Thus he thought also that "the division of labour in the mechanical factory" is characterized by "having lost every specialized character. ... The automatic factory abolishes the specialist and the one-track mind." And he blames Proudhon, "who did not understand even this one revolutionary side of the automatic factory." Marx, *Das Elend der Philosophie*, p. 129.

[31][August] Bebel, *Die Frau und der Sozialismus*, pp. 283ff.

object at all. To satisfy needs would not be work but play. This, however, is not possible. Even the self-sufficient worker, for the most part, must labour far beyond the point where the effort is agreeable. One may assume that work is less unpleasant to him than to the worker who is tied to a definite task, as he finds at the beginning of each job he tackles fresh sensations of pleasure in the activity itself. If, nevertheless, man has given himself up more and more to the division of labour, it is because he has recognized that the higher productivity of labour thus specialized more than repays him for the loss of pleasure. The extent of the division of labour cannot be curtailed without reducing the productivity of labour. This is true of all kinds of labour. It is an illusion to believe that one can maintain productivity and reduce the division of labour.

Abolition of the division of labour would be no remedy for the injuries inflicted on the individual, body and soul, by specialized labour, unless we are prepared to set back social development. It is for the individual himself to set about becoming a complete human being. The remedy lies in reforming consumption, not in "reforming" labour. Play and sport, the pleasure of art, reading are the obvious way of escape.

It is futile to look for the harmoniously developed man at the outset of economic evolution. The almost self-sufficient economic subject as we know him in the solitary peasant of remote valleys shows none of that noble, harmonious development of body, mind, and feeling which the romantics ascribe to him. Civilization is a product of leisure and the peace of mind that only the division of labour can make possible. Nothing is more false than to assume that man first appeared in history with an independent individuality and that only during the evolution which led to the Great Society did he lose, together with material freedom, his spiritual independence. All history, evidence and observation of the lives of primitive peoples is directly contrary to this view. Primitive man lacks all individuality in our sense. Two South Sea Islanders resemble each other far more closely than two twentieth-century Londoners. Personality was not bestowed upon man at the outset. It has been acquired in the course of evolution of society.[32] ◗

---

[32]Durkheim, *De la division du travail social*, pp. 452 ff.

CHAPTER 5

Capitalism:
The Market Economy

Economic Policy:
Thoughts for Tomorrow and Today[1]

"Capitalism"

D escriptive terms which people use are often quite misleading. In talking about modern captains of industry and leaders of big business, for instance, they call a man a "chocolate king" or a "cotton king" or an "automobile king." Their use of such terminology implies that they see practically no difference between the modern heads of industry and those feudal kings, dukes or lords of earlier days. But the difference is in fact very great, for a chocolate king does not rule at all, he *serves*. He does not reign over conquered territory, independent of the market, independent of his customers. The chocolate king — or the steel king or the automobile king or any other king of modern industry — depends on the industry he operates and on the customers he serves. This "king" must stay

---

[1][Ludwig von Mises, *Economic Policy: Thoughts for Tomorrow and Today* (1979; Washington, D.C.: Regnery Gateway, 2006), Lecture 1, pp. 1–15.]

in the good graces of his subjects, the consumers; he loses his "kingdom" as soon as he is no longer in a position to give his customers better service and provide it at lower cost than others with whom he must compete.

Two hundred years ago, before the advent of capitalism, a man's social status was fixed from the beginning to the end of his life; he inherited it from his ancestors, and it never changed. If he was born poor, he always remained poor, and if he was born rich — a lord or a duke — he kept his dukedom and the property that went with it for the rest of his life.

As for manufacturing, the primitive processing industries of those days existed almost exclusively for the benefit of the wealthy. Most of the people (ninety percent or more of the European population) worked the land and did not come in contact with the city-oriented processing industries. This rigid system of feudal society prevailed in the most developed areas of Europe for many hundreds of years.

However, as the rural population expanded, there developed a surplus of people on the land. For this surplus of population without inherited land or estates, there was not enough to do, nor was it possible for them to work in the processing industries; the kings of the cities denied them access. The numbers of these "outcasts" continued to grow, and still no one knew what to do with them. They were, in the full sense of the word, "proletarians," outcasts whom the government could only put into the workhouse or the poorhouse. In some sections of Europe, especially in the Netherlands and in England, they became so numerous that, by the eighteenth century, they were a real menace to the preservation of the prevailing social system.

Today, in discussing similar conditions in places like India or other developing countries, we must not forget that, in eighteenth-century England, conditions were much worse. At that time, England had a population of six or seven million people, but of those six or seven million people, more than one million, probably two million, were simply poor outcasts for whom the existing social system made no provision. What to do with these outcasts was one of the great problems of eighteenth-century England.

Another great problem was the lack of raw materials. The British, very seriously, had to ask themselves this question: what are we going to do in the future, when our forests will no longer give us the wood we need for our industries and for heating our houses? For the ruling classes it was a desperate situation. The statesmen did not know what to do, and the ruling gentry were absolutely without any ideas on how to improve conditions.

Out of this serious social situation emerged the beginnings of modern capitalism. There were some persons among those outcasts, among those poor people, who tried to organize others to set up small shops which could produce something. This was an innovation. These innovators did not produce expensive goods suitable only for the upper classes; they produced cheaper products for everyone's needs. And this was the origin of capitalism as it operates today. It was *the beginning of mass production*, the fundamental principle of capitalistic industry. Whereas the old processing industries serving the rich people in the cities had existed almost exclusively for the demands of the upper classes, the new capitalist industries began to produce things that could be purchased by the general population. It was mass production to satisfy the needs of the masses.

This is the fundamental principle of capitalism as it exists today in all of those countries in which there is a highly developed system of mass production: Big business, the target of the most fanatic attacks by the so-called leftists, produces almost exclusively to satisfy the wants of the masses. Enterprises producing luxury goods solely for the well-to-do can never attain the magnitude of big businesses. And today, it is the people who work in large factories who are the main consumers of the products made in those factories. This is the fundamental difference between the capitalistic principles of production and the feudalistic principles of the preceding ages.

When people assume, or claim, that there is a difference between the producers and the consumers of the products of big businesses, they are badly mistaken. In American department stores you hear the slogan, "the customer is always right." And this customer is the same man who produces in the factory those things which are sold in the department stores. The people who think that the power of big business is enormous are mistaken also, since big business depends entirely on the patronage of those who buy its products: the biggest enterprise loses its power and its influence when it loses its customers.

Fifty or sixty years ago it was said in almost all capitalist countries that the railroad companies were too big and too powerful; they had a monopoly; it was impossible to compete with them. It was alleged that, in the field of transportation, capitalism had already reached a stage at which it had destroyed itself, for it had eliminated competition. What people overlooked was the fact that the power of the railroads depended on their ability to serve people better than any other method of transportation. Of course it would have been ridiculous to compete with one of these big railroad companies by building another railroad parallel to the old line, since the old line was sufficient to serve existing needs. But very soon there came other competitors. Freedom of competition does not mean that you can succeed simply by imitating or copying precisely what someone else has done. Freedom of the press does not mean that you have the right to copy what another man has written and thus to acquire the success which this other man has duly merited on account of his achievements. It means that you have the right to write something different. Freedom of competition concerning railroads, for example, means that you are free to invent something, to do something, which will challenge the railroads and place them in a very precarious competitive situation.

In the United States the competition to the railroads — in the form of buses, automobiles, trucks, and airplanes — has caused the railroads to suffer and to be almost completely defeated, as far as passenger transportation is concerned.

The development of capitalism consists in everyone's having the right to serve the customer better and/or more cheaply. And this method, this principle, has, within a comparatively short time, transformed the whole world. It has made possible an unprecedented increase in world population.

In eighteenth-century England, the land could support only six million people at a very low standard of living. Today more than fifty million people enjoy a much higher standard of living than even the rich enjoyed during the eighteenth-century. And today's standard of living in England would probably be still higher, had not a great deal of the energy of the British been wasted in what were, from various points of view, avoidable political and military "adventures."

These are the facts about capitalism. Thus, if an Englishman — or, for that matter, any other man in any country of the world — says today to his friends that he is opposed to capitalism, there is a wonderful way to answer him: "You know that the population of this planet is now ten times greater than it was in the ages preceding capitalism; you know that all men today enjoy a higher standard of living than your ancestors did before the age of capitalism. But how do you know that you are the one out of ten who would have lived in the absence of capitalism? The mere fact that you are living today is proof that capitalism has succeeded, whether or not you consider your own life very valuable."

In spite of all its benefits, capitalism has been furiously attacked and criticized. It is necessary that we understand the origin of this antipathy. It is a fact that the hatred of capitalism originated *not* with the masses, *not* among the workers themselves, but among the landed aristocracy — the gentry, the nobility, of England and the European continent. They blamed capitalism for something that was not very pleasant for them: at the beginning of the nineteenth century, the higher wages paid by industry to its workers forced the landed gentry to pay equally higher wages to their *agricultural* workers. The aristocracy attacked the industries by criticising the standard of living of the masses of the workers.

Of course — from our viewpoint, the workers' standard of living was extremely low; conditions under early capitalism were absolutely shocking, but not because the newly developed capitalistic industries had harmed the workers. The people hired to work in factories had already been existing at a virtually subhuman level.

The famous old story, repeated hundreds of times, that the factories employed women and children and that these women and children, before they were working in factories, had lived under satisfactory conditions, is one of the greatest falsehoods of history. The mothers who worked in the factories had nothing to cook with; they did not leave their homes and their kitchens to go into the factories, they went into factories because they had no kitchens, and if they had a kitchen they had no food to cook in those kitchens. And the children did not come from comfortable nurseries. They were starving and dying. And all the talk about the so-called unspeakable horror of early capitalism can be refuted by a single statistic: precisely in these years in which British capitalism developed, precisely in the age called the Industrial Revolution in England, in the years from 1760 to 1830, precisely in those years the population of England doubled, which means that hundreds or thousands of children — who would have died in preceding times — survived and grew to become men and women.

There is no doubt that the conditions of the preceding times were very unsatisfactory. It was capitalist business that improved them. It was precisely those early factories that provided for the needs of their workers, either directly or indirectly by exporting products and importing food and raw materials from other countries. Again and again, the early historians of capitalism have — one can hardly use a milder word — falsified history.

One anecdote they used to tell, quite possibly invented, involved Benjamin Franklin. According to the story, Ben Franklin visited a cotton mill in England, and the owner of the mill told him, full of pride: "Look, here are cotton goods for Hungary." Benjamin Franklin, looking around, seeing that the workers were shabbily dressed, said: "Why don't you produce also for your own workers?"

But those exports of which the owner of the mill spoke really meant that he *did* produce for his own workers, because England had to import all its raw materials. There was no cotton either in England or in continental Europe.

There was a shortage of food in England, and food had to be imported from Poland, from Russia, from Hungary. These exports were the payment for the imports of the food which made the survival of the British population possible. Many examples from the history of those ages will show the attitude of the gentry and aristocracy toward the workers. I want to cite only two examples. One is the famous British "Speenhamland" system. By this system, the British government paid all workers who did not get the minimum wage (determined by the government) the difference between the wages they received and this minimum wage. This saved the landed aristocracy the trouble of paying higher wages. The gentry would pay the traditionally low agricultural wage, and the government would supplement it, thus keeping workers from leaving rural occupations to seek urban factory employment.

Eighty years later, after capitalism's expansion from England to continental Europe, the landed aristocracy again reacted against the new production system. In Germany the Prussian Junkers, having lost many workers to the higher-paying capitalistic industries, invented a special term for the problem: "flight from the countryside" — *Landflucht*. And in the German Parliament, they discussed what might be done against this *evil*, as it was seen from the point of view of the landed aristocracy.

Prince Bismarck, the famous chancellor of the German Reich, in a speech one day said, "I met a man in Berlin who once had worked on my estate, and I asked this man, 'Why did you leave the estate; why did you go away from the country; why are you now living in Berlin?'" And according to Bismarck, this man answered, "You don't have such a nice *Biergarten* in the village as we have here in Berlin, where you can sit, drink beer, and listen to music." This is, of course, a story told from the point of view of Prince Bismarck, the employer. It was not the point of view of all his employees. They went into industry because industry paid them higher wages and raised their standard of living to an unprecedented degree.

Today, in the capitalist countries, there is relatively little difference between the basic life of the so-called higher and lower classes; both have food, clothing, and shelter. But in the eighteenth century and earlier, the difference between the man of the middle class and the man of the lower class was that the man of the middle class had shoes and the man of the lower class did *not* have shoes. In the United States today the difference between a rich man and a poor man means very often only the difference between a Cadillac and a Chevrolet. The Chevrolet may be bought secondhand, but basically it renders the same services to its owner: he, too, can drive from one point to another. More than fifty percent of the people in the United States are living in houses and apartments they own themselves.

The attacks against capitalism — especially with respect to the higher wage rates — start from the false assumption that wages are ultimately paid by people who are different from those who are employed in the factories. Now it is all right for economists and for students of economic theories to distinguish between the worker and the consumer and to make a distinction between them. But the fact is that every consumer must, in some way or the other, earn the money he spends, and the immense majority of the consumers are precisely the same people who work as employees in the enterprises that produce the things which they consume. Wage rates under capitalism are not set by a class of people different from the class of people who earn the wages; they are the *same* people. It is *not* the Hollywood film corporation that pays the wages of a movie star; it is the people who pay admission to the movies. And it is *not* the entrepreneur of a boxing match who pays the enormous demands of the prize fighters; it is the people who pay admission to the fight. Through the distinction between the employer and the employee, a distinction is drawn in economic theory, but it is not a distinction in real life; here, the employer and the employee ultimately are one and the same person.

There are people in many countries who consider it very unjust that a man who has to support a family with several children will receive the same salary as a man who has only himself to take care of. But the question is not whether the employer should bear greater responsibility for the size of a worker's family.

The question we must ask in this case is: Are you, as an individual, prepared to pay *more* for something, let us say, a loaf of bread, if you are told that the man who produced this loaf of bread has six children? The honest man will certainly answer in the negative and say, "In principle I would, but in fact if it costs less I would rather buy the bread produced by a man without any children." The fact is that, if the buyers do not pay the employer enough to enable him to pay his workers, it becomes impossible for the employer to remain in business.

The capitalist system was termed "capitalism" not by a friend of the system, but by an individual who considered it to be the worst of all historical systems, the greatest evil that had ever befallen mankind. That man was Karl Marx. Nevertheless, there is no reason to reject Marx's term, because it describes clearly the source of the great social improvements brought about by capitalism. Those improvements are the result of capital accumulation; they are based on the fact that people, as a rule, do not consume everything they have produced, that they save — and invest — a part of it. There is a great deal of misunderstanding about this problem and — in the course of these lectures — I will have the opportunity to deal with the most fundamental misapprehensions which people have concerning the accumulation of capital, the use of capital, and the universal advantages to be gained from such use. I will deal with capitalism particularly in my lectures about foreign investment and about that most critical problem of present-day politics, inflation. You know, of course, that inflation exists not only in this country. It is a problem all over the world today.

An often unrealized fact about capitalism is this: savings mean benefits for all those who are anxious to produce or to earn wages. When a man has accrued a certain amount of money — let us say, one thousand dollars — and, instead of spending it, entrusts these dollars to a savings bank or an insurance company, the money goes into the hands of an entrepreneur, a businessman, enabling him to go out and embark on a project which could not have been embarked on yesterday, because the required capital was unavailable.

What will the businessman do now with the additional capital? The first thing he must do, the first use he will make of this additional capital, is to go out and hire workers and buy raw materials — in turn causing a *further* demand for workers and raw materials to develop, as well as a tendency toward higher wages and higher prices for raw materials. Long before the saver or the entrepreneur obtains any profit from all of this, the unemployed worker, the producer of raw materials, the farmer, and the wage-earner are all sharing in the benefits of the additional savings.

When the entrepreneur will get something out of the project depends on the future state of the market and on his ability to anticipate correctly the future state of the market. But the workers as well as the producers of raw materials get the benefits immediately. Much was said, thirty or forty years ago, about the "wage policy," as they called it, of Henry Ford. One of Mr. Ford's great accomplishments was that he paid higher wages than did other industrialists or factories. His wage policy was described as an "invention," yet it is not enough to say that this new "invented" policy was the result of the liberality of Mr. Ford. A new branch of business, or a new factory in an already existing branch of business, has to attract workers from *other* employments, from other parts of the country, even from other countries. And the only way to do this is to offer the workers higher wages for their work. This is what took place in the early days of capitalism, and it is still taking place today.

When the manufacturers in Great Britain first began to produce cotton goods, they paid their workers more than they had earned before. Of course, a great percentage of these new workers had earned nothing at all before that and were prepared to take anything they were offered. But after a short time — when more and more capital was accumulated and more and more new enterprises were developed — wage rates went up, and the result was the unprecedented increase in British population which I spoke of earlier.

The scornful depiction of capitalism by some people as a system designed to make the rich become richer and the poor become poorer is wrong from beginning to end. Marx's thesis regarding the coming of socialism was based on the assumption that workers *were* getting poorer, that the masses *were* becoming more destitute, and that finally all the wealth of a country would be concentrated in a few hands or in the hands of one man only. And then the masses of impoverished workers would finally rebel and expropriate the riches of the wealthy proprietors. According to this doctrine of Karl Marx, there can be no opportunity, no possibility within the capitalistic system for any improvement of the conditions of the workers.

In 1864, speaking before the International Workingmen's Association in England, Marx said the belief that labor unions could improve conditions for the working population was "absolutely in error." The union policy of asking for higher wage rates and shorter work hours he called *conservative* — conservatism being, of course, the most condemnatory term which Karl Marx could use. He suggested that the unions set themselves a new, *revolutionary* goal: that they "do away with the wage system altogether," that they substitute "socialism" — government ownership of the means of production — for the system of private ownership.

If we look upon the history of the world, and especially upon the history of England since 1865, we realize that Marx was wrong in every respect. There is no western, capitalistic country in which the conditions of the masses have not improved in an unprecedented way. All these improvements of the last eighty or ninety years were made *in spite of* the prognostications of Karl Marx. For the Marxian socialists believed that the conditions of the workers could never be ameliorated. They followed a false theory, the famous "iron law of wages" — the law which stated that a worker's wages, under capitalism, would not exceed the amount he needed to sustain his life for service to the enterprise.

The Marxians formulated their theory in this way: if the workers' wage rates go up, raising wages above the subsistence level, they will have more children; and these children, when they enter the labor force, will increase the number of workers to the point where the wage rates will drop, bringing the workers once more down to the subsistence level — to that minimal sustenance level which will just barely prevent the working population from dying out. But this idea of Marx, and of many other socialists, is a concept of the working man precisely like that which biologists use — and rightly so — in studying the life of animals. Of mice, for instance.

If you increase the quantity of food available for animal organisms or for microbes, then more of them will survive. And if you restrict their food, then you will restrict their numbers. But man is different. Even the worker — in spite of the fact that Marxists do not acknowledge it — has human wants other than food and reproduction of his species. An increase in real wages results not only in an increase in population, it results also, and first of all, in an *improvement in the average standard of living.* That is why today we have a higher standard of living in Western Europe and in the United States than in the developing nations of, say, Africa.

We must realize, however, that this higher standard of living depends on the supply of capital. This explains the difference between conditions in the United States and conditions in India; modern methods of fighting contagious diseases have been introduced in India — at least, to some extent — and the effect has been an unprecedented increase in population but, since this increase in population has not been accompanied by a corresponding increase in the amount of capital invested, the result has been an increase in poverty. *A country becomes more prosperous in proportion to the rise in the invested capital per unit of its population.*

I hope that in my other lectures I will have the opportunity to deal in greater detail with these problems and will be able to clarify them, because some terms — such as "the capital invested per capita" — require a rather detailed explanation.

But you have to remember that, in economic policies, there are no miracles. You have read in many newspapers and speeches, about the so-called German economic miracle — the recovery of Germany after its defeat and destruction in the Second World War. But this was no miracle. It was the application of the *principles of the free market economy*, of the methods of capitalism, even though they were not applied completely in all respects. Every country can experience the same "miracle" of economic recovery, although I must insist that economic recovery does *not* come from a miracle; it comes from the adoption of — and is the result of — sound economic policies. ◗

CHAPTER 6

Economic Calculation

ECONOMIC CALCULATION IN THE SOCIALIST COMMONWEALTH[1]

2. The Nature of Economic Calculation

Every man who, in the course of economic life, takes a choice between the satisfaction of one need as against another, *eo ipso* makes a judgment of value. Such judgments of value at once include only the very satisfaction of the need itself; and from this they reflect back upon the goods of a lower, and then further upon goods of a higher order. As a rule, the man who knows his own mind is in a position to value goods of a lower order. Under simple conditions it is also possible for him without much ado to form some judgment of the significance to him of goods of a higher order. But where the state of affairs is more involved and their interconnections not so easily discernible, subtler means must be employed to accomplish a correct[2] valuation of the means of production. It would not be difficult

---

[1][Ludwig von Mises, *Economic Calculation in the Socialist Commonwealth* (1920; Auburn, Ala.: Mises Institute, 1990), pp. 10–26.]

[2]Using that term, of course, in the sense only of the valuating subject, and not in an objective and universally applicable sense.

for a farmer in economic isolation to come by a distinction between the expansion of pasture-farming and the development of activity in the hunting field. In such a case the processes of production involved are relatively short and the expense and income entailed can be easily gauged. But it is quite a different matter when the choice lies between the utilization of a water-course for the manufacture of electricity or the extension of a coal mine or the drawing up of plans for the better employment of the energies latent in raw coal. Here the roundabout processes of production are many and each is very lengthy; here the conditions necessary for the success of the enterprises which are to be initiated are diverse, so that one cannot apply merely vague valuations, but requires rather more exact estimates and some judgment of the economic issues actually involved.

Valuation can only take place in terms of units, yet it is impossible that there should ever be a unit of subjective use value for goods. Marginal utility does not posit any unit of value, since it is obvious that the value of two units of a given stock is necessarily greater than, but less than double, the value of a single unit. Judgments of value do not measure; they merely establish grades and scales.[3] Even Robinson Crusoe, when he has to make a decision where no ready judgment of value appears and where he has to construct one upon the basis of a more or less exact estimate, cannot operate solely with subjective use value, but must take into consideration the intersubstitutability of goods on the basis of which he can then form his estimates. In such circumstances it will be impossible for him to refer all things back to one unit. Rather will he, so far as he can, refer all the elements which have to be taken into account in forming his estimate to those economic goods which can be apprehended by an obvious judgment of value — that is to say, to goods of a lower order and to pain-cost. That this is only possible in very simple conditions is obvious. In the case of more complicated and more lengthy processes of production it will, plainly, not answer.

In an exchange economy the objective exchange value of commodities enters as the unit of economic calculation. This entails a threefold advantage. In the first place, it renders it possible to base the calculation upon the valuations of all participants in trade. The subjective use value of each is not immediately comparable as a purely individual phenomenon with the subjective use value of other men. It only becomes so in exchange value,

---

[3]Franz Čuhel, *Zur Lehre von den Bedürfnissen* (Innsbruck: Wagner'sche Universität-Buchhandlung, 1907), pp. 198 f.

which arises out of the interplay of the subjective valuations of all who take part in exchange. But in that case calculation by exchange value furnishes a control over the appropriate employment of goods. Anyone who wishes to make calculations in regard to a complicated process of production will immediately notice whether he has worked more economically than others or not; if he finds, from reference to the exchange relations obtaining in the market, that he will not be able to produce profitably, this shows that others understand how to make a better use of the goods of higher order in question. Lastly, calculation by exchange value makes it possible to refer values back to a unit. For this purpose, since goods are mutually substitutable in accordance with the exchange relations obtaining in the market, any possible good can be chosen. In a monetary economy it is money that is so chosen.

Monetary calculation has its limits. Money is no yardstick of value, nor yet of price. Value is not indeed measured in money, nor is price. They merely consist in money. Money as an economic good is not of stable value as has been naïvely, but wrongly, assumed in using it as a "standard of deferred payments." The exchange-relationship which obtains between money and goods is subjected to constant, if (as a rule) not too violent, fluctuations originating not only from the side of other economic goods, but also from the side of money. However, these fluctuations disturb value calculations only in the slightest degree, since usually, in view of the ceaseless alternations in other economic data — these calculations will refer only to comparatively short periods of time — periods in which "good" money, at least normally, undergoes comparatively trivial fluctuations in regard to its exchange relations. The inadequacy of the monetary calculation of value does not have its mainspring in the fact that value is then calculated in terms of a universal medium of exchange, namely money, but rather in the fact that in this system it is exchange value and not subjective use value on which the calculation is based. It can never obtain as a measure for the calculation of those value determining elements which stand outside the domain of exchange transactions. If, for example, a man were to calculate the profitability of erecting a waterworks, he would not be able to include in his calculation the beauty of the waterfall which the scheme might impair, except that he may pay attention to the diminution of tourist traffic or similar changes, which may be valued in terms of money. Yet these considerations might well prove one of the factors in deciding whether or not the building is to go up at all.

It is customary to term such elements "extra-economic." This perhaps is appropriate; we are not concerned with disputes over terminology; yet the considerations themselves can scarcely be termed irrational. In any place where men regard as significant the beauty of a neighborhood or of a building, the health, happiness and contentment of mankind, the honor of individuals or nations, they are just as much motive forces of rational conduct as are economic factors in the proper sense of the word, even where they are not substitutable against each other on the market and therefore do not enter into exchange relationships.

That monetary calculation cannot embrace these factors lies in its very nature; but for the purposes of our everyday economic life this does not detract from the significance of monetary calculation. For all those ideal goods are goods of a lower order, and can hence be embraced straightway within the ambit of our judgment of values. There is therefore no difficulty in taking them into account, even though they must remain outside the sphere of monetary value. That they do not admit of such computation renders their consideration in the affairs of life easier and not harder. Once we see clearly how highly we value beauty, health, honor and pride, surely nothing can prevent us from paying a corresponding regard to them. It may seem painful to any sensitive spirit to have to balance spiritual goods against material. But that is not the fault of monetary calculation; it lies in the very nature of things themselves. Even where judgments of value can be established directly without computation in value or in money, the necessity of choosing between material and spiritual satisfaction cannot be evaded. Robinson Crusoe and the socialist state have an equal obligation to make the choice.

Anyone with a genuine sense of moral values experiences no hardship in deciding between honor and livelihood. He knows his plain duty. If a man cannot make honor his bread, yet can he renounce his bread for honor's sake. Only they who prefer to be relieved of the agony of this decision, because they cannot bring themselves to renounce material comfort for the sake of spiritual advantage, see in the choice a profanation of true values.

Monetary calculation only has meaning within the sphere of economic organization. It is a system whereby the rules of economics may be applied in the disposition of economic goods. Economic goods only have part in this system in proportion to the extent to which they may be exchanged for money. Any extension of the sphere of monetary calculation causes misunderstanding. It cannot be regarded as constituting a kind of yardstick for the valuation of goods, and cannot be so treated in historical investigations into the development of social relationships; it cannot be used as a criterion of national wealth and income, nor as a means of gauging the value of goods which stand outside the sphere of exchange, as who should seek to estimate the extent of human losses through emigrations or wars in terms of money?[4] This is mere sciolistic tomfoolery, however much it may be indulged in by otherwise perspicacious economists.

Nevertheless within these limits, which in economic life it never oversteps, monetary calculation fulfils all the requirements of economic calculation. It affords us a guide through the oppressive plenitude of economic potentialities. It enables us to extend to all goods of a higher order the judgment of value, which is bound up with and clearly evident in, the case of goods ready for consumption, or at best of production goods of the lowest order. It renders their value capable of computation and thereby gives us the primary basis for all economic operations with goods of a higher order. Without it, all production involving processes stretching well back in time and all the longer roundabout processes of capitalistic production would be gropings in the dark.

There are two conditions governing the possibility of calculating value in terms of money. Firstly, not only must goods of a lower, but also those of a higher order, come within the ambit of exchange, if they are to be included. If they do not do so, exchange relationships would not arise. True enough, the considerations which must obtain in the case of Robinson Crusoe prepared, within the range of his own hearth, to exchange, by production, labor and flour for bread, are indistinguishable from those which obtain when he is prepared to exchange bread for clothes in the open market, and, therefore, it is to some extent true to say that every economic action, including Robinson Crusoe's own production, can be termed *exchange*.[5] Moreover, the mind of one man alone — be it ever so cunning, is too weak to grasp the importance of any single one among the countlessly many goods of a higher order. No single man can ever master all the possibilities of production, innumerable as they are, as to be in

---

4Cf. Friedrich von Wieser, *Über den Ursprung und die Hauptgesetze des wirtschaftlichen Eertes* (Vienna: A. Hölder, 1884), pp. 185 f.

5Cf. [Ludwig von] Mises, *Theorie des Geldes und der Umlaufsmittel* (Munich and Leipzig: Duncker & Humblot, 1912), p. 16, with the references there given. [See the English translation by H.E. Batson, *The Theory of Money and Credit* (Indianapolis: Liberty Classics, 1980), p. 52.]

a position to make straightway evident judgments of value without the aid of some system of computation. The distribution among a number of individuals of administrative control over economic goods in a community of men who take part in the labor of producing them, and who are economically interested in them, entails a kind of intellectual division of labor, which would not be possible without some system of calculating production and without economy.

The second condition is that there exists in fact a universally employed medium of exchange — namely, money — which plays the same part as a medium in the exchange of production goods also. If this were not the case, it would not be possible to reduce all exchange-relationships to a common denominator.

Only under simple conditions can economics dispense with monetary calculation. Within the narrow confines of household economy, for instance, where the father can supervise the entire economic management, it is possible to determine the significance of changes in the processes of production, without such aids to the mind, and yet with more or less of accuracy. In such a case the process develops under a relatively limited use of capital. Few of the capitalistic roundabout processes of production are here introduced: what is manufactured is, as a rule, consumption goods or at least such goods of a higher order as stand very near to consumption-goods. The division of labor is in its rudimentary stages: one and the same laborer controls the labor of what is in effect, a complete process of production of goods ready for consumption, from beginning to end. All this is different, however, in developed communal production. The experiences of a remote and bygone period of simple production do not provide any sort of argument for establishing the possibility of an economic system without monetary calculation.

In the narrow confines of a closed household economy, it is possible throughout to review the process of production from beginning to end, and to judge all the time whether one or another mode of procedure yields more consumable goods. This, however, is no longer possible in the incomparably more involved circumstances of our own social economy. It will be evident, even in the socialist society, that 1,000 hectolitres of wine are better than 800, and it is not difficult to decide whether it desires 1,000 hectolitres of wine rather than 500 of oil. There is no need for any system of calculation to establish this fact: the deciding element is the will of the economic subjects involved. But once this decision has been taken, the real task of rational economic direction only commences, i.e., economically, to place the means at the service of the end. That can only be done with some kind of economic calculation. The human mind cannot orientate itself properly among the bewildering mass of intermediate products and potentialities of production without such aid. It would simply stand perplexed before the problems of management and location.[6]

It is an illusion to imagine that in a socialist state calculation *in natura* can take the place of monetary calculation. Calculation *in natura*, in an economy without exchange, can embrace consumption goods only; it completely fails when it comes to dealing with goods of a higher order. And as soon as one gives up the conception of a freely established monetary price for goods of a higher order, rational production becomes completely impossible. Every step that takes us away from private ownership of the means of production and from the use of money also takes us away from rational economics.

It is easy to overlook this fact, considering that the extent to which socialism is in evidence among us constitutes only a socialistic oasis in a society with monetary exchange, which is still a free society to a certain degree. In one sense we may agree with the socialists' assertion which is otherwise entirely untenable and advanced only as a demagogic point, to the effect that the nationalization and municipalization of enterprise is not really socialism, since these concerns in their business organizations are so much dependent upon the environing economic system with its free commerce that they cannot be said to partake today of the really essential nature of a socialist economy. In state and municipal undertakings technical improvements are introduced because their effect in similar private enterprises, domestic or foreign, can be noticed, and because those private industries which produce the materials for these improvements give the impulse for their introduction. In these concerns the advantages of reorganization can be established, because they operate within the sphere of a society based upon private ownership of the means of production and upon the system of monetary exchange, being thus capable of computation and account. This state of affairs, however, could not obtain in the case of socialist concerns operating in a purely socialistic environment.

Without economic calculation there can be no economy. Hence, in a socialist state wherein the pursuit of economic calculation is impossible, there can be — in our sense of the term — no economy whatsoever.

---

[6]Friedrich von Gottl-Ottlilienfeld, *Wirtschaft und technik* (Grundriss der Sozialökonomik, Section 2; Tübingen: J.C.B. Mohr, 1914), p. 216.

In trivial and secondary matters rational conduct might still be possible, but in general it would be impossible to speak of rational production any more. There would be no means of determining what was rational, and hence it is obvious that production could never be directed by economic considerations. What this means is clear enough, apart from its effects on the supply of commodities. Rational conduct would be divorced from the very ground which is its proper domain. Would there, in fact, be any such thing as rational conduct at all, or, indeed, such a thing as rationality and logic in thought itself? Historically, human rationality is a development of economic life. Could it then obtain when divorced therefrom?

For a time the remembrance of the experiences gained in a competitive economy, which has obtained for some thousands of years, may provide a check to the complete collapse of the art of economy. The older methods of procedure might be retained not because of their rationality but because they appear to be hallowed by tradition. Actually, they would meanwhile have become irrational, as no longer comporting with the new conditions. Eventually, through the general reconstruction of economic thought, they will experience alterations which will render them in fact uneconomic. The supply of goods will no longer proceed anarchically of its own accord; that is true. All transactions which serve the purpose of meeting requirements will be subject to the control of a supreme authority. Yet in place of the economy of the "anarchic" method of production, recourse will be had to the senseless output of an absurd apparatus. The wheels will turn, but will run to no effect.

One may anticipate the nature of the future socialist society. There will be hundreds and thousands of factories in operation. Very few of these will be producing wares ready for use; in the majority of cases what will be manufactured will be unfinished goods and production goods. All these concerns will be interrelated. Every good will go through a whole series of stages before it is ready for use. In the ceaseless toil and moil of this process, however, the administration will be without any means of testing their bearings. It will never be able to determine whether a given good has not been kept for a superfluous length of time in the necessary processes of production, or whether work and material have not been wasted in its completion. How will it be able to decide whether this or that method of production is the more profitable? At best it will only be able to compare the quality and quantity of the consumable end product produced, but will in the rarest cases be in a position to compare the expenses entailed in production. It will know, or think it knows, the ends to be achieved by economic organization, and will have to regulate its activities accordingly, i.e., it will have to attain those ends with the least expense. It will have to make its computations with a view to finding the cheapest way. This computation will naturally have to be a value computation. It is eminently clear, and requires no further proof, that it cannot be of a technical character, and that it cannot be based upon the objective use value of goods and services.

Now, in the economic system of private ownership of the means of production, the system of computation by value is necessarily employed by each independent member of society. Everybody participates in its emergence in a double way: on the one hand as a consumer and on the other as a producer. As a consumer he establishes a scale of valuation for goods ready for use in consumption. As a producer he puts goods of a higher order into such use as produces the greatest return. In this way all goods of a higher order receive a position in the scale of valuations in accordance with the immediate state of social conditions of production and of social needs. Through the interplay of these two processes of valuation, means will be afforded for governing both consumption and production by the economic principle throughout. Every graded system of pricing proceeds from the fact that men always and ever harmonized their own requirements with their estimation of economic facts.

All this is necessarily absent from a socialist state. The administration may know exactly what goods are most urgently needed. But in so doing, it has only found what is, in fact, but one of the two necessary prerequisites for economic calculation. In the nature of the case it must, however, dispense with the other — the valuation of the means of production. It may establish the value attained by the totality of the means of production; this is obviously identical with that of all the needs thereby satisfied. It may also be able to calculate the value of any means of production by calculating the consequence of its withdrawal in relation to the satisfaction of needs. Yet it cannot reduce this value to the uniform expression of a money price, as can a competitive economy, wherein all prices can be referred back to a common expression in terms of money. In a socialist commonwealth which, whilst it need not of necessity dispense with money altogether, yet finds it impossible to use money as an expression of the price of the factors of production (including labor), money can play no role in economic calculation.[7]

---

[7]This fact is also recognized by Otto Neurath (*Durch die Kriegswirtschaft zur Natural-wirtschaft* [Munich: G.D.W. Callwey, 1919], pp. 216f.). He advances the view that every

Picture the building of a new railroad. Should it be built at all, and if so, which out of a number of conceivable roads should be built? In a competitive and monetary economy, this question would be answered by monetary calculation. The new road will render less expensive the transport of some goods, and it may be possible to calculate whether this reduction of expense transcends that involved in the building and upkeep of the next line. That can only be calculated in money. It is not possible to attain the desired end merely by counterbalancing the various physical expenses and physical savings. Where one cannot express hours of labor, iron, coal, all kinds of building material, machines and other things necessary for the construction and upkeep of the railroad in a common unit it is not possible to make calculations at all. The drawing up of bills on an economic basis is only possible where all the goods concerned can be referred back to money. Admittedly, monetary calculation has its inconveniences and serious defects, but we have certainly nothing better to put in its place, and for the practical purposes of life monetary calculation as it exists under a sound monetary system always suffices. Were we to dispense with it, any economic system of calculation would become absolutely impossible.

The socialist society would know how to look after itself. It would issue an edict and decide for or against the projected building. Yet this decision would depend at best upon vague estimates; it would never be based upon the foundation of an exact calculation of value.

The static state can dispense with economic calculation. For here the same events in economic life are ever recurring; and if we assume that the first disposition of the static socialist economy follows on the basis of the final state of the competitive economy, we might at all events conceive of a socialist production system which is rationally controlled from an economic point of view. But this is only conceptually possible. For the moment, we leave aside the fact that a static state is impossible in real life, as our economic data are forever changing, so that the static nature of economic activity is only a theoretical assumption corresponding to no real state of affairs, however necessary it may be for our thinking and for the perfection of our knowledge of economics. Even so, we must assume that the transition to socialism must, as a consequence of the levelling

complete administrative economy is, in the final analysis, a natural economy. "Socialization," he says, "is thus the pursuit of natural economy." Neurath merely overlooks the insuperable difficulties that would have to develop with economic calculation in the socialist commonwealth.

out of the differences in income and the resultant readjustments in consumption, and therefore production, change all economic data in such a way that a connecting link with the final state of affairs in the previously existing competitive economy becomes impossible. But then we have the spectacle of a socialist economic order floundering in the ocean of possible and conceivable economic combinations without the compass of economic calculation.

Thus in the socialist commonwealth every economic change becomes an undertaking whose success can be neither appraised in advance nor later retrospectively determined. There is only groping in the dark. Socialism is the abolition of rational economy. ❯

HUMAN ACTION[8]

1. Monetary Calculation as a Method of Thinking

Monetary calculation is the guiding star of action under the social system of division of labor. It is the compass of the man embarking upon production. He calculates in order to distinguish the remunerative lines of production from the unprofitable ones, those of which the sovereign consumers are likely to approve from those of which they are likely to disapprove. Every single step of entrepreneurial activities is subject to scrutiny by monetary calculation. The premeditation of planned action becomes commercial precalculation of expected costs and expected proceeds. The retrospective establishment of the outcome of past action becomes accounting of profit and loss.

The system of economic calculation in monetary terms is conditioned by certain social institutions. It can operate only in an institutional setting of the division of labor and private ownership of the means of production in which goods and services of all orders are bought and sold against a generally used medium of exchange, i.e., money.

Monetary calculation is the method of calculating employed by people acting within the frame of society based on private control of the means of production. It is a device of acting individuals; it is a mode of computation designed for ascertaining private wealth and income and private profits

---

[8][Ludwig von Mises, *Human Action* (1949; Auburn, Ala.: Mises Institute, 1998), chap. 13: "Monetary Calculation as a Tool of Action," pp. 230–32.]

and losses of individuals acting on their own behalf within a free enter-prise society.[9] All its results refer to the actions of individuals only. When statisticians summarize these results, the outcome shows the sum of the autonomous actions of a plurality of self-directing individuals, but not the effect of the action of a collective body, of a whole, or of a totality. Mon-etary calculation is entirely inapplicable and useless for any consideration which does not look at things from the point of view of individuals. It involves calculating the individuals' profits, not imaginary "social" values and "social" welfare.

Monetary calculation is the main vehicle of planning and acting in the social setting of a society of free enterprise directed and controlled by the market and its prices. It developed in this frame and was gradually perfected with the improvement of the market mechanism and with the expansion of the scope of things which are negotiated on markets against money. It was economic calculation that assigned to measurement, num-ber, and reckoning the role they play in our quantitative and computing civilization. The measurements of physics and chemistry make sense for practical action only because there is economic calculation. It is monetary calculation that made arithmetic a tool in the struggle for a better life. It provides a mode of using the achievements of laboratory experiments for the most efficacious removal of uneasiness.

Monetary calculation reaches its full perfection in capital accounting. It establishes the money prices of the available means and confronts this total with the changes brought about by action and by the operation of other factors. This confrontation shows what changes occurred in the state of the acting men's affairs, and the magnitude of those changes; it makes success and failure, profit and loss ascertainable. The system of free enter-prise has been dubbed capitalism in order to deprecate and to smear it. However, this term can be considered very pertinent. It refers to the most characteristic feature of the system, its main eminence, viz. the role the notion of capital plays in its conduct.

There are people to whom monetary calculation is repulsive. They do not want to be roused from their daydreams by the voice of critical rea-son. Reality sickens them, they long for a realm of unlimited opportunity. They are disgusted by the meanness of a social order in which everything is nicely reckoned in dollars and pennies. They call their grumbling the

---

[9]In partnerships and corporations it is always individuals who act, although not only one individual.

noble deportment worthy of the friends of the spirit, of beauty, and virtue as opposed to the ignoble baseness and villainy of Babbittry. However, the cult of beauty and virtue, wisdom and the search for truth are not hindered by the rationality of the calculating and computing mind. It is only romantic reverie that cannot thrive in a milieu of sober criticism. The cool-headed reckoner is the stern chastiser of the ecstatic visionary.

Our civilization is inseparably linked with our methods of economic calculation. It would perish if we were to abandon this most precious intellectual tool of acting. Goethe was right in calling bookkeeping by double entry "one of the finest inventions of the human mind."[10]

2. Economic Calculation and the Science of Human Action

The evolution of capitalist economic calculation was the necessary condition for the establishment of a systematic and logically coherent science of human action. Praxeology and economics have a definite place in the evolution of human history and in the process of scientific research. They could only emerge when acting man had succeeded in creating methods of thinking that made it possible to calculate his actions. The science of human action was at the beginning merely a discipline dealing with those actions which can be tested by monetary calculation. It dealt exclusively with what we may call the orbit of economics in the narrower sense, that is, with those actions which within a market society are transacted by the intermediary of money. The first steps on the way to its elaboration were odd investigations concerning currency, moneylending, and the prices of various goods. The knowledge conveyed by Gresham's Law, the first crude formulations of the quantity theory of money — such as those of Bodin and Davanzati — and the Law of Gregory King mark the first dawn of the cognition that regularity of phenomena and inevitable necessity prevail in the field of action. The first comprehensive system of economic theory, that brilliant achievement of the classical economists, was essentially a theory of calculated action. It drew implicitly the borderline between what is to be considered economic and what extra-economic along the line which separates action calculated in monetary terms from other action. Starting from this basis the economists were bound to widen step

---

[10]Cf. [Johann Wolfgang von] Goethe, *Wilhelm Meister's Apprenticeship* (1795), Bk. 1, chap. 10.

by step the field of their studies until they finally developed a system dealing with all human choices, a general theory of action. ❯

CHAPTER 7

Profit and Loss

*PLANNING FOR FREEDOM
AND OTHER ESSAYS AND ADDRESSES*[1]

"PROFIT AND LOSS"

1. The Emergence of Profit and Loss

In the capitalist system of society's economic organization the entrepreneurs determine the course of production. In the performance of this function they are unconditionally and totally subject to the sovereignty of the buying public, the consumers. If they fail to produce in the cheapest and best possible way those commodities which the consumers are asking for most urgently, they suffer losses and are finally eliminated from their entrepreneurial position. Other men who know better how to serve the consumers replace them.

---

[1][Ludwig von Mises, *Planning for Freedom and Sixteen Other Essays and Addresses* (1952; South Holland, Ill.: Libertarian Press, 1980), chap. 9: "Profit and Loss," section A: "The Economic Nature of Profit and Loss," pp. 108–28.]

If all people were to anticipate correctly the future state of the market, the entrepreneurs would neither earn any profits nor suffer any losses. They would have to buy the complementary factors of production at prices which would, already at the instant of the purchase, fully reflect the future prices of the products. No room would be left either for profit or for loss. What makes profit emerge is the fact that the entrepreneur who judges the future prices of the products more correctly than other people do buys some or all of the factors of production at prices which, seen from the point of view of the future state of the market, are too low. Thus the total costs of production — including interest on the capital invested — lag behind the prices which the entrepreneur receives for the product. This difference is entrepreneurial profit.

On the other hand, the entrepreneur who misjudges the future prices of the products allows for the factors of production prices which, seen from the point of view of the future state of the market, are too high. His total costs of production exceed the prices at which he can sell the product. This difference is entrepreneurial loss.

Thus profit and loss are generated by success or failure in adjusting the course of production activities to the most urgent demand of the consumers. Once this adjustment is achieved, they disappear. The prices of the complementary factors of production reach a height at which total costs of production coincide with the price of the product. Profit and loss are ever-present features only on account of the fact that ceaseless change in the economic data makes again and again new discrepancies, and consequently the need for new adjustments originate.

2. The Distinction Between Profits and Other Proceeds

Many errors concerning the nature of profit and loss were caused by the practice of applying the term profit to the totality of the residual proceeds of an entrepreneur.

Interest on the capital employed is not a component part of profit. The dividends of a corporation are not profit. They are interest on the capital invested plus profit or minus loss.

The market equivalent of work performed by the entrepreneur in the conduct of the enterprise's affairs is entrepreneurial quasi-wages but not profit.

If the enterprise owns a factor on which it can earn monopoly prices, it makes a monopoly gain. If this enterprise is a corporation, such gains increase the dividend. Yet they are not profit proper.

Still more serious are the errors due to the confusion of entrepreneurial activity and technological innovation and improvement.

The maladjustment, the removal of which is the essential function of entrepreneurship, may often consist in the fact that new technological methods have not yet been utilized to the full extent to which they should be in order to bring about the best possible satisfaction of consumers' demand. But this is not necessarily always the case. Changes in the data, especially in consumers' demand, may require adjustments which have no reference at all to technological innovations and improvements. The entrepreneur who simply increases the production of an article by adding to the existing production facilities a new outfit without any change in the technological method of production is no less an entrepreneur than the man who inaugurates a new way of producing. The business of the entrepreneur is not merely to experiment with new technological methods, but to select from the multitude of technologically feasible methods those which are best fit to supply the public in the cheapest way with the things they are asking for most urgently. Whether a new technological procedure is or is not fit for this purpose is to be provisionally decided by the entrepreneur and will be finally decided by the conduct of the buying public. The question is not whether a new method is to be considered as a more "elegant" solution of a technological problem. It is whether, under the given state of economic data, it is the best possible method of supplying the consumers in the cheapest way.

The activities of the entrepreneur consist in making decisions. He determines for what purpose the factors of production should be employed. Any other acts which an entrepreneur may perform are merely accidental to his entrepreneurial function. It is this that laymen often fail to realize. They confuse the entrepreneurial activities with the conduct of the technological and administrative affairs of a plant. In their eyes not the stockholders, the promoters and speculators, but hired employees are the real entrepreneurs. The former are merely idle parasites who pocket the dividends.

Now nobody ever contended that one could produce without working. But neither is it possible to produce without capital goods, the previously produced factors of further production. These capital goods are scarce, i.e., they do not suffice for the production of all things which one would like to have produced. Hence the economic problem arises: to employ them in such a way that only those goods should be produced which are fit to satisfy the most urgent demands of the consumers. No good should remain unproduced on account of the fact that the factors required for its production were used — wasted — for the production of another good for which the demand of the public is less intense. To achieve this is, under capitalism, the function of entrepreneurship that determines the allocation of capital to the various branches of production. Under socialism it would be a function of the state, the social apparatus of coercion and oppression. The problem whether a socialist directorate, lacking any method of economic calculation, could fulfill this function is not to be dealt with in this essay.

There is a simple rule of thumb to tell entrepreneurs from non-entrepreneurs. The entrepreneurs are those on whom the incidence of losses on the capital employed falls. Amateur-economists may confuse profits with other kinds of intakes. But it is impossible to fail to recognize losses on the capital employed.

3. Non-Profit Conduct of Affairs

What has been called the democracy of the market manifests itself in the fact that profit-seeking business is unconditionally subject to the supremacy of the buying public.

Non-profit organizations are sovereign unto themselves. They are, within the limits drawn by the amount of capital at their disposal, in a position to defy the wishes of the public.

A special case is that of the conduct of government affairs, the administration of the social apparatus of coercion and oppression, viz., the police power. The objectives of government, the protection of the inviolability of the individuals' lives and health and of their efforts to improve the material conditions of their existence, are indispensable. They benefit all and are the necessary prerequisite of social cooperation and civilization. But they cannot be sold and bought in the way merchandise is sold and bought; they have therefore no price on the market. With regard to them there cannot be any economic calculation. The costs expended for their conduct cannot be confronted with a price received for the product. This state of affairs would make the officers entrusted with the administration of governmental activities irresponsible despots if they were not curbed by the budget system. Under this system the administrators are forced to comply with detailed instructions enjoined upon them by the sovereign, be it a self-appointed autocrat or the whole people acting through elected representatives. To the officers limited funds are assigned which they are bound to spend only for those purposes which the sovereign has ordered. Thus the management of public administration becomes bureaucratic, i.e., dependent on definite detailed rules and regulations.

Bureaucratic management is the only alternative available where there is no profit and loss management.

4. The Ballot of the Market

The consumers by their buying and abstention from buying elect the entrepreneurs in a daily repeated plebiscite as it were. They determine who should own and who not, and how much each owner should own.

As is the case with all acts of choosing a person — choosing holders of public office, employees, friends or a consort — the decision of the consumers is made on the ground of experience and thus necessarily always refers to the past. There is no experience of the future. The ballot of the market elevates those who in the immediate past have best served the consumers. However, the choice is not unalterable and can daily be corrected. The elected who disappoints the electorate is speedily reduced to the ranks.

Each ballot of the consumers adds only a little to the elected man's sphere of action. To reach the upper levels of entrepreneurship he needs a great number of votes, repeated again and again over a long period of time, a protracted series of successful strokes. He must stand every day a new trial, must submit anew to reelection as it were.

It is the same with his heirs. They can retain their eminent position only by receiving again and again confirmation on the part of the public. Their office is revocable. If they retain it, it is not on account of the deserts of their predecessor, but on account of their own ability to employ the capital for the best possible satisfaction of the consumers.

The entrepreneurs are neither perfect nor good in any metaphysical sense. They owe their position exclusively to the fact that they are better fit for the performance of the functions incumbent upon them than other people are. They earn profit not because they are clever in performing their tasks, but because they are more clever or less clumsy than other people are. They are not infallible and often blunder. But they are less liable to error and blunder less than other people do. Nobody has the right to take offense at the errors made by the entrepreneurs in the conduct of affairs and to stress the point that people would have been better supplied if the entrepreneurs had been more skillful and prescient. If the grumbler knew better, why did he not himself fill the gap and seize the opportunity to earn profits? It is easy indeed to display foresight after the event. In retrospect all fools become wise.

A popular chain of reasoning runs this way: The entrepreneur earns profit not only on account of the fact that other people were less successful than he in anticipating correctly the future state of the market. He himself contributed to the emergence of profit by not producing more of the article concerned; but for intentional restriction of output on his part, the supply of this article would have been so ample that the price would have dropped to a point at which no surplus of proceeds over costs of production expended would have emerged. This reasoning is at the bottom of the spurious doctrines of imperfect and monopolistic competition. It was resorted to a short time ago by the American Administration when it blamed the enterprises of the steel industry for the fact that the steel production capacity of the United States was not greater than it really was.

Certainly those engaged in the production of steel are not responsible for the fact that other people did not likewise enter this field of production. The reproach on the part of the authorities would have been sensible if they had conferred on the existing steel corporations the monopoly of steel production. But in the absence of such a privilege, the reprimand given to the operating mills is not more justified than it would be to censure the nation's poets and musicians for the fact that there are not more and better poets and musicians. If somebody is to blame for the fact that the number of people who joined the voluntary civilian defense organization is not larger, then it is not those who have already joined but only those who have not.

That the production of a commodity p is not larger than it really is, is due to the fact that the complementary factors of production required for an expansion were employed for the production of other commodities. To speak of an insufficiency of the supply of p is empty rhetoric if it does not indicate the various products m which were produced in too large quantities with the effect that their production appears now, i.e., after the event, as a waste of scarce factors of production. We may assume that the entrepreneurs who instead of producing additional quantities of p turned to the production of excessive amounts of m and consequently suffered losses did not intentionally make their mistake.

Neither did the producers of p intentionally restrict the production of p. Every entrepreneur's capital is limited; he employs it for those projects which, he expects, will, by filling the most urgent demand of the public, yield the highest profit.

An entrepreneur at whose disposal are 100 units of capital employs, for instance, 50 units for the production of p and 50 units for the production of q. If both lines are profitable, it is odd to blame him for not having employed more, e.g., 75 units, for the production of p. He could increase the production of p only by curtailing correspondingly the production of q. But with regard to q the same fault could be found by the grumblers. If one blames the entrepreneur for not having produced more p, one must blame him also for not having produced more q. This means: one blames the entrepreneur for the facts that there is a scarcity of the factors of production and that the earth is not a land of Cockaigne.

Perhaps the grumbler will object on the ground that he considers p a vital commodity, much more important than q, and that therefore the production of p should be expanded and that of q restricted. If this is really the meaning of his criticism, he is at variance with the valuations of the consumers. He throws off his mask and shows his dictatorial aspirations. Production should not be directed by the wishes of the public but by his own despotic discretion.

But if our entrepreneur's production of q involves a loss, it is obvious that his fault was poor foresight and not intentional.

Entrance into the ranks of the entrepreneurs in a market society, not sabotaged by the interference of government or other agencies resorting to violence, is open to everybody. Those who know how to take advantage of any business opportunity cropping up will always find the capital required. For the market is always full of capitalists anxious to find the most promising employment for their funds and in search of the ingenious newcomers, in partnership with whom they could execute the most remunerative projects.

People often failed to realize this inherent feature of capitalism because they did not grasp the meaning and the effects of capital scarcity. The task of the entrepreneur is to select from the multitude of technologically feasible projects those which will satisfy the most urgent of the not yet satisfied needs of the public. Those projects for the execution of which the capital supply does not suffice must not be carried out. The market is always crammed with visionaries who want to float such impracticable and unworkable schemes. It is these dreamers who always complain about the blindness of the capitalists who are too stupid to look after their own interests. Of course, the investors often err in the choice of their investments. But these faults consist precisely in the fact that they preferred an unsuitable project to another that would have satisfied more urgent needs of the buying public.

People often err very lamentably in estimating the work of the creative genius. Only a minority of men are appreciative enough to attach the right value to the achievement of poets, artists and thinkers. It may happen that the indifference of his contemporaries makes it impossible for a genius to accomplish what he would have accomplished if his fellow-men had displayed better judgment. The way in which the poet laureate and the philosopher *à la mode* are selected is certainly questionable.

But it is impermissible to question the free market's choice of the entrepreneurs. The consumers' preference for definite articles may be open to condemnation from the point of view of a philosopher's judgment. But judgments of value are necessarily always personal and subjective. The consumer chooses what, as he thinks, satisfies him best. Nobody is called upon to determine what could make another man happier or less unhappy. The popularity of motor cars, television sets and nylon stockings may be criticized from a "higher" point of view. But these are the things that people are asking for. They cast their ballots for those entrepreneurs who offer them this merchandise of the best quality at the cheapest price.

In choosing between various political parties and programs for the commonwealth's social and economic organization most people are uninformed and groping in the dark. The average voter lacks the insight to distinguish between policies suitable to attain the ends he is aiming at and those unsuitable. He is at a loss to examine the long chains of aprioristic reasoning which constitute the philosophy of a comprehensive social program. He may at best form some opinion about the short-run effects of the policies concerned. He is helpless in dealing with the long-run effects. The socialists and communists in principle often assert the infallibility of majority decisions. However, they belie their own words in criticizing parliamentary majorities rejecting their creed, and in denying to the people, under the one-party system, the opportunity to choose between different parties.

But in buying a commodity or abstaining from its purchase there is nothing else involved than the consumer's longing for the best possible satisfaction of his instantaneous wishes. The consumer does not — like the voter in political voting — choose between different means whose effects appear only later. He chooses between things which immediately provide satisfaction. His decision is final.

An entrepreneur earns profit by serving the consumers, the people, as they are and not as they should be according to the fancies of some grumbler or potential dictator.

5. The Social Function of Profit and Loss

Profits are never normal. They appear only where there is a maladjustment, a divergence between actual production and production as it should be in order to utilize the available material and mental resources for the best possible satisfaction of the wishes of the public. They are the prize of those who remove this maladjustment; they disappear as soon as the maladjustment is entirely removed. In the imaginary construction of an evenly rotating economy there are no profits. There the sum of the prices of the complementary factors of production, due allowance being made for time preference, coincides with the price of the product.

The greater the preceding maladjustments, the greater the profit earned by their removal. Maladjustments may sometimes be called excessive. But it is inappropriate to apply the epithet "excessive" to profits.

People arrive at the idea of excessive profits by confronting the profit earned with the capital employed in the enterprise and measuring the profit as a percentage of the capital. This method is suggested by the customary procedure applied in partnerships and corporations for the assignment of quotas of the total profit to the individual partners and shareholders. These men have contributed to a different extent to the realization of the project and share in the profits and losses according to the extent of their contribution.

But it is not the capital employed that creates profits and losses. Capital does not "beget profit" as Marx thought. The capital goods as such are dead things that in themselves do not accomplish anything. If they are utilized according to a good idea, profit results. If they are utilized according to a mistaken idea, no profit or losses result. It is the entrepreneurial decision that creates either profit or loss. It is mental acts, the mind of the entrepreneur, from which profits ultimately originate. Profit is a product of the mind, of success in anticipating the future state of the market. It is a spiritual and intellectual phenomenon.

The absurdity of condemning any profits as excessive can easily be shown. An enterprise with a capital of the amount c produced a definite quantity of p which it sold at prices that brought a surplus of proceeds over costs of s and consequently a profit of n per cent. If the entrepreneur had been less capable, he would have needed a capital of $2c$ for the production of the same quantity of p. For the sake of argument we may even neglect the fact that this would have necessarily increased costs of production as it would have doubled the interest on the capital employed, and we may assume that s would have remained unchanged. But at any rate s would have been confronted with $2c$ instead of c and thus the profit would have been only $n/2$ per cent of the capital employed. The "excessive" profit would have been reduced to a "fair" level. Why? Because the entrepreneur was less efficient and because his lack of efficiency deprived his fellow-men of all the advantages they could have got if an amount c of capital goods had been left available for the production of other merchandise.

In branding profits as excessive and penalizing the efficient entrepreneurs by discriminatory taxation, people are injuring themselves. Taxing profits is tantamount to taxing success in best serving the public. The only goal of all production activities is to employ the factors of production in such a way that they render the highest possible output. The smaller the input required for the production of an article becomes, the more of the scarce factors of production is left for the production of other articles. But the better an entrepreneur succeeds in this regard, the more is he vilified and the more is he soaked by taxation. Increasing costs per unit of output, that is, waste, is praised as a virtue.

The most amazing manifestation of this complete failure to grasp the task of production and the nature and functions of profit and loss is shown in the popular superstition that profit is an addendum to the costs of production, the height of which depends uniquely on the discretion of the seller. It is this belief that guides governments in controlling prices. It is the same belief that has prompted many governments to make arrangements with their contractors according to which the price to be paid for an article delivered is to equal costs of production expended by the seller increased by a definite percentage. The effect was that the purveyor got a surplus the higher, the less he succeeded in avoiding superfluous costs. Contracts of this type enhanced considerably the sums the United States had to expend in the two world wars. But the bureaucrats, first of all the professors of economics who served in the various war agencies, boasted of their clever handling of the matter.

All people, entrepreneurs as well as non-entrepreneurs, look askance upon any profits earned by other people. Envy is a common weakness of men. People are loath to acknowledge the fact that they themselves could have earned profits if they had displayed the same foresight and judgment the successful businessman did. Their resentment is the more violent the more they are subconsciously aware of this fact.

There would not be any profits but for the eagerness of the public to acquire the merchandise offered for sale by the successful entrepreneur. But the same people who scramble for these articles vilify the businessman and call his profit ill got.

The semantic expression of this enviousness is the distinction between earned and unearned income. It permeates the textbooks, the language of the laws and administrative procedure. Thus, for instance, the official Form 201 for the New York state income tax return calls "earnings" only the compensation received by employees and, by implication, all other income, also that resulting from the exercise of a profession, unearned income. Such is the terminology of a state whose governor is a Republican and whose state assembly has a Republican majority.

Public opinion condones profits only as far as they do not exceed the salary paid to an employee. All surplus is rejected as unfair. The objective of taxation is, under the ability-to-pay principle, to confiscate this surplus.

Now one of the main functions of profits is to shift the control of capital to those who know how to employ it in the best possible way for the satisfaction of the public. The more profits a man earns, the greater his wealth consequently becomes, the more influential does he become in the conduct of business affairs. Profit and loss are the instruments by means of which the consumers pass the direction of production activities into the hands of those who are best fit to serve them. Whatever is undertaken to curtail or to confiscate profits impairs this function. The result of such measures is to loosen the grip the consumers hold over the course of production. The economic machine becomes, from the point of view of the people, less efficient and less responsive.

The jealousy of the common man looks upon the profits of the entrepreneurs as if they were totally used for consumption. A part of them is, of course, consumed. But only those entrepreneurs attain wealth and influence in the realm of business who consume merely a fraction of their proceeds and plough back the much greater part into their enterprises. What makes small business develop into big business is not spending, but saving and capital accumulation.

6. Profit and Loss in the Progressing and in the Retrogressing Economy

We call a stationary economy an economy in which the per head quota of the income and wealth of the individuals remains unchanged. In such an economy what the consumers spend more for the purchase of some articles must be equal to what they spend less for other articles. The total amount of the profits earned by one part of the entrepreneurs equals the total amount of losses suffered by other entrepreneurs.

A surplus of the sum of all profits earned in the whole economy above the sum of all losses suffered emerges only in a progressing economy, that is, in an economy in which the per head quota of capital increases. This increment is an effect of saving that adds new capital goods to the quantity already previously available. The increase of capital available creates maladjustments insofar as it brings about a discrepancy between the actual state of production and that state which the additional capital makes possible. Thanks to the emergence of additional capital, certain projects which hitherto could not be executed become feasible. In directing the new capital into those channels in which it satisfies the most urgent among the previously not satisfied wants of the consumers, the entrepreneurs earn profits which are not counterbalanced by the losses of other entrepreneurs.

The enrichment which the additional capital generates goes only in part to those who have created it by saving. The rest goes, by raising the marginal productivity of labor and thereby wage rates, to the earners of wages and salaries and, by raising the prices of definite raw materials and foodstuffs, to the owners of land, and, finally, to the entrepreneurs who integrate this new capital into the most economical production processes. But while the gain of the wage earners and of the landowners is permanent, the profits of the entrepreneurs disappear once this integration is accomplished. Profits of the entrepreneurs are, as has been mentioned already, a permanent phenomenon only on account of the fact that maladjustments appear daily anew by the elimination of which profits are earned.

Let us for the sake of argument resort to the concept of national income as employed in popular economics. Then it is obvious that in a stationary economy no part of the national income goes into profits. Only in a progressing economy is there a surplus of total profits over total losses. The popular belief that profits are a deduction from the income of workers and consumers is entirely fallacious. If we want to apply the term deduction to the issue, we have to say that this surplus of profits over losses as well as the increments of the wage earners and the landowners is deducted from the gains of those whose saving brought about the additional capital. It is their saving that is the vehicle of economic improvement, that makes the employment of technological innovations possible and raises productivity and the standard of living. It is the entrepreneurs whose activity takes care of the most economical employment of the additional capital. As far as they themselves do not save, neither the workers nor the landowners contribute anything to the emergence of the circumstances which generate what is called economic progress and improvement. They are benefited by other peoples' saving that creates additional capital on the one hand and by the entrepreneurial action that directs this additional capital toward the satisfaction of the most urgent wants on the other hand.

A retrogressing economy is an economy in which the per head quota of capital invested is decreasing. In such an economy the total amount of losses incurred by entrepreneurs exceeds the total amount of profits earned by other entrepreneurs.

7. The Competition of Profit and Loss

The originary praxeological categories of profit and loss are psychic qualities and not reducible to any interpersonal description in quantitative terms. They are intensive magnitudes. The difference between the value of the end attained and that of the means applied for its attainment is profit if it is positive and loss if it is negative.

Where there are social division of efforts and cooperation as well as private ownership of the means of production, economic calculation in terms of monetary units becomes feasible and necessary. Profit and loss are computable as social phenomena. The psychic phenomena of profit and loss, from which they are ultimately derived, remain, of course, incalculable intensive magnitudes.

The fact that in the frame of the market economy entrepreneurial profit and loss are determined by arithmetical operations has misled many people. They fail to see that essential items that enter into this calculation are estimates emanating from the entrepreneur's specific understanding of the future state of the market. They think that these computations are open to examination and verification or alteration on the part of a disinterested expert. They ignore the fact that such computations are as a rule an inherent part of the entrepreneur's speculative anticipation of uncertain future conditions.

For the task of this essay it suffices to refer to one of the problems of cost accounting. One of the items of a bill of costs is the establishment of the difference between the price paid for the acquisition of what is commonly called durable production equipment and its present value. This present value is the money equivalent of the contribution this equipment will make to future earnings. There is no certainty about the future state of the market and about the height of these earnings. They can only be determined by a speculative anticipation on the part of the entrepreneur. It is preposterous to call in an expert and to substitute his arbitrary judgment for that of the entrepreneur. The expert is objective insofar as he is not affected by an error made. But the entrepreneur exposes his own material well-being.

Of course, the law determines magnitudes which it calls profit and loss. But these magnitudes are not identical with the economic concepts of profit and loss and must not be confused with them. If a tax law calls a magnitude profit, it in effect determines the height of taxes due. It calls this magnitude profit because it wants to justify its tax policy in the eyes of the public. It would be more correct for the legislator to omit the term profit and simply to speak of the basis for the computation of the tax due.

The tendency of the tax laws is to compute what they call profit as high as possible in order to increase immediate public revenue. But there are other laws which are committed to the tendency to restrict the magnitude they call profit. The commercial codes of many nations were and are guided by the endeavor to protect the rights of creditors. They aimed at restricting what they called profit in order to prevent the entrepreneur from withdrawing to the prejudice of creditors too much from the firm or corporation for his own benefit. It was these tendencies which were operative in the evolution of the commercial usages concerning the customary height of depreciation quotas.

There is no need today to dwell upon the problem of the falsification of economic calculation under inflationary conditions. All people begin to comprehend the phenomenon of illusory profits, the offshoot of the great inflations of our age.

Failure to grasp the effects of inflation upon the customary methods of computing profits originated the modern concept of *profiteering*. An entrepreneur is dubbed a profiteer if his profit and loss statement, calculated in terms of a currency subject to a rapidly progressing inflation, shows profits which other people deem "excessive." It has happened very often in many countries that the profit and loss statement of such a profiteer, when calculated in terms of a non-inflated or less inflated currency, showed not only no profit at all but considerable losses.

Even if we neglect for the sake of argument any reference to the phenomenon of merely inflation-induced illusory profits, it is obvious that the epithet profiteer is the expression of an arbitrary judgment of value. There is no other standard available for the distinction between profiteering and earning fair profits than that provided by the censor's personal envy and resentment. ...

2. The Consequences of the Abolition of Profit[2]

The idea to abolish profit for the advantage of the consumers involves that the entrepreneur should be forced to sell the products at prices not exceeding the costs of production expended. As such prices are, for all articles the sale of which would have brought profit, below the potential market price, the available supply is not sufficient to make it possible for all those who want to buy at these prices to acquire the articles. The market is paralyzed by the maximum price decree. It can no longer allocate the products to the consumers. A system of rationing must be adopted.

The suggestion to abolish the entrepreneur's profit for the benefit of the employees aims not at the abolition of profit. It aims at wresting it from the hands of the entrepreneur and handing it over to his employees.

Under such a scheme the incidence of losses incurred falls upon the entrepreneur, while profits go to the employees. It is probable that the effect of this arrangement would consist in making losses increase and profits dwindle. At any rate, a greater part of the profits would be consumed and less would be saved and ploughed back into the enterprise. No capital would be available for the establishment of new branches of production and for the transfer of capital from branches which — in compliance with the demand of the customers — should shrink into branches which should expand. For it would harm the interests of those employed in a definite enterprise or branch to restrict the capital employed in it and to transfer it into another enterprise or branch. If such a scheme had been adopted half a century ago, all the innovations accomplished in this period would have been rendered impossible. If, for the sake of argument, we were prepared

---

2[Ibid., section B: "The Condemnation of Profit," pp. 132–34.]

to neglect any reference to the problem of capital accumulation, we would still have to realize that giving profit to the employees must result in rigidity of the once attained state of production and preclude any adjustment, improvement and progress.

In fact, the scheme would transfer ownership of the capital invested into the hands of the employees. It would be tantamount to the establishment of syndicalism and would generate all the effects of syndicalism, a system which no author or reformer ever had the courage to advocate openly.

A third solution of the problem would be to confiscate all the profits earned by the entrepreneurs for the benefit of the state. A one hundred per cent tax on profits would accomplish this task. It would transform the entrepreneurs into irresponsible administrators of all plants and workshops. They would no longer be subject to the supremacy of the buying public. They would just be people who have the power to deal with production as it pleases them.

The policies of all contemporary governments which have not adopted outright socialism apply all these three schemes jointly. They confiscate by various measures of price control a part of the potential profits for the alleged benefit of the consumers. They support the labor unions in their endeavors to wrest, under the ability-to-pay principle of wage determination, a part of the profits from the entrepreneurs. And, last but not least, they are intent upon confiscating, by progressive income taxes, special taxes on corporation income, and "excess profits" taxes, an ever-increasing part of profits for public revenue. It can easily be seen that these policies if continued will very soon succeed in abolishing entrepreneurial profit altogether.

The joint effect of the application of these policies is already today rising chaos. The final effect will be the full realization of socialism by smoking out the entrepreneurs. Capitalism cannot survive the abolition of profit. It is profit and loss that force the capitalists to employ their capital for the best possible service to the consumers. It is profit and loss that make those people supreme in the conduct of business who are best fit to satisfy the public. If profit is abolished, chaos results. ◗

CHAPTER 8

The Nature of Money

MONEY, METHOD, AND THE MARKET PROCESS[1]

"THE POSITION OF MONEY AMONG ECONOMIC GOODS"

Karl Knies has recommended to replace the traditional division of economic goods into consumer goods and producer goods with a threefold classification: producer goods, consumer goods, and means of exchange.[2] Terminological questions of this kind, however, should be decided solely on the basis of their usefulness for furthering scientific work; definitions, concepts, and the taxonomy of phenomena have to prove their usefulness in the results of the research which makes use of them. When these criteria are applied to the classification and terminology suggested by Knies, it becomes apparent that they are extremely appropriate. Indeed, there is no theory of catallactics which does not make

---

[1][Ludwig von Mises, *Money, Method, and the Market Process: Essays by Ludwig von Mises*, ed. Richard M. Ebeling (1932; Norwell, Mass. and Auburn, Ala.: Kluwer Academic Publishers and Mises Institute, 1990), chap. 4, pp. 55–64.]

[2]Karl Knies, *Geld und Kredit*, 2d. (Berlin: Weidmann, 1885), pp. 20ff.

use of them. The theory of the value of money is always reserved for special treatment and separated for the explanation of the price formation of producer goods as well as consumer goods, although it is obviously part of a uniform theory of value and price. Even if we do not use the Kniesian terminology and classification consciously, in all significant discussions we act as if we had adopted them completely.

But it is also necessary to note that the special role of money among economic goods has, if anything, been over-emphasized. The problems of the determination of the purchasing power of money have mostly been treated as if they had nothing or very little in common with the problems of non-monetary exchange. This led to a special status of monetary theory and has been detrimental to the development of economic understanding. Even today, we continually encounter attempts to defend certain unjustified peculiarities of monetary theory.

Roscher's often quoted remark, "[that] the wrong definitions of money can be divided into two main groups: Those which think of it as more and those which think of it as less than the most saleable good,"[3] applies not only to the question of the definition of money. Even a number of those who consider the theory of money a part of catallactics go too far in emphasizing its special position. This branch of our science offers plenty of difficulties and it is not necessary to construct artificial problems; the existing ones provide enough challenge.

1. Monetary Services and the Value of Money

It is clear that the naive conception of the layman that things have value in themselves, i.e., intrinsic value, necessarily leads to a position which draws the dividing line between money and money substitutes differently from the position according to which the value of a thing is derived from its usefulness. Those who conceive of value as the result of properties inherent in things must necessarily make a distinction between physically valuable money and means of exchange which provide monetary services but are without material value. This approach inescapably leads to a contrasting of normal money with bad and abnormal money, which, in reality, is not money at all.

---

[3]Wilhelm Roscher, *Gundlagen der Nationalökonomie,* 25th ed. (Stuttgart and Berlin: J.G. Cotta'sche Buchhandlung Nachtfolger, 1918), p. 340.

Today there is no need to deal with this theory. For the modern subjective theory of value, the question has long been decided. No one would still openly defend a concept according to which the whole or a portion of value and price theory was based upon intrinsic exchange value, i.e., independent of the valuations of acting men. Once this is admitted, one has already adopted the fundamental principle of subjective value theory, i.e., the theory of marginal utility.

For prescientific economists — the predecessors of the Physiocrats and the Classical Economists — it was a significant problem to integrate the theory of the value of money with that of the value of other goods. Holding a crudely materialistic bias, they saw the source of value in the "objective" usefulness of goods. From this point of view, it is obvious why bread, which can still hunger, and cloth, which can protect from the cold, will have value. But from where does money, which can neither nourish people nor keep them warm, derive its value? Some responded that it arose "from convention" and others maintained that the value of money was "imaginary."

The error in this view was discovered early. John Law had put it most succinctly. If all value is derived from usefulness, then it must be true that the adoption of the precious metals as means of exchange must generate a value for it. If one wishes to call the value of the metal used as money, insofar as it is derived from its monetary services, imaginary, one has to regard all value as imaginary,

> Car aucune chose n'a de valeur que par l'usage auquel on l'applique, et a raison des demandes qu'on en fait, proportionellement a sa quantite.[4]

With these words, Law anticipated the subjective theory of value; he should not be denied the place he deserves in the history of our science. The importance of his accomplishment is not reduced by his inability to develop all the implications from his fundamental idea or that he got lost in the impenetrable thicket of error or, perhaps, even of guilt.

Researchers who came after him were also unable to make full use of the content of the clearly developed fundamental idea advanced by Law. In three respects we still encounter misconceptions.

---

[4]John Law, *Considerations sur le Numeraire et le Commerce* (Paris: Buisson, 1851), pp. 447ff. The passage translates as: The value of a thing is only in the use we make of it and the expectations we put into it, proportional to its quantity.

First, some writers categorically deny that the service provided by money can generate value. Unfortunately, they do not provide a justification why monetary services should be different from the services provided by food and clothing. The difficulty posed by "paper money" is circumvented by viewing "paper money" as a claim on genuine, i.e., "materially" valuable, metallic money. Fluctuations in the rate of exchange of "paper money" are explained by changes in the probability of payment in species. In view of the development of monetary theory during the last decades, I consider it superfluous to challenge this theory. I have attempted an empirical refutation and have not encountered adequate opposition.[5]

In a way, the second error is connected with the first: the denial of the possibility of there being a money whose "substance" only produces monetary services and nothing else. It is usually granted that monetary services can generate value, just as every other service, in general. Without reservation, we have to agree with Knies when he argues, "[that] gold and silver would have been as unsuitable for the purpose of performing the functions of money as any other commodity, if they had not previously — before their adoption for monetary services — served as economic goods for the satisfaction of human wants, a 'general' economic need, a need that was widely felt and persistent."[6] But Knies is in error when he continues, "it is not sufficient that this primary use of the precious metals has preceded their use for monetary services; it is necessary that this use continues, lest the pieces of precious metal lose their usefulness as money. ... If people ceased to use gold and silver to satisfy their desire for jewelry or ornamentation, etc., then the other use of the precious metals, their use as a means of exchange, would be eliminated, also."[7] Knies did not succeed in proving the validity of this assertion. It is by no means evident why an economic good, which performs the services of a commonly used means of exchange, should lose its ability to serve as money simply because its use for other purposes are gradually discontinued.

That the adoption of a good as a medium of exchange requires the goods' previous use or consumption for other purposes results from the fact that the specific demand for its services as a means of exchange presupposes an already existing objective exchange value. This objective exchange

---

[5]See [Ludwig von] Mises, *The Theory of Money and Credit*, pp. 146–53.

[6]Knies, *Geld und Kredit*, p. 322.

[7]Ibid., pp. 322 ff.

value, which subsequently will be modified by the demand for the good as a medium of exchange in addition to the demand for it in its "other" use, will be based exclusively upon its "other" use when it begins to be used as a means of exchange. But once an economic good has become money, then the specific demand for money can tie into an already existing exchange relationship between money and goods in the market, even if the demand for the money-good, as motivated by the other use, disappears.

Only very slowly and with difficulty has the human spirit freed itself from the crude materialistic mode of thought that has resulted in a prolonged resistance to the idea that the use of a good as a medium of exchange, like any other possible use for the good, generates a demand that establishes a price and is capable of changing that price. If the ability of a thing to satisfy a human need, as well as the *recognition* of this ability, are made the prerequisites for establishing the goods-quality of a thing,[8] then one comes close to distinguishing between "real" and "unreal" goods among the objects of economic action. As soon as the economist steps upon this ground, he loses his footing and slides unintentionally out of the domain of scientific objectivity; he enters the realm of ethical valuations, morality, and policy. There, he will compare the "objectively useful" things to those which are merely "thought to be useful." He will examine whether and to what extent the things which are thought to be useful (and therefore are treated accordingly) are indeed so in an "objective" sense. As soon as one has come this far, it is only logical to ask whether the usefulness provided by a good satisfies a genuine need or merely a fictitious one. This way of thinking may subsequently lead to the view that the value of precious metals (which serve "only" the desire for jewelry and do not satisfy a physiological need as, e.g., food and clothing undeniably do from a crude materialistic point-of-view) is entirely imaginary, a result of inappropriate social institutions and human vanity. On the other hand, the result can be that the value of precious metals is admitted as legitimate since even the desire for jewelry is "genuine" and "justified." The objective utility of the precious metals is not denied; rather, the general validity of the requirement for the services of money is questioned since society had once existed without money and, in any case, such a society is imaginable. It is an untenable assumption that the "goods-quality" requires a "natural" utility not limited to the particular requirements of any presupposed social order.

---

[8]This is even done by [Carl] Menger; see, his *Principles of Economics* (1871) (New York: New York University Press, 1981), pp. 52–53.

But an even cruder materialism was the view which wanted to deny monetary services their value-creating power because money in its performance of this service did not lose its ability to serve other purposes; in other words, because its "substance" was not used up in its services as money.

All of those who denied the ability of the services of money to determine its exchange value failed to recognize that the only decisive element is demand. The fact that there exists a demand for money — the most marketable (most saleable) good, for which the owners of other goods are prepared to exchange — means that the monetary function is capable of creating value.

2. Money Supply and Money Demand: The "Velocity of Circulation" of Money

The most disastrous of the unjustified deviations of monetary theory from the theory of direct exchange was the failure to base the analysis of the fundamental problem of the theory of the value of money on the relation between the stock of money and the demand for it by the individual economic units, or between the demand for money and the supply of money on the market. Rather, the analysis began with the objective usefulness of the monetary unit for the aggregate economy, which was expressed as the velocity of money relative to the money stock and which was then compared to the sum of transactions.

The old tendency, taken over from the Cameralists, to base the analysis of economic problems of the "national economy," on the "totality" and not on the acting human subjects, seems hard to eradicate. In spite of all the warnings of the subjective economists, we continue to observe relapses. It is one of the lesser evils that ethical judgments regarding phenomena are presented under the guise of scientific objectivity. For example, productive activity (i.e., activity carried out in an imagined socialist community led by the critic) is contrasted with profit-seeking activity (i.e., the activity of individuals in a society based on private property in the means of production). The former will be viewed as the "just" and the latter as the "unjust" mode of production. Much more important is the fact that if one thinks in terms of the totality of a society's economy, one can never understand the operation of a society based on private property in the means of production. It is erroneous to maintain that the necessity for the collectivist method can be proved by showing that actions of the individuals can only be understood within the framework of that individual's environment.

This is so because economic analysis does not depend on the psychological understanding of the motives of action, but only an understanding of action itself. It is unimportant for catallactics why bread, clothes, books, cannons or religious items are desired on the market; it is only important that a certain demand does exist. The mechanism of the market and, therefore, the laws of the capitalistic economy can only be grasped if one begins with the forces operating on the market. But on the market there are only individuals acting as buyers and sellers, never the "totality." In economic theory, the totality can be taken only in the sense of an economic collective where the means of production are entirely outside the orbit of exchange and, therefore, cannot be sold for money. Here there is neither room for price theory nor a theory of money. But if we wish to grasp the value problems of a collective economy, we can — ironically — only use that method of analysis which has come to be known as the "individualistic method."

The attempts to solve the problem of the value of money with reference to the aggregate economy, rather than through market factors, culminated in a tautological equation without any epistemological value. Only a theory which shows how subjective value judgments of buyers and sellers are influenced by changes in the different elements of the equation of exchange can legitimately be called a theory of the value of money.

Buyers and sellers on the market never concern themselves with the elements in the equation of exchange, of which two — velocity of circulation and the price level — do not even exist before market parties act and the other two — the quantity of money (in the whole economy) and the sum of transactions — could not possibly be known to the parties in the market. Only the importance which the various actors in the market attach, on the one hand, to the maintenance of a cash balance of a certain magnitude and, on the other hand, to the ownership of the various goods in question determines the formation of the exchange relationship between money and goods.

Connected with the concept of the velocity of circulation of money is the mental image that money generates its usefulness only at the instant of transaction, but is "idle" and useless at other times. A distinction between active and idle money is also made when one speaks of money hoarding and proceeds to a comparison between the "hoarded" quantity of money and the quantity of money that would be necessary to perform the monetary services; what distinguishes this from the previous case is the way in which the boundary between active and idle money is drawn. Both distinctions must be rejected.

The service of money is not confined to transactions. It fulfills its task not only at the moment it passes from one hand to the next. It also performs services when it rests in the till, as the most marketable good, in anticipation of its future use in trade as a generally used means of exchange. The demand for money of individuals, as well as the entire economy, is determined by the desire to maintain a cash balance and not by the aggregate of transactions to be carried out during a certain time period.[9]

It is an arbitrary procedure to divide the money stock into two parts: that which is designated to perform money services proper and that which serves as a money hoard. Of course, no damage will be done if, on the one hand, the demand for money is separated into a demand for hoarding and a demand to perform the monetary service proper. But a formula which portrays and solves only an arbitrarily delineated part of the problem must be rejected if we are able to show another one which will deal with and solve the whole problem in a uniform fashion.

3. Fluctuations in the Value of Money

One of the most peculiar phenomena in the history of monetary theory is the stubborn resistance encountered by the quantity theory. The imperfect formulation given to it by many of its advocates inevitably ran into opposition, with many — as, for example, Benjamin Anderson[10] — ascribing to the concept a meaning quite different from that commonly accepted. As a result, what they call the quantity theory, and oppose as such, is not the theory itself but only a variation of it. This is not particularly astonishing. But what is quite surprising is that an attempt was made and sometimes is still made today to deny that changes in the relation between money supply and money demand will modify the purchasing power of the monetary unit. It is not sufficient to base an explanation on the special interests of inflationists, statists and socialists, of civil servants and politicians who would be harmed by a spreading of knowledge concerning monetary policy. We will never arrive at an answer by following the path of the Historical-Realistic School, which (following the Marxian example) explains all ideas by ideologies. It had never been a problem to explain why a particular ideology

---

[9]Also see, Edwin Cannan, *Money,* 4th ed. (Westminster: P.S. King and Son, 1932), pp. 72ff.

[10]Benjamin Anderson, *The Value of Money* (New York: Macmillan, 1917).

is developed and advocated by certain classes who believe they can benefit from it directly (even if this direct advantage is more than outweighed by indirect disadvantages). What has to be explained, however, is rather how incorrect theories come about and find followers. How does it come about that many people, without justification, come to assume that a certain policy benefits either the entire society or many groups in that society?

However, the theory of money as such is not interested in these psychological aspects which explain the reasons for the unpopularity of the quantity theory and the tendency to adopt other explanations for the value of money. Rather, it is interested in the question: which elements of the doctrines opposing the quantity theory could be useful? Since it was equally inadmissible to deny the importance of changes in supply for the formation of exchange relations in the area of indirect exchange as it was in the area of direct exchange, one could oppose the quantity theory only by admitting its correctness in principle, but arguing that notwithstanding its general validity another principle would regularly eliminate its effectiveness. This attempt was made by the Banking School with its famous theory of hoarding, and its offshoot, the theory of the automatic adjustment of the circulation of money substitutes to the demand for money in the broader sense. Today, both theories are overthrown.

As is the case with so many theories, the advocates of the quantity theory have harmed it more than its enemies. We have already mentioned the inadequacy of those theories based on the concept of the velocity of circulation of money. It was not any less erroneous to interpret the quantity theory as saying that the changes in the quantity of money resulted in proportional changes in the prices of goods. It was overlooked that every change in the relationship between the supply of money and the demand for money would necessarily bring about a shift in the distribution of wealth and income and that, therefore, the prices of the different goods and services could not be effected proportionally and simultaneously.

Nowhere has the practice of working with formulas modeled after mechanics, instead of paying attention to the problem of the influence of market factors, taken a greater toll than in this case. Economists wanted to operate with the equation of exchange without noticing that the changes in the volume of money and the demand for money can come about in only one way: at first, the evaluations and with them the actions of only a few economic subjects will be influenced, with the resulting changes in the purchasing power of the monetary unit only spreading through the economy in a step-by-step pattern. In other words, the problem of changes in the value of money have been treated with the method of "statics," although there should never have been any doubt concerning the dynamic character of the problem.

4. Money Substitutes

The most difficult and most important special problem of monetary theory is that of money substitutes. The fact that money services can also be rendered by secure money claims redeemable on demand, presents considerable difficulties to the monetary theorists' attempt to define the supply of money and the demand for money. This difficulty could not be overcome as long as money substitutes were not clearly defined and separated into money certificates and fiduciary media, in order to treat the granting of credit through the issue of fiduciary media separately from all other types of credit.

Loans which do not involve the issuing of fiduciary media (i.e., bank notes or deposits which are not backed by money) is of no consequence for the volume of money. The demand for money can be influenced by lending as much as by any other institution of the economic order. Without knowledge of the data of the specific case, we cannot say in which direction this influence will operate. The widely-held opinion that an expansion of credit will always lead to a reduction in the demand for money is not correct. If many of the loan contracts provide for large repayments on certain days (for example, at the end of the month or quarter), the result will be an increase and not a reduction in the demand for money. The consequences of this increase in the demand for money will be expressed in prices, if it were not for clearing arrangements, on the one hand, and the practice of banks to increase the volume of fiduciary media on critical days, on the other hand.

Everything depends on the clear separation of money from money substitutes and within the category of money substitutes a distinction between money certificates (a money substitute fully backed by money) and the fiduciary medium (the money substitute not backed by money). But this is above all a question of terminological appropriateness. However, this question gains in importance in view of the difficulty and complexity of the problems. It is not — as so often is still maintained — the "granting of credit" but the issuing of fiduciary media which causes those effects on prices, wages, and interest rates, which banking theory has to deal with. It is, therefore, not inappropriate to refer to banking theory as the theory of fiduciary media. ▶

CHAPTER 9

Monetary Theory and Policy

SELECTED WRITINGS OF LUDWIG VON MISES[1]

"THE MAIN ISSUES IN PRESENT-DAY MONETARY CONTROVERSIES"

Introductory Remarks

This is not a systematic presentation of the problems of money and credit. Neither is it a complete exposition of the theories and doctrines dealt with. The aim of this paper is merely to enumerate certain topics that should not be neglected in a discussion of money and credit.

1. THE PURCHASING POWER CONTROVERSY

A. Is Money "Neutral"?

The older economists believed that — other things being equal — changes in the supply or demand of money make all commodity prices and wage

---

[1][In *Selected Writings of Ludwig von Mises*, vol. 3: *The Political Economy of International Reform and Reconstruction*, ed. Richard M. Ebeling (1946; Indianapolis, Ind.: Liberty Fund, 2000), pp. 119–32.]

rates simultaneously rise or fall in exact proportion to these changes. The price "level" changes, but the relations among the prices of individual commodities and services remain the same. Those mathematical economists whose theorizing culminates in the formulation of an equation of exchange still maintain this thesis.

Modern economic analysis rejects this assumption. The changes in the supply or demand of money do not affect all individuals at the same time and to the same extent. In the case of inflation, for instance, the additional quantity of money does not find its way at first into the pockets of all individuals, nor does every individual of those benefited first with the increase in the quantity of money get the same amount; and not every individual reacts to the same additional quantity in the same way. Consequently, the prices of various commodities and services rise neither at the same time nor to the same extent. The nonsimultaneous appearance and unevenness of the price changes brought about by increases in the quantity of money results in a shift of income and wealth from some groups of the population to other groups. Monetary fluctuations are not neutral, even apart from their repercussions on all contracts stipulating some form of deferred payments. Monetary changes are a source of economic and social change.

B. Are Changes in the Purchasing Power of Money Measurable?

Even if we were prepared to leave out consideration of the nonsimultaneous appearance and unevenness of the price changes brought about by changes in the supply of or demand for money, we must realize that the index-number method does not provide a faithful criterion for the measurement of changes in the purchasing power of the monetary unit. Economic conditions are not rigid; they are — also apart from any changes occurring in monetary matters — continuously changing. New commodities appear, old commodities disappear. The quality of the various commodities is subject to change. Tastes, wants, and desires are changing and with them the valuation of the various goods offered on the market. A motorcar of 1920 and a motorcar of 1940 are entirely different things. Twenty-five years ago, where were vitamins, refrigerators, and talking pictures? How different is the role played today in the average American household by canned food, rayon, and radio sets? How much do clothes and shoes change from one year to the next? Even standard foods like milk, butter, meat, and vegetables have in the last decades improved in quality to such an extent that it is impermissible to take them as equivalent with those marketed in the past. A method which tacitly assumes that nothing else had changed in the economic system than the available quantity of money is utterly illusory. The chairman of our committee has provided us with the results of an investigation undertaken in his corporation. According to this information, only a fraction of the products manufactured today are of the same kind as the goods manufactured a few years ago. This is a typical case, more or less representative for all American processing industries.

Besides, mathematics provides us with various methods for the computation of averages from a given set of figures. Each of these methods has, with regard to the problem in question, some merits and some defects. Each of them yields different results. As it is impossible to declare one of these methods as the only adequate one and to discard all the others as manifestly unsuitable, it is obvious that the index-number approach does not provide an indisputable and uncontested solution that could command general acceptance.

C. Is It Possible to Adjust Monetary Manipulation to a Nonarbitrary Standard?

The advocates of a manipulated currency pretend to aim at the stability of the monetary unit's purchasing power. They fail, however, to realize that in a changing economic world, the concept of a stable purchasing power is devoid of any real meaning.

There are three main objections to be raised against the proposals for a manipulated currency.

1. The various methods suggested for a measurement of changes in the monetary unit's purchasing power are arbitrary. Their results are contested by all those whose material interests would be hurt if they were to be used as a basis of monetary manipulation. In advocating the application of a certain index-number system, the results of which happen at the moment to provide a quasi-scientific justification of their particular interests, every pressure group and political party will always be in a position to cite the doctrine of some economists and statisticians. On the other hand, their adversaries will quote dissenting opinions of no less renowned experts. There is no means to free a tabular standard from the faults of purely arbitrary and party-ridden bias.

2. It is impossible to know beforehand to what extent and at what date a definite amount of inflation or deflation (an increase or a reduction

in the quantity of money and credit) will increase or reduce the prices of various commodities and services.

3. Apart from other deficiencies, the proposals for stabilization are faulty because they are based on the idea of money's neutrality. They all suggest methods to undo changes in the purchasing power of money that have already had their effects. If there has been an inflation, they wish to deflate to the same extent and vice versa. They do not realize that by this procedure, they do not undo the social consequences of monetary changes (that is, the shift of income and wealth from some groups to others), but simply add to them the social consequences of a new change. If a man has been hurt by being run over by an automobile, it is no remedy to let the car go back over him in the opposite direction.

D. The Case Against Flexible Foreign Exchange Parities

If the purchasing power of an individual country's domestic currency changes, while the other countries' currencies do not change at all or not to the same extent, foreign trade is affected. As a rule, foreign exchange rates are adjusted at an early stage of the inflationary or deflationary process to the new state of the domestic money supply, even while the prices of some commodities and services still lag behind and are not fully adjusted for a time. As long as the inflationary or deflationary changes have not exhausted all their effects on the structure of prices, the comparatively low or high state of some prices results — in the case of inflation — in encouraging exports and discouraging imports. From the viewpoint of mercantilist fallacies, a fall of the domestic monetary unit's purchasing power is, therefore, considered as a very fortunate occurrence.

What really happens is this: The country exports more than it did before, and it gets, as compensation for these increased exports, a smaller amount of foreign products. Exports are, as it were, subsidized and imports penalized to the burden of the natives. The inflation is, by and large, tantamount to a tax imposed upon the domestic consumers in order to cheapen the consumption of domestic products by foreigners.

Nowadays, currency devaluation is mostly advocated as a remedy against the rigidity of wage rates. People are afraid of fighting openly the inappropriate policies of labor unions. They resort to an indirect attack. They hope that currency devaluation will, notwithstanding the rise of domestic commodity prices, not raise money wage rates and thus reduce real wage rates. Lord Keynes believes that "a gradual and automatic lowering or real wages as a result of rising prices" would not be "strongly resisted" by labor. He does not see that wage rates are rigid only on the downside, not on the upside, too.

E. The Case for the Gold Standard

The gold standard is not perfect. No human institution is.

The main argument in favor of the gold standard is that it renders the formation of the monetary unit's purchasing power independent of arbitrary action on the part of governments, political parties, and pressure groups. It places a check upon inflationary policies, and is the only standard which can possibly become an international, a world standard.

2. THE CREDIT CONTROVERSY

A. The Banking Principle

Some economists of the "Banking School" ventured to deny flatly that changes in the quantity of money available can affect prices and interest rates. They introduced into their reasoning the idea of monetary "hoards" as a *deus ex machina*. The amount of money kept in these mythical hoards changes in such a way as to neutralize automatically changes in the quantity of money. A surplus of money is swallowed by these hoards; a deficiency of money is made good by a restriction of the amount hoarded. This fable has long since been abandoned.

The bulk of the older Banking School economists and all contemporary representatives of this school do not deny that an increase in the quantity of money (metallic money, government paper money, irredeemable bank notes, and deposit currency) must — other things being equal — result in a general rise of prices. The core of their teachings is: Short-term credits granted by commercial banks in the form of bank notes or deposits created for this purpose do not affect prices and interest rates, provided they do not exceed "the needs of trade." Such loans provide the debtor with the funds required for the production and the marketing of goods. They are self-liquidating. If the purchased raw materials are made up and sold, or if the buyer of products settles his balance, the loan is paid off, and the bank notes or deposits disappear again. An actual need has brought them into existence. With the cessation of this need, they go off the stage. The amount of credit of this type which the market can absorb is determined by the volume of production and business activity. It is beyond the power of the banks to alter this volume. No credit expansion is to be feared if the banks strictly abide by the rule to limit their lending to satisfy the demand of producers or merchants for short-term credit.

The reasoning of the Banking School misses the essential problem. It is obvious that no credit expansion takes place if the banks keep the total amount of their lending at the same level. But if a new bank enters the field or if an existing bank embarks upon the granting of additional credit above the amount of its previous credits, credit expansion results.

It is not true that the volume of credit that the banks are in a position to grant, if strictly abiding by the aforementioned rules, is independent of the bank's policy. The market is always in a position to absorb a surplus of credit supply. An increase in the supply of credit brings about a tendency toward a lowering of the rate of interest. With the lower rate of interest, many projects appear attractive that did not appear so with a higher rate. The lowering of the rate of interest encourages the expansion of precisely those business activities that — according to the banking doctrine — are viewed as proper instances for the granting of bank credit. Thus the credit expansion automatically increases the "needs of trade." It stimulates business activities because it cheapens the exchange of future purchasing power for present purchasing power. While the supply of capital goods remained unaltered, there is now a greater demand for them on the part of business. Prices must, consequently, rise. A boom starts.

B. The Currency Principle

The "Currency School" intended to provide an explanation of the recurrence of economic crises. Its proponents first observed that the root cause of the depression is the preceding boom and substituted for the study of crises the study of the trade cycle.

Their reasoning ran this way: If the British banks expanded credit while conditions in the other countries remained unchanged, British prices would begin to rise, and these on the world market would lag behind them. Consequently, there would be an excess of British imports over exports. As the surplus of imported goods could not be paid for by shipping bank notes, the importers would have to export gold. Hence, gold would be withdrawn from the banks; their reserves would dwindle. This "external drain" would force upon the banks a restriction of their lending activities. The artificial boom would come to an end and give way to a depression.

The main fault of the Currency School was that it dealt with bank notes only and did not realize that deposits subject to check are only technically different from bank notes, while their economic significance is equal to that of bank notes. This failure vitiated the British Bank Act of 1844. But it is easy to rectify this error by a simple extension of the theory.

C. Austrian Theory of the Trade Cycle

Currency theory did not consider the problem of the consequences of credit expansion within an isolated country or of a synchronous credit expansion in all countries. It did not enter into a discussion of the way in which the market and the whole apparatus of production and distribution react to credit expansion. This task was accomplished by Austrian theory.

The rate of interest established on a market not hampered by credit expansion, says Austrian theory, separates those business projects that can be carried out under the existing state of the supply of capital goods and consumers' preferences from those that cannot. With the lowering of the rate of interest brought about by credit expansion, the entrepreneurs embark upon projects for the realization of which the available amount of factors of production does not suffice.[2] They are deceived by the appearance of a nonexistent richness in the supply of material factors of production. They behave like a master builder who has overestimated the amount of building material available, has used up too much for the foundations and cannot complete his plan on account of a lack of material. Some of the new projects will never be finished; others, when finished, will be useless for lack of the plants producing the required complementary producers' goods; others will not yield an adequate return on the capital invested.

It is true, the banks (or the governments) are in a position to prolong the boom for some time by injecting progressively increasing quantities of bank notes and deposits into the market. But the artificially created prosperity cannot last forever. Sooner or later it must come to an end. There are only two alternatives:

---

[2]It is necessary to keep in mind that interest rates, in the course of a credit expansion, are — with the exception of the very beginning of the process — not always low when compared with the level which business used to consider as normal. But they are always low when measured by the standard that they would have to reach in a period of progressive inflation and its corollary, a general rise of prices, since they would have to include at such a time a compensation for the depreciation of the money unit going on in the period of the loan.

1. The banks do not stop and go on expanding credit at a progressively accelerated pace. But the spell of inflation breaks once the public has the conviction that the banks and the authorities are resolved not to stop. If no limit of the inflation and, consequently, of the general rise of prices can be foreseen, a general *Flucht in die Sachwerte* starts. Everybody becomes aware of the fact that to hold cash and deposit balances with the banks involves loss, and that he does better to buy and store goods. Everybody is anxious to get rid of money and to exchange it for some other commodities, no matter how much he must pay for them. Prices are running away, and the purchasing power of the monetary unit drops to zero. The national currency system cracks up.

2. As a rule, the banks do not let things go so far. They stop sooner by restricting credit. Then the day of reckoning dawns. The illusions disappear, people begin again to see reality as it is. The blunders committed in the boom become visible.

In every case, the slump is unavoidable. There is no means to make permanent a boom created by credit expansion and inflation.

The slump does not destroy values, but merely illusions. It does not make people poorer, it merely makes them aware of the impoverishment brought about by the malinvestment of the boom. It is not the depression that is an evil, but the preceding boom. The depression is the process of adjustment of economic conditions to the real market state-of-affairs. The fall in prices and wage rates is the preliminary step toward recovery and future real prosperity. He who wants to prevent the recurrence of economic crises must prevent the resumption of credit expansion.

In short, credit expansion is doomed to failure at any rate. There is no means to substitute fictitious capital created by monetary and credit manipulation for nonexisting capital goods. The only method to increase a nation's wealth and income is to save and to accumulate more real capital goods.

The rate of interest is a market phenomenon. In the long run, its height does not depend on the supply of money and credit. It is determined by the difference in the valuation of present goods and future goods. An increase in the supply of money and credit only temporarily lowers the rate of interest. In bringing about malinvestments, it finally results in a reduction in the amount of capital goods available. The economy has to pay heavily for the orgy of the artificial boom.

D. The Socialists' Rejection of Austrian Theory

In the eyes of the socialists, there is no such thing as a scarcity of material factors of production. Mankind could enjoy a life in plenty. Scarcity is merely an outcome of the capitalist mode of production and distribution. Economic crises are an evil inherent in capitalism. They have nothing at all to do with the endeavors to expand credit and to lower the rate of interest by bank manipulation.

The consistent supporters of these tenets blithely assert that interest is a purely monetary phenomenon that could not exist in a barter economy. (Such were, for instance, the ideas of Silvio Gesell, the minister of finance of the short-lived communist Soviet regime in Munich; Lord Keynes is full of praise for Gesell and calls him an "unduly neglected prophet.") Others are less outspoken and cling to a more cautious language. But a faulty doctrine does not gain anything from the fact that its advocates lack the courage to profess frankly all the conclusions which must be drawn logically from the principles they have espoused.

Whoever does not share the opinion that the rate of interest is only a monetary phenomenon is under the necessity to demonstrate the mechanism by which that level of the rate of interest, which corresponds to the whole structure of market conditions, reestablishes itself when temporarily disarranged by an easy money policy. The only solution of this problem provided up to now is that of the Austrian theory.

All those economists who want to explain the trade cycle as being caused by factors other than credit expansion must admit that no boom could arise if the amount of money and credit available were not increased. This implies that they cannot help admitting the fundamental thesis of Austrian theory.

E. Salvation Through Credit Manipulation

Consistent supporters of the doctrine that the rate of interest is a monetary phenomenon only and that there is no harm in the endeavors to abolish it by credit manipulation cannot help approving plans to establish the millennium by a reform of the monetary and banking system. The best known of the older projects of this type was that of the French socialist Proudhon, the man who coined the phrase "Property is theft."

Such ideas are very popular with many successful businessmen. The Belgian Ernest Solvay advocated "social compatabilism," a system hardly distinguished from that of Proudhon. More than twenty years ago, Thomas

A. Edison and Henry Ford suggested that the construction of roads be financed by the issue of additional paper money in order to avoid the payment of interest to the banks or the public.

The present-day variety of this old superstition is embodied in the doctrine of unbalanced budgets and government spending. As far as the government procures the means required for spending by taxing the citizens and by borrowing from the public, its spending curtails individuals' capacity to invest to the same extent that it increases that of the government. As far as the government borrows from the commercial banks or issues additional paper money, it embarks upon credit expansion and inflation.

In the early stages of every instance of credit expansion and inflation, there is always optimism. People do not want to pay attention to the warning voices of economists. They stubbornly insist that their present situation has nothing in common with the boom periods of the past, and that the theorists are wrong in predicting the breakdown of the "prosperity." But when the crisis comes, people become desperate; then they impeach not the faulty monetary and credit policies but the capitalist system as such.

3. The Foreign Exchange Controversy

A. Purchasing Power Parity Theory

The exchange ratio between two different kinds of money tends to correspond to the exchange ratio between each of them and commodities and services. It is usual to call this ratio the static or natural ratio. If this exchange ratio between two kinds of money is disturbed, people will start operations — buying and selling — in order to profit from existing discrepancies. These transactions tend to reestablish the natural ratio.

It does not make any difference whether the two kinds of money are used in the same country simultaneously (as was the case under the old parallel gold and silver standard) or whether each country uses one of them only. The natural rate of foreign exchange is determined by the purchasing power of each of the two kinds of money.

If a payment has to be effected in a distant place, the transaction is burdened with the cost of shipping the money. These costs are avoided if claims and debts of various people in the two places can be cleared. If complete settlement of all payments due can be achieved in this way, no actual shipping of money is required. If an unsettled surplus turns up, it must be settled by transfers from place to place.

The balance of payments does not determine the exchange ratio. It only determines how much of the cost of shipping money can be saved. If the two places or countries in question use the same precious metal as the standard, the balance of payments determines the fluctuations of the rate-of-exchange *within the rigid limits set by the cost of shipping money* (gold points or shipping points).

B. Balance of Payment Theory

Balance of payment theory asserts that foreign exchange rates are determined by the balance of payments.

This doctrine fails to realize that the amount of foreign trade depends on the structure of prices. If Atlantis imports from Thule a commodity A, for the unit of which two ducats must be paid in Atlantis, the commodity must be sold in Thule at the equivalent of two ducats in its local currency, that is, ten florins. If, without any inflation in Thule, the price of the ducat goes up to three florins, the importation of A must drop or stop altogether because at the price of fifteen florins, the demand for A in Thule shrinks or disappears altogether. A rise of foreign exchange rates that does not correspond to a rise of domestic prices (a fall of the purchasing power of the domestic currency) thus has the tendency to render the country's balance of payment "favorable,"

But, object the supporters of balance of payment theory, things are certainly different if A is a vital necessity for the citizens of Thule. Then, they must import A, no matter how much its price goes up. This, too, is a fallacy. If the individual citizens of Thule spend more florins for the purchase of A, they must, if there is no domestic inflation, restrict their buying of other commodities, either domestic or imported. In the first case, the prices of these domestic commodities drop, and they become available for export. In the second case, the amount of foreign exchange that would have been absorbed by the importation of other goods becomes available for the purchase of A.

If there is domestic inflation in Thule, then — and only then — a rise of the price of A (in florins) will not hinder the importation of A, as soon as the price of A (in Thule) is affected by the general rise of prices.

C. The Requirements of Foreign Exchange Stability

There is but one means to keep a nation's domestic currency at par with gold and the sound currency of other countries: to abstain from credit expansion and inflation. ◗

MONEY, METHOD, AND THE MARKET PROCESS[3]

"THE NON-NEUTRALITY OF MONEY"

The monetary economists of the sixteenth and seventeenth centuries succeeded in dissipating the popular fallacies concerning an alleged stability of money. The old error disappeared, but a new one originated, the illusion of money's neutrality.

Of course, classical economics did its best to dispose of these mistakes. David Hume, the founder of British Political Economy, and John Stuart Mill, the last in the line of classical economists, both dealt with the problem in a masterful way. And then we should not forget Cairnes, who in his essay on the course of depreciation paved the way for a realistic view of the issue involved.

Notwithstanding these first steps towards a more correct grasp, modern economists incorporated the fallacy of money neutrality into their system of thought.

The reasoning of modern marginal utility economics begins from the assumption of a state of pure barter. The mechanism of exchanging commodities and of market transactions is considered on the supposition that direct exchange alone prevails. The economists depict a purely hypothetical entity, a market without indirect exchange, without a medium of exchange, without money. There is no doubt that this method is the only possible one, that the elimination of money is necessary and that we cannot do without this concept of a market with direct exchange only. But we have to realize that it is a hypothetical concept which has no counterpart in reality. The

---

[3][Ludwig von Mises, *Money, Method, and the Market Process: Essays by Ludwig von Mises*, ed. Richard M. Ebeling (1938; Boston: Kluwer, 1990), pp. 69–77.]

actual market is necessarily a market of indirect exchange and money transactions.

From this assumption of a market without money, the fallacious idea of neutral money is derived. The economists were so fond of the tool which this hypothetical concept provided that they overestimated the extent of its applicability. They began to believe that all problems of catallactics could be analyzed by means of this fictitious concept. In accordance with this view, they considered that the main work of economic analysis was the study of direct exchange. After that all that was left was to introduce the monetary terms into the formulas obtained. But this was, in their eyes, a work of only secondary importance, because, as they were convinced, the introduction of monetary terms did not affect the substantial operation of the mechanism they had described. The functioning of the market mechanism as demonstrated by the concept of pure barter was not affected by monetary factors.

Of course, the economists knew that the exchange ratio between money and commodities was subject to change. But they believed — and this is exactly the essence of the fallacy of money's neutrality — that these changes in purchasing power were brought about simultaneously in the whole market and that they affected all commodities to the same extent. The most striking expression of this point of view is to be found in the current metaphorical use of the term "level" in reference to prices. Changes in the supply or demand of money — other things remaining equal — make all prices and wages simultaneously rise or fall. The purchasing power of the monetary unit changes, but the relations among the prices of individual commodities remain the same.

Of course, economists have developed for more than a hundred years the method of index numbers in order to measure changes in purchasing power in a world where the ratios between the prices of individual commodities are in continuous transition. But in doing so, they did not give up the assumption that the consequences of a change in the supply or demand of money were a proportional and simultaneous modification of prices. The method of index numbers was designed to provide them with a means of distinguishing between the consequences of those changes in prices which take their origins from the side of the demand for or supply of individual commodities and those which start from the side of demand for or supply of money.

The erroneous assumption of money neutrality is at the root of all endeavors to establish the formula of a so-called equation of exchange. In dealing with such an equation the mathematical economist assumes that something — one of the elements of the equation — changes and that corresponding changes in the other values must needs follow. These elements of the equation are not items in the individual's economy, but items of the whole economic system, and consequently the changes occur not with individuals but with the whole economic system, with the *Volkswirtschaft* as a whole. Proceeding thus, the economists apply unawares for the treatment of monetary problems a method radically different from the modern catallactic method. They revert to the old manner of reasoning which doomed to failure the work of older economists. In those early days philosophers dealt in their speculations with universal concepts, such as mankind and other generic notions. They asked: What is the value of gold or of iron, that is: value in general, for all times and for all people, and again gold or iron in general, all the gold or iron available or even not yet mined. They could not succeed in this way; they discovered only alleged autinomies which were insoluble for them.

All the successful achievements of modern economic theory have to be ascribed to the fact that we have learned to proceed in a different way. We realize that individuals acting in the market are never presented with the choice between all the gold existing and all the iron existing. They do not have to decide whether gold or iron is more useful for mankind as a whole, but they have to choose between two limited quantities both of which they cannot have together. They decide which of these two alternatives is more favorable for them under the conditions and at the moment when they make their decision. These acts of choice performed by individuals faced with alternatives are the ultimate causes of the exchange ratios established in the market. We have to direct our attention to these acts of choice and are not at all interested in the metaphysical and purely academic, nay, vain question of which commodity in general appears more useful in the eyes of a superhuman intelligence surveying earthly conditions from a transcendental point of view.

Monetary problems are economic problems and have to be dealt with in the same way as all other economic problems. The monetary economist does not have to deal with universal entities like volume of trade meaning total volume of trade or quantity of money meaning all the money current in the whole economic system. Still less can he make use of the nebulous metaphor "velocity of circulation." He has to realize that the demand for money arises from the preferences of individuals within a market society. Because everybody wishes to have a certain amount of cash, sometimes more, sometimes less, there is a demand for money.

Money is never simply in the economic system, in the *Volkswirtschaft*, money is never simply circulating. All the money available is always in the cash holdings of somebody. Every piece of money may one day — sometimes oftener, sometimes more seldom — pass from one man's cash holding to another man's. But at every moment it is owned by somebody and is a part of his cash holdings. The decisions of individuals regarding the magnitude of their cash holdings constitute the ultimate factor in the formation of purchasing power.

Changes in the quantity of money and in the demand for money for cash holding do not occur in the economic system as a whole if they do not occur in the households of individuals. These changes in the households of individuals never occur for all individuals at the same time and to the same degree and they therefore never affect their judgments of value to the same extent and at the same time. It is exactly the merit of Hume and Mill that they tried to construct a hypothetical case where the changes in the supply of money could affect all individuals in such a way that the prices of all commodities would rise or fall at the same time and in the same proportion. The failure of their attempts provided a negative proof, and modern economics has added to this the positive proof that the prices of different commodities are not influenced at the same time and to the same extent. The oversimple formula both of the old quantity theory and of contemporary mathematical economists according to which prices, that is all prices, rise or fall in the proportion of the increase or decrease in the quantity of money, is disproved.

To simplify and to shorten our analysis let us look at the case of inflation only. The additional quantity of money does not find its way at first into the pockets of all individuals; not every individual of those benefited first gets the same amount and not every individual reacts to the same additional quantity in the same way. Those first benefited — in the case of gold, the owners of the mines, in the case of government paper money, the treasury — now have greater cash holdings and they are now in a position to offer more money on the market for goods and services they wish to buy. The additional amount of money offered by them on the market makes prices and wages go up. But not all the prices and wages rise, and those which do rise do not rise to the same degree. If the additional money is spent for military purposes, the prices of some commodities only and the wages of only some kinds of labor rise, others remain unchanged or may even temporarily fall. They may fall because there are now on the market some groups of men whose incomes have not risen but who nevertheless are obliged to pay more for some commodities, namely for those asked by the men first benefited by the inflation. Thus, price changes which are the result of the inflation start with some commodities and services only, and are diffused more or less slowly from one group to the others. It takes time till the additional quantity of money has exhausted all its price changing possibilities. But even in the end the different commodities are not affected to the same extent. The process of progressive depreciation has changed the income and the wealth of the different social groups. As long as this depreciation is still going on, as long as the additional quantity of money has not yet exhausted all its possibilities of influencing prices, as long as there are still prices left unchanged at all or not yet changed to the extent that they will be, there are in the community some groups favored and some at a disadvantage. Those selling the commodities or services whose prices rise first are in a position to sell at the new higher prices and to buy what they want to buy at the old still unchanged prices. On the other hand, those who sell commodities or services whose prices remain for some time unchanged are selling at the old prices whereas they already have to buy at the new higher prices. The former are making a specific gain, they are profiteers, the latter are losing, they are the losers, out of whose pockets the extra-gains of the profiteers must come. As long as the inflation is in progress, there is a perpetual shift in income and wealth from some social group, to other social groups. When all price consequences of the inflation are consummated, a transfer of wealth between social groups has taken place. The result is that there is in the economic system a new dispersion of wealth and income and in this new social order the wants of individuals are satisfied to different relative degrees, than formerly. Prices in this new order cannot simply be a multiple of the previous prices.

The social consequences of a change in the purchasing power of money are twofold: first, as money is the standard of deferred payments, the relations between creditors and debtors is changed. Second, as the changes in purchasing power do not affect all prices and wages at the same moment and to the same extent, there is a shift of wealth and income between different social groups. It was one of the errors of all proposals to stabilize purchasing power that they did not take into account this second consequence. We may say that economic theory in general did not pay enough attention to this matter. As far as it did, it principally considered it only in reference to the reaction of a change in a country's currency on its foreign trade. But this is only a special application of a problem which has a much wider scope.

What is fundamental for economic theory is that there is no constant relation between changes in the quantity of money and in prices. Changes in the supply of money affect individual prices and wages in different ways. The metaphorical use of the term price level is misleading.

The erroneous opinion to the contrary was based on a consideration which may be represented thus: let us think of two absolutely independent systems of static equilibrium A and B. Both are in every respect alike except that to the total quantity of money (M) in A and to every individual cash holding (m) in A there correspond in B a total quantity of Mn and individual cash holdings mn. On these assumptions of course all the prices and wages in B are n times those in A. But they are exactly thus because these are our hypothetical assumptions. But nobody can devise a way by which the system A can be transformed into the system B. Of course it is unpermissible to operate with static equilibrium if we wish to approach a dynamic problem.

Setting aside all qualms about the use of the terms dynamic and static, I wish to say: money is necessarily a dynamic agent and it was a mistake to deal with monetary problems in a static way.

Of course there is no room left for money in a concept of static equilibrium. In forming the concept of a static society we assume that no changes are taking place. Everything is going on in the same old manner. Today is like yesterday and tomorrow will be like today. But under these conditions nobody needs a cash holding. Cash holding is necessary only when the individual does not know what situation he will have to face in an uncertain future. If everybody knows when and what he will have to buy, he does not need a private cash holding and can entrust all his money to the central bank as time deposits due on the dates and in the amounts necessary for his future payments. As everybody would proceed in the same way, the central bank does not need any reserves to meet its obligations. Of course, the total amount which it has to pay out to the buyers every day exactly balances the amount which it receives as deposits from the sellers. If we assume that in this world of static equilibrium once, before the equilibrium was attained, there was metallic currency only, let us say gold, we have to assume that with the gradual approach towards conditions of equilibrium the citizens deposited more and more of their gold and that the bank, which had no need for it, sold the gold to jewelers and others for industrial consumption. With the advent of equilibrium there is no more metallic money, there is in fact no more money at all, but an unsubstantial and immaterial clearing system, which cannot be considered as money in the ordinary sense. It is rather an unrealizable and even unthinkable system of accounting, a numeraire as some economists believed ideal money ought to be. This, if it could be called money, would be neutral money. But we should never forget, that the state of equilibrium is purely hypothetical, that this concept is nothing but a tool for our mental work. Not being able to make experiments, the social sciences have to forge such tools. But we must be very careful in their use. We have to be aware that the state of static equilibrium can never be attained in real life. Still more important is the fact, that in this hypothetical state the individual does not make choices, does not act and does not have to decide between incompatible alternatives. Life in this hypothetical state is therefore robbed of its essential element. In constructing this hypothetical state we want merely to understand the incentives of action, which always implies change, by conceiving conditions, in which no action takes place. But a changeless world would be a dead world. We do not just have to deal with death, but with life, action, and change. In a living world there is no room for neutrality of money.

Money, of course, is a dynamic factor and as such cannot be discussed in terms of static equilibrium.

Let me now briefly point out some of the major conclusions derived from an insight into the non-neutrality of money.

First we have to realize that the abandonment of the fallacious concept of neutral money destroys the last stronghold of the advocates of quantitative economics. For a very long time eminent economists have believed that it will be possible one day to replace qualitative economics by quantitative economics. What renders these hopes vain, is the fact, that in economic quantities we never have any constant ratios among magnitudes. What the economist discovers when he studies relations between demand and prices is not comparable with the work of the natural scientist who determines by experiments in his laboratory constant relations, e.g., the specific gravity of different substances. What the economist determines is of historical value only; he is in his statistical work a historian, but not an experimenter. The work of the late lamented Henry Schultz was economic history; what we learn from his research is what happened with some commodities in a limited period of the past in the United States and Canada. It tells us nothing about what happened with the same commodities elsewhere or in another period or what will happen in the future.

But there still has remained the belief that it is different with money. I may cite, for example, Professor Fisher's book on the *Purchasing Power of Money*, which is founded on the assumption that the purchasing power of the monetary unit changes in inverse proportion to the quantity of money. I think that this assumption is arbitrary and fallacious.

The second conclusion which we have to draw is the futility of all endeavors to make money stable in purchasing power. It is beyond the scope of my short address to explain the advantages of a sound money policy and the disadvantages of both inflation and deflation. But we should not confuse the political concept of sound money with the theoretical concept of stable money. I do not wish to discuss the inner contradictions of this stability concept. From the point of view of the present subject it is more important to emphasize that all proposals for stabilization, apart from other deficiencies, are based on the idea of money's neutrality. They all suggest methods to undo changes in purchasing power already effected if there has been an inflation they wish to deflate to the same extent and vice versa. They do not realize that by this procedure they do not undo the social consequences of the first change, but simply add to it the social consequences of a new change. If a man has been hurt by being run over by an automobile, it is no remedy to let the car go back over him in the opposition direction.

The popularity of all schemes for stabilization invites us to a philosophical consideration. It is a general weakness of the human mind to regard the state of rest and absence of change as more perfect than the state of motion. The absolute, that old phantom of misguided philosophical speculation, is still with us; its modern name is stability. But stability, e.g., absence of change, is, we have to repeat, absence of life.

The third conclusion which we may draw is the futility of the distinction between statics and dynamics and between short-run and long-run economics. The way in which we have to study monetary changes provides us with the best evidence that every correct economic consideration has to be dynamic and that static concepts are only instrumental. And at the same time we have to realize that all correct economic theorizing is a gradual progress from short-run to long-run effects.

But the most important value of the theory of money's dynamism is its use for the development of the monetary theory of the trade cycle. The old British Currency-Theory was already in a restricted sense a monetary explanation of the cycle. It studied the consequences of credit expansion on the assumption only that there is credit expansion in one country whereas in the rest of the world things are left unchanged. This seemed to be enough for the explanation of the business cycle in Great Britain in the first half of the nineteenth century. But the explanation of an external drain does not provide an answer to the question what may happen in a completely isolated country or in the case of a simultaneous credit expansion all over the world. But only the answer to this second question could be considered satisfactory under the conditions prevailing in the twentieth century. Only the answer to this second question is important, if we have to consider the proposals for eliminating the cyclical changes either by loosening the international ties of the national economy or by making credit expansion international in the way the Bretton Woods Agreements provide. It is the boast of the monetary theory of the trade cycle that it provides us with a satisfactory answer to these and to some other serious problems.

I do not wish to infringe more upon your time and so I wish only to add some remarks on the treatment of the problem by certain younger economists. I myself am not responsible for the term "neutral money." I have developed a theory of the changes in purchasing power and its social consequences. I have demonstrated that money acts as a dynamic agent and that the assumption that the changes in purchasing power are inversely proportional to the changes in the relation of demand for to the supply of money is fallacious. The term "neutral money" was coined by later authors. I do not wish to consider the question of whether it was a happy choice. But in any case I must protest against the belief that it has to be a goal of monetary policy to make money neutral and that it is the duty of the economists to determine a method of doing so. I wish to emphasize that in a living and changing world, in a world of action, there is no room left for a neutral money. Money is non-neutral or it does not exist. ▶

ECONOMIC POLICY:
THOUGHTS FOR TOMORROW AND TODAY[4]

"INFLATION"

If the supply of caviar were as plentiful as the supply of potatoes, the price of caviar — that is, the exchange ratio between caviar and money or caviar and other commodities — would change considerably. In that

---

[4][Ludwig von Mises, *Economic Policy: Thoughts for Tomorrow and Today* (1979; Washington, D.C.: Regnery Gateway, 2006), Lecture 4, pp. 55–73.]

case, one could obtain caviar at a much smaller sacrifice than is required today. Likewise, if the quantity of money is increased, the purchasing power of the monetary unit decreases, and the quantity of goods that can be obtained for one unit of this money decreases also.

When, in the sixteenth century, American resources of gold and silver were discovered and exploited, enormous quantities of the precious metals were transported to Europe. The result of this increase in the quantity of money was a general tendency toward an upward movement of prices in Europe. In the same way, today, when a government increases the quantity of paper money, the result is that the purchasing power of the monetary unit begins to drop, and so prices rise. This is called *inflation*.

Unfortunately, in the United States, as well as in other countries, some people prefer to attribute the cause of inflation not to an increase in the quantity of money but, rather, to the rise in prices.

However, there has never been any serious argument against the economic interpretation of the relationship between prices and the quantity of money, or the exchange ratio between money and other goods, commodities, and services. Under present day technological conditions there is nothing easier than to manufacture pieces of paper upon which certain monetary amounts are printed. In the United States, where all the notes are of the same size, it does not cost the government more to print a bill of a thousand dollars than it does to print a bill of one dollar. It is purely a printing procedure that requires the same quantity of paper and ink.

In the eighteenth century, when the first attempts were made to issue bank notes and to give these bank notes the quality of legal tender — that is, the right to be honored in exchange transactions in the same way that gold and silver pieces were honored — the governments and nations believed that bankers had some secret knowledge enabling them to produce wealth out of nothing. When the governments of the eighteenth century were in financial difficulties, they thought all they needed was a clever banker at the head of their financial management in order to get rid of all their difficulties.

Some years before the French Revolution, when the royalty of France was in financial trouble, the king of France sought out such a clever banker, and appointed him to a high position. This man was, in every regard, the opposite of the people who, up to that time, had ruled France. First of all he was not a Frenchman, he was a foreigner — a Swiss from Geneva, Jacques Necker. Secondly, he was not a member of the aristocracy, he was a simple commoner. And what counted even more in eighteenth century

France, he was not a Catholic, but a Protestant. And so Monsieur Necker, the father of the famous Madame de Staël, became the minister of finance, and everyone expected him to solve the financial problems of France. But in spite of the high degree of confidence Monsieur Necker enjoyed, the royal cashbox remained empty — Necker's greatest mistake having been his attempt to finance aid to the American colonists in their war of independence against England *without raising taxes.* That was certainly the wrong way to go about solving France's financial troubles.

There can be no secret way to the solution of the financial problems of a government; if it needs money, it has to obtain the money by taxing its citizens (or, under special conditions, by borrowing it from people who have the money). But many governments, we can even say *most* governments, think there is another method for getting the needed money; simply to print it.

If the government wants to do something beneficial — if, for example, it wants to build a hospital — the way to find the needed money for this project is to tax the citizens and build the hospital out of tax revenues. Then no special "price revolution" will occur, because when the government collects money for the construction of the hospital, the citizens — having paid the taxes — are forced to reduce their spending. The individual taxpayer is forced to restrict either his consumption, his investments or his savings. The government, appearing on the market as a buyer, *replaces* the individual citizen: the citizen buys less, but the government buys more. The government, of course, does not always buy the same goods which the citizens would have bought; but on the average there occurs no rise in prices due to the government's construction of a hospital.

I choose this example of a hospital precisely because people sometimes say: "It makes a difference whether the government uses its money for good or for bad purposes." I want to assume that the government *always* uses the money which it has printed for the best possible purposes-purposes with which we all agree. For it is not the *way* in which the money is spent, it is the way in which the government *obtains* this money that brings about those consequences we call inflation and which most people in the world today do not consider as beneficial.

For example, without inflating, the government could use the tax-collected money for hiring new employees or for raising the salaries of those who are already in government service. Then these people, whose salaries have been increased, are in a position to buy more. When the government taxes the citizens and uses this money to increase the salaries of government employees, the taxpayers have less to spend, but the government employees have more. Prices in general will not increase.

But if the government does not use tax money for this purpose, if it uses freshly printed money instead, it means that there will be people who now have more money while all other people still have as much as they had before. So those who received the newly-printed money will be competing with those people who were buyers before. And since there are no more commodities than there were previously, but there *is* more money on the market — and since there are now people who can buy more today than they could have bought yesterday — there will be an additional demand for that same quantity of goods. Therefore prices will tend to go up. This cannot be avoided, no matter what the use of this newly-issued money will be.

And more importantly, this tendency for prices to go up will develop step by step; it is not a general upward movement of what has been called the "price level." The metaphorical expression "price level" must never be used.

When people talk of a "price level," they have in mind the image of a level of a liquid which goes up or down according to the increase or decrease in its quantity, but which, like a liquid in a tank, always rises evenly. But with prices, there is no such thing as a "level." Prices do not change to the same extent at the same time. There are always prices that are changing more rapidly, rising or falling more rapidly than other prices. There is a reason for this.

Consider the case of the government employee who received the new money added to the money supply. People do not buy today precisely the same commodities and in the same quantities as they did yesterday. The additional money which the government has printed and introduced into the market is not used for the purchase of *all* commodities and services. It is used for the purchase of certain commodities, the prices of which will rise, while other commodities will still remain at the prices that prevailed before the new money was put on the market. Therefore, when inflation starts, different groups within the population are affected by this inflation in different ways. Those groups who get the new money first gain a temporary benefit.

When the government inflates in order to wage a war, it has to buy munitions, and the first to get the additional money are the munitions industries and the workers within these industries. These groups are now in a very favorable position. They have higher profits and higher wages;

their business is moving. Why? Because they were the first to receive the additional money. And having now more money at their disposal, they are buying. And they are buying from other people who are manufacturing and selling the commodities that these munitions makers want.

These other people form a second group. And this second group considers inflation to be very good for business. Why not? Isn't it wonderful to sell more? For example, the owner of a restaurant in the neighborhood of a munitions factory says: "It is really marvelous! The munitions workers have more money; there are many more of them now than before; they are all patronizing my restaurant; I am very happy about it." He does not see any reason to feel otherwise.

The situation is this: those people to whom the money comes first now have a higher income, and they can still buy many commodities and services at prices which correspond to the previous state of the market, to the condition that existed on the eve of inflation. Therefore, they are in a very favorable position. And thus inflation continues step by step, from one group of the population to another. And all those to whom the additional money comes at the early state of inflation are benefited because they are buying some things at prices still corresponding to the previous stage of the exchange ratio between money and commodities.

But there are other groups in the population to whom this additional money comes much, much later. These people are in an *unfavorable* position. Before the additional money comes to them they are forced to pay higher prices than they paid before for some — or for practically all — of the commodities they wanted to purchase, while their income has remained the same, or has not increased proportionately with prices.

Consider for instance a country like the United States during the Second World War; on the one hand, inflation at that time favored the munitions workers, the munitions industries, the manufacturers of guns, while on the other hand it worked against other groups of the population. And the ones who suffered the greatest disadvantages from inflation were the teachers and the ministers.

As you know, a minister is a very modest person who serves God and must not talk too much about money. Teachers, likewise, are dedicated persons who are supposed to think more about educating the young than about their salaries. Consequently, the teachers and ministers were among those who were most penalized by inflation, for the various schools and churches were the last to realize that they must raise salaries. When the church elders and the school corporations finally discovered that after all, one should also raise the salaries of those dedicated people, the earlier losses they had suffered still remained.

For a long time, they had to buy less than they did before, to cut down their consumption of better and more expensive foods, and to restrict their purchase of clothing — because prices had already adjusted upward, while their incomes, their salaries, had not yet been raised. (This situation has changed considerably today, at least for teachers.)

There are therefore always different groups in the population being affected differently by inflation. For some of them, inflation is not so bad; they even ask for a continuation of it because they are the first to profit from it. We will see, in the next lecture, how this unevenness in the consequences of inflation vitally affects the politics that lead toward inflation.

Under these changes brought about by inflation, we have groups who are favored and groups who are directly profiteering. I do not use the term "profiteering" as a reproach to these people, for if there is someone to blame, it is the government that established the inflation. And there are always people who *favor* inflation, because they realize what is going on sooner than other people do. Their special profits are due to the fact that there will necessarily be unevenness in the process of inflation.

The government may think that inflation — as a method of raising funds — is better than taxation, which is always unpopular and difficult. In many rich and great nations, legislators have often discussed, for months and months, the various forms of new taxes that were necessary because the parliament had decided to increase expenditures. Having discussed various methods of getting the money by taxation, they finally decided that perhaps it was better to do it by inflation.

But of course, the word "inflation" was not used. The politician in power who proceeds toward inflation does not announce: "I am proceeding toward inflation." The technical methods employed to achieve the inflation are so complicated that the average citizen does not realize inflation has begun.

One of the biggest inflations in history was in the German Reich after the First World War. The inflation was not so momentous *during* the war; it was the inflation *after* the war that brought about the catastrophe. The government did not say: "We are proceeding toward inflation." The government simply borrowed money very indirectly from the central bank. The government did not have to ask how the central bank would find and deliver the money. The central bank simply printed it.

Today the techniques for inflation are complicated by the fact that there is checkbook money. It involves another technique, but the result is the same. With the stroke of a pen, the government creates *fiat* money, thus increasing the quantity of money and credit. The government simply issues the order, and the fiat money is there.

The government does not care, at first, that some people will be losers, it does not care that prices will go up. The legislators say: "This is a wonderful system!" But this wonderful system has one fundamental weakness: it cannot last. If inflation could go on forever, there would be no point in telling governments they should not inflate. But the certain fact about inflation is that, sooner or later, it must come to an end. It is a policy that cannot last.

In the long run, inflation comes to an end with the breakdown of the currency; it comes to a catastrophe, to a situation like the one in Germany in 1923. On August 1, 1914, the value of the dollar was four marks and twenty pfennigs. Nine years and three months later, in November 1923, the dollar was pegged at 4.2 trillion marks. In other words, the mark was worth nothing. It no longer had *any* value.

Some years ago, a famous author, John Maynard Keynes, wrote: "In the long run we are all dead." This is certainly true, I am sorry to say. But the question is, how short or long will the short run be? In the eighteenth century there was a famous lady, Madame de Pompadour, who is credited with the dictum: "Après nous le déluge" ("After us will come the flood"). Madame de Pompadour was happy enough to die in the short run. But her successor in office, Madame du Barry, outlived the short run and was beheaded in the long run. For many people the "long run" quickly becomes the "short run" — and the longer inflation goes on the sooner the "short run."

How long can the short run last? How long can a central bank continue an inflation? Probably as long as people are convinced that the government, sooner or later, but certainly not too late, will stop printing money and thereby stop decreasing the value of each unit of money.

When people no longer believe this, when they realize that the government will go on and on without any intention of stopping, then they begin to understand that prices tomorrow will be higher than they are today. Then they begin buying at any price, causing prices to go up to such heights that the monetary system breaks down.

I refer to the case of Germany, which the whole world was watching. Many books have described the events of that time. (Although I am not a German, but an Austrian, I saw everything from the inside: in Austria, conditions were not very different from those in Germany; nor were they much different in many other European countries.) For several years, the German people believed that their inflation was just a temporary affair, that it would soon come to an end. They believed it for almost nine years, until the summer of 1923. Then, finally, they began to doubt. As the inflation continued, people thought it wiser to buy anything available, instead of keeping money in their pockets. Furthermore, they reasoned that one should not give loans of money, but on the contrary, that it was a very good idea to be a debtor. Thus inflation continued feeding on itself.

And it went on in Germany until exactly November 20, 1923. The masses had believed inflation money to be real money, but then they found out that conditions had changed. At the end of the German inflation, in the fall of 1923, the German factories paid their workers every morning in advance for the day. And the workingman who came to the factory with his wife, handed his wages — all the millions he got — over to her immediately. And the lady immediately went to a shop to buy something, no matter what. She realized what most people knew at that time- that overnight, from one day to another, the mark lost 50% of its purchasing power. Money, like chocolate in a hot oven, was melting in the pockets of the people. This last phase of German inflation did not last long; after a few days, the whole nightmare was over: the mark was valueless and a new currency had to be established.

Lord Keynes, the same man who said that in the long run we are all dead, was one of a long line of inflationist authors of the twentieth century. They all wrote against the gold standard. When Keynes attacked the gold standard, he called it a "barbarous relic." And most people today consider it ridiculous to speak of a return to the gold standard. In the United States, for instance, you are considered to be more or less a dreamer if you say: "Sooner or later, the United States will have to return to the gold standard."

Yet the gold standard has one tremendous virtue: the quantity of money under the gold standard is independent of the policies of governments and political parties. This is its advantage. It is a form of protection against spendthrift governments. If, under the gold standard, a government is asked to spend money for something new, the minister of finance can say: "And where do I get the money? Tell me, first, how I will find the money for this additional expenditure."

Under an inflationary system, nothing is simpler for the politicians to do than to order the government printing office to provide as much money as they need for their projects. Under a gold standard, sound government has a much better chance; its leaders can say to the people and to the politicians: "We can't do it unless we increase taxes."

But under inflationary conditions, people acquire the habit of looking upon the government as an institution with limitless means at its disposal: the state, the government, can do anything. If, for instance, the nation wants a new highway system, the government is expected to build it. But where will the government get the money?

One could say that in the United States today — and even in the past, under McKinley — the Republican party was more or less in favor of sound money and of the gold standard, and the Democratic party was in favor of inflation, of course not a paper inflation, but a silver inflation.

It was, however, a Democratic president of the United States, President Cleveland, who at the end of the 1880s vetoed a decision of Congress, to give a small sum — about $10,000 — to help a community that had suffered some disaster. And President Cleveland justified his veto by writing: "While it is the duty of the citizens to support the government, it is not the duty of the government to support the citizens." This is something which every statesman should write on the wall of his office to show to people who come asking for money.

I am rather embarrassed by the necessity to simplify these problems. There are so many complex problems in the monetary system, and I would not have written volumes about them if they were as simple as I am describing them here. But the fundamentals are precisely these: if you increase the quantity of money, you bring about the lowering of the purchasing power of the monetary unit. This is what people whose private affairs are unfavorably affected do not like. People who do not benefit from inflation are the ones who complain.

If inflation is bad and if people realize it, why has it become almost a way of life in all countries? Even some of the richest countries suffer from this disease. The United States today is certainly the richest country in the world, with the highest standard of living. But when you travel in the United States, you will discover that there is constant talk about inflation and about the necessity to stop it. But they only talk; they do not act.

To give you some facts: after the First World War, Great Britain returned to the prewar gold parity of the pound. That is, it revalued the pound upward. This increased the purchasing power of every worker's wages. In an unhampered market the nominal *money* wage would have fallen to compensate for this and the workers' *real* wage would not have suffered. We do not have time here to discuss the reasons for this. But the unions in Great Britain were unwilling to accept an adjustment of money wage rates downward as the purchasing power of the monetary unit rose. Therefore *real* wages were raised considerably by this monetary measure. This was a serious catastrophe for England, because Great Britain is a predominantly industrial country that has to import its raw materials, half-finished goods, and food stuffs in order to live, and has to export manufactured goods to pay for these imports. With the rise in the international value of the pound, the price of British goods rose on foreign markets and sales and exports declined. Great Britain had, in effect, priced itself out of the world market.

The unions could not be defeated. You know the power of a union today. It has the right, practically the privilege, to resort to violence. And a union order is, therefore, let us say, not less important than a government decree. The government decree is an order for the enforcement of which the enforcement apparatus of the government — the police — is ready. You must obey the government decree, otherwise you will have difficulties with the police.

Unfortunately, we have now, in almost all countries all over the world, a second power that is in a position to exercise force: the labor unions. The labor unions determine wages and then strike to enforce them in the same way in which the government might decree a minimum wage rate. I will not discuss the union question now; I shall deal with it later. I only want to establish that it is the union policy to raise wage rates *above* the level they would have on an unhampered market. As a result a considerable part of the potential labor force can be employed only by people or industries that are prepared to suffer losses. And, since businesses are not able to keep on suffering losses, they close their doors and people become unemployed. The setting of wage rates above the level they would have on the unhampered market always results in the unemployment of a considerable part of the potential labor force.

In Great Britain, the result of high wage rates enforced by the labor unions was lasting unemployment, prolonged year after year. Millions of workers were unemployed, production figures dropped. Even experts were perplexed. In this situation the British government made a move which it considered an indispensable, emergency measure: it *devalued* its currency.

The result was that the purchasing power of the money wages, upon which the unions had insisted, was no longer the same. The *real* wages, the commodity wages, were reduced. Now the worker could not buy as much as he had been able to buy before, even though the nominal wage rates remained the same. In this way, it was thought, *real* wage rates would return to free market levels and unemployment would disappear.

This measure — devaluation — was adopted by various other countries, by France, the Netherlands, and Belgium. One country even resorted twice to this measure within a period of one year and a half. That country was Czechoslovakia. It was a surreptitious method, let us say, to thwart the power of the unions. You could not call it a real success, however.

After a few years, the people, the workers, even the unions, began to understand what was going on. They came to realize that currency devaluation had reduced their real wages. The unions had the power to oppose this. In many countries they inserted a clause into wage contracts providing that money wages must go up automatically with an increase in prices. This is called *indexing*. The unions became index conscious. So, this method of reducing unemployment that the government of Great Britain started in 1931 — which was later adopted by almost all important governments — this method of "solving unemployment" no longer works today.

In 1936, in his *General Theory of Employment, Interest and Money*, Lord Keynes unfortunately elevated this method — the emergency measures of the period between 1929 and 1933 — to a *principle*, to a fundamental system of policy. And he justified it by saying, in effect: "Unemployment is bad. If you want unemployment to disappear you must inflate the currency."

He realized very well that wage rates can be too high for the market, that is, too high to make it profitable for an employer to increase his work force, thus too high from the point of view of the total working population, for with wage rates imposed by unions above the market only a part of those anxious to earn wages can obtain jobs.

And Keynes said, in effect: "Certainly mass unemployment prolonged year after year, is a very unsatisfactory condition." But instead of suggesting that wage rates could and should be adjusted to market conditions, he said, in effect: "If one devalues the currency and the workers are not clever enough to realize it, they will not offer resistance against a drop in real wage rates, as long as nominal wage rates remain the same." In other words, Lord Keynes was saying that if a man gets the same amount of sterling today as he got before the currency was devalued, he will not realize that he is, in fact, now getting less.

In old fashioned language, Keynes proposed cheating the workers. Instead of declaring openly that wage rates must be adjusted to the conditions of the market — because, if they are not, a part of the labor force will inevitably remain unemployed — he said, in effect: "Full employment can be reached only if you have inflation. Cheat the workers." The most interesting fact, however, is that when his *General Theory* was published, it was no longer possible to cheat, because people had already become index conscious. But the goal of full employment remained.

What does "full employment" mean? It has to do with the unhampered labor market, which is not manipulated by the unions or by the government. On this market, wage rates for every type of labor tend to reach a point at which everybody who wants a job can get one and every employer can hire as many workers as he needs. If there is an increase in the demand for labor, the wage rate will tend to be greater, and if fewer workers are needed, the wage rate will tend to fall.

The only method by which a "full employment" situation can be brought about is by the maintenance of an unhampered labor market. This is valid for every kind of labor and for every kind of commodity.

What does a businessman do who wants to sell a commodity for five dollars a unit? When he cannot sell it at that price, the technical business expression in the United States is, "the inventory does not move." But it *must* move. He cannot retain things because he must buy something new; fashions are changing. So he sells at a lower price. If he cannot sell the merchandise at five dollars, he must sell it at four. If he cannot sell it at four, he must sell it at three. There is no other choice as long as he stays in business. He may suffer losses, but these losses are due to the fact that his anticipation of the market for his product was wrong.

It is the same with the thousands and thousands of young people who come every day from the agricultural districts into the city trying to earn money. It happens so in every industrial nation. In the United States they come to town with the idea that they should get, say, a hundred dollars a week. This may be impossible. So if a man cannot get a job for a hundred dollars a week, he must try to get a job for ninety or eighty dollars, and perhaps even less. But if he were to say — as the unions do — "one hundred dollars a week or nothing," then he might have to remain unemployed. (Many do not mind being unemployed, because the government pays unemployment benefits — out of special taxes levied on the employers — which are sometimes nearly as high as the wages the man would receive if he were employed.)

Because a certain group of people believes that full employment can be attained only by inflation, inflation is accepted in the United States. But people are discussing the question: Should we have a sound currency with unemployment, or inflation with full employment? This is in fact a very vicious analysis.

To deal with this problem we must raise the question: How can one improve the condition of the workers and of all other groups of the population? The answer is: by maintaining an unhampered labor market and thus achieving full employment. Our dilemma is, shall the market determine wage rates or shall they be determined by union pressure and compulsion? The dilemma is *not* "shall we have inflation or unemployment?"

This mistaken analysis of the problem is argued in England, in European industrial countries and even in the United States. And some people say: "Now look, even the United States is inflating. Why should we not do it also."

To these people one should answer first of all: "One of the privileges of a rich man is that he can afford to be foolish much longer than a poor man." And this is the situation of the United States. The financial policy of the United States is very bad and is getting worse. Perhaps the United States can afford to be foolish a bit longer than some other countries.

The most important thing to remember is that inflation is not an act of God; inflation is not a catastrophe of the elements or a disease that comes like the plague. Inflation is a *policy* — a deliberate policy of people who resort to inflation because they consider it to be a lesser evil than unemployment. But the fact is that, in the not very long run, inflation does *not* cure unemployment.

Inflation is a policy. And a policy can be changed. Therefore, there is no reason to give in to inflation. If one regards inflation as an evil, then one has to stop inflating. One has to balance the budget of the government. Of course, public opinion must support this; the intellectuals must help the people to understand. Given the support of public opinion, it is certainly possible for the people's elected representatives to abandon the policy of inflation.

We must remember that, in the long run, we may all be dead and certainly will be dead. But we should arrange our earthly affairs, for the short run in which we have to live, in the best possible way. And one of the measures necessary for this purpose is to abandon inflationary policies. ❱

CHAPTER 10

Time and Time Preference

HUMAN ACTION[1]

1. Perspective in the Valuation of Time Periods

Acting man distinguishes the time before satisfaction of a want is attained and the time for which the satisfaction continues.

Action always aims at the removal of future uneasiness, be it only the future of the impending instant. Between the setting in of action and the attainment of the end sought there always elapses a fraction of time, viz., the maturing time in which the seed sown by the action grows to maturity. The most obvious example is provided by agriculture. Between the tilling of the soil and the ripening of the fruit there passes a considerable period of time. Another example is the improvement of the quality of wine by aging. In some cases, however, the maturing time is so short that ordinary speech may assert that the success appears instantly.

As far as action requires the employment of labor, it is concerned with the working time. The performance of every kind of labor absorbs time. In

---

[1][Ludwig von Mises, *Human Action* (1949; Auburn, Ala.: Mises Institute, 1998), chap. 18: "Action in the Passing of Time," pp. 476–85, 496–99.]

some cases the working time is so short that people say the performance requires no time at all.

Only in rare cases does a simple, indivisible and nonrepeated act suffice to attain the end aimed at. As a rule what separates the actor from the goal of his endeavors is more than one step only. He must make many steps. And every further step to be added to those previously made raises anew the question whether or not he should continue marching toward the goal once chosen. Most goals are so far away that only determined persistence leads to them. Persevering action, unflinchingly directed to the end sought, is needed in order to succeed. The total expenditure of time required, i.e., working time plus maturing time, may be called the period of production. The period of production is long in some cases and short in other cases. It is sometimes so short that it can be entirely neglected in practice.

The increment in want-satisfaction which the attainment of the end brings about is temporally limited. The result produced extends services only over a period of time which we may call the duration of serviceableness. The duration of serviceableness is shorter with some products and longer with other goods which are commonly called durable goods. Hence acting man must always take into account the period of production and the duration of serviceableness of the product. In estimating the disutility of a project considered he is not only concerned with the expenditure of material factors and labor required, but also with the period of production. In estimating the utility of the expected product he is concerned with the duration of its serviceableness. Of course, the more durable a product is, the greater is the amount of services it renders. But if these services are not cumulatively available on the same date, but extended piecemeal over a certain period of time, the time element, as will be shown, plays a particular role in their evaluation. It makes a difference whether n units of service are rendered on the same date or whether they are stretched over a period of n days in such a way that only one unit is available daily.

It is important to realize that the period of production as well as the duration of serviceableness are categories of human action and not concepts constructed by philosophers, economists, and historians as mental tools for their interpretation of events. They are essential elements present in every act of reasoning that precedes and directs action. It is necessary to stress this point because Böhm-Bawerk, to whom economics owes the discovery of the role played by the period of production, failed to comprehend the difference.

Acting man does not look at his condition with the eyes of a historian. He is not concerned with how the present situation originated. His only concern is to make the best use of the means available today for the best possible removal of future uneasiness. The past does not count for him. He has at his disposal a definite quantity of material factors of production. He does not ask whether these factors are nature-given or the product of production processes accomplished in the past. It does not matter for him how great a quantity of nature-given, i.e., original material factors of production and labor, was expended in their production and how much time these processes of production have absorbed. He values the available means exclusively from the aspect of the services they can render him in his endeavors to make future conditions more satisfactory. The period of production and the duration of serviceableness are for him categories in planning future action, not concepts of academic retrospection and historical research. They play a role in so far as the actor has to choose between periods of production of different length and between the production of more durable and less durable goods.

Action is not concerned with the future in general, but always with a definite and limited fraction of the future. This fraction is limited, on the one side, by the instant in which the action must take place. Where its other end lies depends on the actor's decision and choice. There are people who are concerned with only the impending instant. There are other people whose provident care stretches far beyond the prospective length of their own life. We may call the fraction of future time for which the actor in a definite action wants to provide in some way and to some extent, the period of provision. In the same way in which acting man chooses among various kinds of want-satisfaction within the same fraction of future time, he chooses also between want-satisfaction in the nearer and in the remoter future. Every choice implies also a choice of a period of provision. In making up his mind how to employ the various means available for the removal of uneasiness, man also determines implicitly the period of provision. In the market economy the demand of the consumers also determines the length of the period of provision.

There are various methods available for a lengthening of the period of provision:

1. The accumulation of larger stocks of consumers' goods destined for later consumption.
2. The production of goods which are more durable.

3. The production of goods requiring a longer period of production.

4. The choice of methods of production consuming more time for the production of goods which could also be produced within a shorter period of production.

The first two methods do not require any further comment. The third and the fourth methods must be scrutinized more closely.

It is one of the fundamental data of human life and action that the shortest processes of production, i.e., those with the shortest period of production, do not remove felt uneasiness entirely. If all those goods which these shortest processes can provide are produced, unsatisfied wants remain and incentive to further action is still present. As acting man prefers those processes which, other things being equal, produce the products in the shortest time,[2] only such processes are left for further action which consume more time. People embark upon these more time-consuming processes because they value the increment in satisfaction expected more highly than the disadvantage of waiting longer for their fruits. Böhm-Bawerk speaks of the higher productivity of roundabout ways of production requiring more time. It is more appropriate to speak of the higher physical productivity of production processes requiring more time. The higher productivity of these processes does not always consist in the fact that they produce — with the same quantity of factors of production expended — a greater quantity of products. More often it consists in the fact that they produce products which could not be produced at all in shorter periods of production. These processes are not roundabout processes. They are the shortest and quickest way to the goal chosen. If one wants to catch more fish, there is no other method available than the substitution of fishing with the aid of nets and canoes for fishing without the aid of this equipment. There is no better, shorter, and cheaper method for the production of aspirin known than that adopted by the chemical plants. If one disregards error and ignorance, there cannot be any doubt about the highest productivity and expediency of the processes chosen. If people had not considered them the most direct processes, viz., those leading by the shortest way to the end sought, they would not have adopted them.

The lengthening of the period of provision through the mere accumulation of stocks of consumers' goods is the outcome of the desire to

---

[2]Why man proceeds in this way, will be shown on the following pages.

provide in advance for a longer period of time. The same is valid for the production of goods the durability of which is greater in proportion to the greater expenditure of factors of production required.[3] But if temporally remoter goals are aimed at, lengthening of the period of production is a necessary corollary of the venture. The end sought cannot be attained in a shorter period of production.

The postponement of an act of consumption means that the individual prefers the satisfaction which later consumption will provide to the satisfaction which immediate consumption could provide. The choice of a longer period of production means that the actor values the product of the process bearing fruit only at a later date more highly than the products which a process consuming less time could provide. In such deliberations and the resulting choices the period of production appears as waiting time. It was the great contribution of Jevons and Böhm-Bawerk to have shown the role played by taking account of waiting time.

If acting men were not to pay heed to the length of the waiting time, they would never say that a goal is temporally so distant that one cannot consider aiming at it. Faced with the alternative of choosing between two processes of production which render different output with the same input, they would always prefer that process which renders the greater quantity of the same products or better products in the same quantity, even if this result could be attained only by lengthening the period of production. Increments in input which result in a more than proportionate increase in the products' duration of serviceableness would unconditionally be deemed advantageous. The fact that men do not act in this way evidences that they value fractions of time of the same length in a different way according as they are nearer or remoter from the instant of the actor's decision. Other things being equal, satisfaction in a nearer period of the future is preferred to satisfaction in a more distant period; disutility is seen in waiting.

This fact is already implied in the statement stressed in the opening of this chapter that man distinguishes the time before satisfaction is attained and the time for the duration of which there is satisfaction. If any role at all is played by the time element in human life, there cannot be any question of equal valuation of nearer and remoter periods of the same length. Such

---

[3]If the lengthening of durability were not at least proportionate to the increment in expenditure needed, it would be more advantageous to increase the quantity of units of a shorter durability.

an equal valuation would mean that people do not care whether success is attained sooner or later. It would be tantamount to a complete elimination of the time element from the process of valuation.

The mere fact that goods with a longer duration of serviceableness are valued more highly than those with a shorter duration does not yet in itself imply a consideration of time. A roof that can protect a house against the weather during a period of ten years is more valuable than a roof which renders this service only for a period of five years. The quantity of service rendered is different in both cases. But the question which we have to deal with is whether or not an actor in making his choices attaches to a service to be available in a later period of the future the same value he attaches to a service available at an earlier period.

2. Time Preference as an Essential Requisite of Action

The answer to this question is that acting man does not appraise time periods merely with regard to their dimension. His choices regarding the removal of future uneasiness are directed by the categories *sooner* and *later*. Time for man is not a homogeneous substance of which only length counts. It is not a *more* or a *less* in dimension. It is an irreversible flux the fractions of which appear in different perspective according to whether they are nearer to or remoter from the instant of valuation and decision. Satisfaction of a want in the nearer future is, other things being equal, preferred to that in the farther distant future. Present goods are more valuable than future goods.

Time preference is a categorial requisite of human action. No mode of action can be thought of in which satisfaction within a nearer period of the future is not — other things being equal — preferred to that in a later period. The very act of gratifying a desire implies that gratification at the present instant is preferred to that at a later instant. He who consumes a nonperishable good instead of postponing consumption for an indefinite later moment thereby reveals a higher valuation of present satisfaction as compared with later satisfaction. If he were not to prefer satisfaction in a nearer period of the future to that in a remoter period, he would never consume and so satisfy wants. He would always accumulate, he would never consume and enjoy. He would not consume today, but he would not consume tomorrow either, as the morrow would confront him with the same alternative.

Not only the first step toward want-satisfaction, but also any further step is guided by time preference. Once the desire *a* to which the scale of values assigns the rank 1 is satisfied, one must choose between the desire b to which the rank 2 is assigned and c that desire of tomorrow to which — in the absence of time preference — the rank 1 would have been assigned. If b is preferred to c, the choice clearly involves time preference. Purposive striving after want-satisfaction must needs be guided by a preference for satisfaction in the nearer future over that in a remoter future.

The conditions under which modern man of the capitalist West must act are different from those under which his primitive ancestors lived and acted. As a result of the providential care of our forebears we have at our disposal an ample stock of intermediate products (capital goods or produced factors of production) and of consumers' goods. Our activities are designed for a longer period of provision because we are the lucky heirs of a past which has lengthened, step by step, the period of provision and has bequeathed to us the means to expand the waiting period. In acting we are concerned with longer periods and are aiming at an even satisfaction in all parts of the period chosen as the period of provision. We are in a position to rely upon a continuing influx of consumers' goods and have at our disposal not only stocks of goods ready for consumption but also stocks of producers' goods out of which our continuous efforts again and again make new consumers' goods mature. In our dealing with this increasing "stream of income," says the superficial observer, there is no heed paid to any considerations related to a different valuation of present and of future goods. We synchronize, he asserts, and thus the time element loses any importance for the conduct of affairs. It is, therefore, pointless, he continues, in the interpretation of modern conditions to resort to time preference.

The fundamental error involved in this popular objection is caused, like so many other errors, by a lamentable misapprehension of the imaginary construction of the evenly rotating economy. In the frame of this imaginary construction no change occurs; there prevails an unvarying course of all affairs. In the evenly rotating economy consequently nothing is altered in the allocation of goods for the satisfaction of wants in nearer and in remoter periods of the future. No one plans any change because — according to our assumptions — the prevailing allocation best serves him and because he does not believe that any possible rearrangement could improve his condition. No one wants to increase his consumption in a nearer period of the future at the expense of his consumption in a more distant period or vice versa because the existing mode of allocation pleases him better than any other thinkable and feasible mode.

The praxeological distinction between capital and income is a category of thought based on a different valuation of want-satisfaction in various periods of the future. In the imaginary construction of the evenly rotating economy it is implied that the whole income but not more than the income is consumed and that therefore the capital remains unchanged. An equilibrium is reached in the allocation of goods for want-satisfaction in different periods of the future. It is permissible to describe this state of affairs by asserting that nobody wants to consume tomorrow's income today. We have precisely designed the imaginary construction of the evenly rotating economy in such a way as to make it fit just this condition. But it is necessary to realize that we can assert with the same apodictic assurance that, in the evenly rotating economy, nobody wants to have more of any commodity than he really has. These statements are true with regard to the evenly rotating economy because they are implied in our definition of this imaginary construction. They are nonsensical when asserted with regard to a changing economy which alone is real. As soon as a change in the data occurs, the individuals are faced anew with the necessity of choosing both between various modes of want-satisfaction in the same period and between want-satisfaction in different periods. An increment can be either employed for immediate consumption or invested for further production. No matter how the actors employ it, their choice must needs be the result of a weighing of the advantages expected from want-satisfaction in different periods of the future. In the world of reality, in the living and changing universe, each individual in each of his actions is forced to choose between satisfaction in various periods of time. Some people consume all that they earn, others consume a part of their capital, others save a part of their income.

Those contesting the universal validity of time preference fail to explain why a man does not always invest a sum of 100 dollars available today, although these 100 dollars would increase to 104 dollars within a year's time. It is obvious that this man in consuming this sum today is determined by a judgment of value which values 100 present dollars higher than 104 dollars available a year later. But even in case he chooses to invest these 100 dollars, the meaning is not that he prefers satisfaction in a later period to that of today. It means that he values 100 dollars today less than 104 dollars a year later. Every penny spent today is, precisely under the conditions of a capitalist economy in which institutions make it possible to invest even the smallest sums, a proof of the higher valuation of present satisfaction as compared with later satisfaction.

The theorem of time preference must be demonstrated in a double way. First for the case of plain saving in which people must choose between the immediate consumption of a quantity of goods and the later consumption of the same quantity. Second for the case of capitalist saving in which the choice is to be made between the immediate consumption of a quantity of goods and the later consumption either of a greater quantity or of goods which are fit to provide a satisfaction which — except for the difference in time — is valued more highly. The proof has been given for both cases. No other case is thinkable.

It is possible to search for a psychological understanding of the problem of time preference. Impatience and the pains caused by waiting are certainly psychological phenomena. One may approach their elucidation by referring to the temporal limitations of human life, to the individual's coming into existence, his growth and maturing, and his inevitable decay and passing away. There is in the course of man's life a right moment for everything as well as a *too early* and a *too late*. However, the praxeological problem is in no way related to psychological issues. We must conceive, not merely understand. We must conceive that a man who does not prefer satisfaction within a nearer period of the future to that in a remoter period would never achieve consumption and enjoyment at all.

Neither must the praxeological problem be confused with the physiological. He who wants to live to see the later day, must first of all care for the preservation of his life in the intermediate period. Survival and appeasement of vital needs are thus requirements for the satisfaction of any wants in the remoter future. This makes us understand why in all those situations in which bare life in the strict sense of the term is at stake satisfaction in the nearer future is preferred to that in later periods. But we are dealing with action as such, not with the motives directing its course. In the same way in which as economists we do not ask why albumin, carbohydrates, and fat are demanded by man, we do not inquire why the satisfaction of vital needs appears imperative and does not brook any delay. We must conceive that consumption and enjoyment of any kind presuppose a preference for present satisfaction to later satisfaction. The knowledge provided by this insight far exceeds the orbit for which the physiological facts concerned provide explanation. It refers to every kind of want-satisfaction, not only to the satisfaction of the vital necessities of mere survival.

It is important to stress this point because the term "supply of subsistence, available for advances of subsistence," as used by Böhm-Bawerk, can easily be misinterpreted. It is certainly one of the tasks of this stock to provide the means for a satisfaction of the bare necessities of life and thus to secure survival. But besides it must be large enough to satisfy, beyond the requirements of necessary maintenance for the waiting time, all those wants and desires which — apart from mere survival — are considered more urgent than the harvesting of the physically more abundant fruits of production processes consuming more time.

Böhm-Bawerk declared that every lengthening of the period of production depends on the condition that "a sufficient quantity of present goods is available to make it possible to overbridge the lengthened average interval between the starting of preparatory work and the harvesting of its product."[4] The expression "sufficient quantity" needs elucidation. It does not mean a quantity sufficient for necessary sustenance. The quantity in question must be large enough to secure the satisfaction of all those wants the satisfaction of which during the waiting time is considered more urgent than the advantages which a still greater lengthening of the period of production would provide. If the quantity in question were smaller, a shortening of the period of production would appear advantageous; the increase in the quantity of products or the improvement of their quality to be expected from the preservation of the longer period of production would no longer be considered a sufficient remuneration for the restriction of consumption enjoined during the waiting time. Whether or not the supply of subsistence is sufficient, does not depend on any physiological or other facts open to objective determination by the methods of technology and physiology. The metaphorical term "overbridge," suggesting a body of water the breadth of which poses to the bridge builder an objectively determined task, is misleading. The quantity in question is valued by men, and their subjective judgments decide whether or not it is sufficient.

Even in a hypothetical world in which nature provides every man with the means for the preservation of biological survival (in the strict sense of the term), in which the most important foodstuffs are not scarce and action is not concerned with the provision for bare life, the phenomenon of time preference would be present and direct all actions.[5] ▶

---

[4]Cf. [Eugen von] Böhm-Bawerk, *Kleinere Abhandlungen über Kapital und Zins*, vol. 2 in *Gesammelte Schriften*, ed. F.X. Weiss (Vienna, 1926), p. 169.

[5]Time preference is not specifically human. It is an inherent feature of the behavior of all living beings. The distinction of man consists in preference is not inexorable and the lengthening of the period of provision not merely instinctive as with certain animals that store food, but the result of a process of valuation.

CHAPTER 11

The Interest Rate

Human Action[1]

2. Originary Interest

Originary interest is the ratio of the value assigned to want-satisfaction in the immediate future and the value assigned to want-satisfaction in remoter periods of the future. It manifests itself in the market economy in the discount of future goods as against present goods. It is a ratio of commodity prices, not a price in itself. There prevails a tendency toward the equalization of this ratio for all commodities. In the imaginary construction of the evenly rotating economy the rate of originary interest is the same for all commodities.

Originary interest is not "the price paid for the services of capital."[2] The higher productivity of more time-consuming roundabout methods of production which is referred to by Böhm-Bawerk and by some later economists in the explanation of interest, does not explain the phenomenon.

---

[1][Ludwig von Mises, *Human Action* (1949; Auburn, Ala.: Mises Institute, 1998), chap. 19: "Interest," pp. 523–29.]

[2]This is the popular definition of interest as, for instance, given by [Richard T.] Ely, [Thomas] Adams, [Max]Lorenz, and [Allyn] Young, *Outlines of Economics* (3d ed. New York, 1920), p. 493.

It is, on the contrary, the phenomenon of originary interest that explains why less time-consuming methods of production are resorted to in spite of the fact that more time-consuming methods would render a higher output per unit of input. Moreover, the phenomenon of originary interest explains why pieces of usable land can be sold and bought at finite prices. If the future services which a piece of land can render were to be valued in the same way in which its present services are valued, no finite price would be high enough to impel its owner to sell it. Land could neither be bought nor sold against definite amounts of money, nor bartered against goods which can render only a finite number of services. Pieces of land would be bartered only against other pieces of land. A superstructure that can yield during a period of ten years an annual revenue of one hundred dollars would be priced (apart from the soil on which it is built) at the beginning of this period at one thousand dollars, at the beginning of the second year at nine hundred dollars, and so on.

Originary interest is not a price determined on the market by the interplay of the demand for and the supply of capital or capital goods. Its height does not depend on the extent of this demand and supply. It is rather the rate of originary interest that determines both the demand for and the supply of capital and capital goods. It determines how much of the available supply of goods is to be devoted to consumption in the immediate future and how much to provision for remoter periods of the future.

People do not save and accumulate capital because there is interest. Interest is neither the impetus to saving nor the reward or the compensation granted for abstaining from immediate consumption. It is the ratio in the mutual valuation of present goods as against future goods.

The loan market does not determine the rate of interest. It adjusts the rate of interest on loans to the rate of originary interest as manifested in the discount of future goods.

Originary interest is a category of human action. It is operative in any valuation of external things and can never disappear. If one day the state of affairs were to return which was actual at the close of the first millennium of the Christian era when people believed that the ultimate end of all earthly things was impending, men would stop providing for future secular wants. The factors of production would in their eyes become useless and worthless. The discount of future goods as against present goods would not vanish. It would, on the contrary, increase beyond all measure. On the other hand, the fading away of originary interest would mean that people do not care at all for want-satisfaction in nearer periods of the future. It would mean that they prefer to an apple available today, tomorrow, in one year or in ten years, two apples available in a thousand or ten thousand years.

We cannot even think of a world in which originary interest would not exist as an inexorable element in every kind of action. Whether there is or is not division of labor and social cooperation and whether society is organized on the basis of private or of public control of the means of production, originary interest is always present. In a socialist commonwealth its role would not differ from that in the market economy.

Böhm-Bawerk has once for all unmasked the fallacies of the naïve productivity explanations of interest, i.e., of the idea that interest is the expression of the physical productivity of factors of production. However, Böhm-Bawerk has himself based his own theory to some extent on the productivity approach. In referring in his explanation to the technological superiority of more time-consuming, roundabout processes of production, he avoids the crudity of the naïve productivity fallacies. But in fact he returns, although in a subtler form, to the productivity approach. Those later economists who, neglecting the time-preference idea, have stressed exclusively the productivity idea contained in Böhm-Bawerk's theory cannot help concluding that originary interest must disappear if men were one day to reach a state of affairs in which no further lengthening of the period of production could bring about a further increase in productivity.[3] This is, however, utterly wrong. Originary interest cannot disappear as long as there is scarcity and therefore action.

As long as the world is not transformed into a land of Cockaigne, men are faced with scarcity and must act and economize; they are forced to choose between satisfaction in nearer and in remoter periods of the future because neither for the former nor for the latter can full contentment be attained. Then a change in the employment of factors of production which withdraws such factors from their employment for want-satisfaction in the nearer future and devotes them to want-satisfaction in the remoter future must necessarily impair the state of satisfaction in the nearer future and improve it in the remoter future. If we were to assume that this is not the case, we should become embroiled in insoluble contradictions. We

---

[3]Cf. [Friedrich A.] Hayek, "The Mythology of Capital," *The Quarterly Journal of Economics* 50 (1936): 223ff. However Professor Hayek has since partly changed his point of view. (Cf. his article "Time-Preference and Productivity, a Reconsideration," *Economica* 12 [1945]: 22–25.) But the idea criticized in the text is still widely held by economists.

may at best think of a state of affairs in which technological knowledge and skill have reached a point beyond which no further progress is possible for mortal men. No new processes increasing the output per unit of input can henceforth be invented. But if we suppose that some factors of production are scarce, we must not assume that all processes which — apart from the time they absorb — are the most productive ones are fully utilized, and that no process rendering a smaller output per unit of input is resorted to merely because of the fact that it produces its final result sooner than other, physically more productive processes. Scarcity of factors of production means that we are in a position to draft plans for the improvement of our well-being the realization of which is unfeasible because of the insufficient quantity of the means available. It is precisely the unfeasibility of such desirable improvements that constitutes the element of scarcity. The reasoning of the modern supporters of the productivity approach is misled by the connotations of Böhm-Bawerk's term *roundabout methods of production* and the idea of technological improvement which it suggests. However, if there is scarcity, there must always be an unused technological opportunity to improve the state of well-being by a lengthening of the period of production in some branches of industry, regardless of whether or not the state of technological knowledge has changed. If the means are scarce, if the praxeological correlation of ends and means still exists, there are by logical necessity unsatisfied wants with regard both to nearer and to remoter periods of the future. There are always goods the procurement of which we must forego because the way that leads to their production is too long and would prevent us from satisfying more urgent needs. The fact that we do not provide more amply for the future is the outcome of a weighing of satisfaction in nearer periods of the future against satisfaction in remoter periods of the future. The ratio which is the outcome of this valuation is originary interest.

In such a world of perfect technological knowledge a promoter drafts a plan *A* according to which a hotel in picturesque, but not easily accessible, mountain districts and the roads leading to it should be built. In examining the practicability of this plan he discovers that the means available are not sufficient for its execution. Calculating the prospects of the profitability of the investment, he comes to the conclusion that the expected proceeds are not great enough to cover the costs of material and labor to be expended and interest on the capital to be invested. He renounces the execution of project *A* and embarks instead upon the realization of another plan, *B*. According to plan *B* the hotel is to be erected in a more easily accessible location which does not offer all the advantages of the picturesque landscape which plan *A* had selected, but in which it can be built either with lower costs of construction or finished in a shorter time. If no interest on the capital invested were to enter into the calculation, the illusion could arise that the state of the market data — supply of capital goods and the valuations of the public — allows for the execution of plan *A*. However, the realization of plan *A* would withdraw scarce factors of production from employments in which they could satisfy wants considered more urgent by the consumers. It would mean a manifest malinvestment, a squandering of the means available.

A lengthening of the period of production can increase the quantity of output per unit of input or produce goods which cannot be produced at all within a shorter period of production. But it is not true that the imputation of the value of this additional wealth to the capital goods required for the lengthening of the period of production generates interest. If one were to assume this, one would relapse into the crassest errors of the productivity approach, irrefutably exploded by Böhm-Bawerk. The contribution of the complementary factors of production to the result of the process is the reason for their being considered as valuable; it explains the prices paid for them and is fully taken into account in the determination of these prices. No residuum is left that is not accounted for and could explain interest.

It has been asserted that in the imaginary construction of the evenly rotating economy no interest would appear.[4] However, it can be shown that this assertion is incompatible with the assumptions on which the construction of the evenly rotating economy is based.

We begin with the distinction between two classes of saving: plain saving and capitalist saving. Plain saving is merely the piling up of consumers' goods for later consumption. Capitalist saving is the accumulation of goods which are designed for an improvement of production processes. The aim of plain saving is later consumption; it is merely postponement of consumption. Sooner or later the goods accumulated will be consumed and nothing will be left. The aim of capitalist saving is first an improvement in the productivity of effort. It accumulates capital goods which are employed for further production and are not merely reserves for later consumption. The boon derived from plain saving is later consumption of the stock not instantly consumed but accumulated for later use. The boon derived from capitalist saving is the increase of the quantity of goods

---

[4]Cf. [Joseph] Schumpeter, *The Theory of Economic Development*, trans. by R. Opie (Cambridge, 1934), pp. 34–46, 54.

produced or the production of goods which could not be produced at all without its aid. In constructing the image of an evenly rotating (static) economy, economists disregard the process of capital accumulation; the capital goods are given and remain, as, according to the underlying assumptions, no changes occur in the data. There is neither accumulation of new capital through saving, nor consumption of capital available through a surplus of consumption over income, i.e., current production minus the funds required for the maintenance of capital. It is now our task to demonstrate that these assumptions are incompatible with the idea that there is no interest.

There is no need to dwell, in this reasoning, upon plain saving. The objective of plain saving is to provide for a future in which the saver could possibly be less amply supplied than in the present. Yet, one of the fundamental assumptions characterizing the imaginary construction of the evenly rotating economy is that the future does not differ at all from the present, that the actors are fully aware of this fact and act accordingly. Hence, in the frame of this construction, no room is left for the phenomenon of plain saving.

It is different with the fruit of capitalist saving, the accumulated stock of capital goods. There is in the evenly rotating economy neither saving and accumulation of additional capital goods nor eating up of already existing capital goods. Both phenomena would amount to a change in the data and would thus disturb the even rotation of the imaginary system. Now, the magnitude of saving and capital accumulation in the past — i.e., in the period preceding the establishment of the evenly rotating economy — was adjusted to the height of the rate of interest. If — with the establishment of the conditions of the evenly rotating economy — the owners of the capital goods were no longer to receive any interest, the conditions which were operative in the allocation of the available stocks of goods to the satisfaction of wants in the various periods of the future would be upset. The altered state of affairs requires a new allocation. Also in the evenly rotating economy the difference in the valuation of want-satisfaction in various periods of the future cannot disappear. Also in the frame of this imaginary construction, people will assign a higher value to an apple available today as against an apple available in ten or a hundred years. If the capitalist no longer receives interest, the balance between satisfaction in nearer and remoter periods of the future is disarranged. The fact that a capitalist has maintained his capital at just 100,000 dollars was conditioned by the fact that 100,000 present dollars were equal to 105,000 dollars available twelve months later. These 5,000 dollars were in his eyes sufficient to outweigh the advantages to be expected from an instantaneous consumption of a part of this sum. If interest payments are eliminated, capital consumption ensues.

This is the essential deficiency of the static system as Schumpeter depicts it. It is not sufficient to assume that the capital equipment of such a system has been accumulated in the past, that it is now available to the extent of this previous accumulation and is henceforth unalterably maintained at this level. We must also assign in the frame of this imaginary system a role to the operation of forces which bring about such a maintenance. If one eliminates the capitalist's role as receiver of interest, one replaces it by the capitalist's role as consumer of capital. There is no longer any reason why the owner of capital goods should abstain from employing them for consumption. Under the assumptions implied in the imaginary construction of static conditions (the evenly rotating economy) there is no need to keep them in reserve for rainy days. But even if, inconsistently enough, we were to assume that a part of them is devoted to this purpose and therefore withheld from current consumption, at least that part of capital will be consumed which corresponds to the amount that capitalist saving exceeds plain saving.[5]

If there were no originary interest, capital goods would not be devoted to immediate consumption and capital would not be consumed. On the contrary, under such an unthinkable and unimaginable state of affairs there would be no consumption at all, but only saving, accumulation of capital, and investment. Not the impossible disappearance of originary interest, but the abolition of payment of interest to the owners of capital, would result in capital consumption. The capitalists would consume their capital goods and their capital precisely because there is originary interest and present want-satisfaction is preferred to later satisfaction.

Therefore there cannot be any question of abolishing interest by any institutions, laws, and devices of bank manipulation. He who wants to "abolish" interest will have to induce people to value an apple available in a hundred years no less than a present apple. What can be abolished by laws and decrees is merely the right of the capitalists to receive interest. But such laws would bring about capital consumption and would very soon throw mankind back into the original state of natural poverty. ◗

---

[5]Cf. [Lionel] Robbins, "On a Certain Ambiguity in the Conception of Stationary Equilibrium," *The Economic Journal* 40 (1930): 211ff.

CHAPTER 12

The Business Cycle

INTERVENTIONISM: AN ECONOMIC ANALYSIS[1]

2. Credit Expansion

It is a fundamental fact of human behavior that people value present goods higher than future goods. An apple available for immediate consumption is valued higher than an apple which will be available next year. And an apple which will be available in a year is in turn valued higher than an apple which will become available in five years. This difference in valuation appears in the market economy in the form of the discount, to which future goods are subject as compared to present goods. In money transactions this discount is called interest.

Interest therefore cannot be abolished. In order to do away with interest we would have to prevent people from valuing a house, which today is habitable, more highly than a house which will not be ready for use for ten

---

[1][Ludwig von Mises, *Interventionism: An Economic Analysis* (Irvington-on-Hudson, N.Y.: The Foundation for Economic Education, 1998), chap. 3, "Inflation and Credit Expansion," pp. 39–44.]

years. Interest is not peculiar to the capitalistic system only. In a socialist community too the fact will have to be considered that a loaf of bread which will not be ready for consumption for another year does not satisfy present hunger.

Interest does not have its origin in the meeting of supply and demand of money loans in the capital market. It is rather the function of the loan market, which in business terms is called the money market (for short-term credit) and the capital market (for long-term credit), to adjust the interest rates for loans transacted in money to the difference in the valuation of present and future goods. This difference in valuation is the real source of interest. An increase in the quantity of money, no matter how large, cannot in the long run influence the rate of interest.

No other economic law is less popular than this, that interest rates are, in the long run, independent of the quantity of money. Public opinion is reluctant to recognize interest as a market phenomenon. Interest is thought to be an evil, an obstacle to human welfare, and, therefore, it is demanded that it be eliminated or at least considerably reduced. And credit expansion is considered the proper means to bring about "easy money."

There is no doubt that credit expansion leads to a reduction of the interest rate in the short run. At the beginning, the additional supply of credit forces the interest rate for money loans below the point which it would have in an unmanipulated market. But it is equally clear that even the greatest expansion of credit cannot change the difference in the valuation of future and present goods. The interest rate must ultimately return to the point at which it corresponds to this difference in the valuation of goods. The description of this process of adjustment is the task of that part of economics which is called the theory of the business cycle.

At every constellation of prices, wages, and interest rates, there are projects which will not be carried out because a calculation of their profitability shows that there is no chance for the success of such undertakings. The businessman does not have the courage to start the enterprise because his calculations convince him that he will not gain, but will lose by it.

This unattractiveness of the project is not a consequence of money or credit conditions; it is due to the scarcity of economic goods and labor and to the fact that they have to be devoted to more urgent and therefore more attractive uses.

When the interest rate is artificially lowered by credit expansion the false impression is created that enterprises which previously had been regarded as unprofitable now become profitable. Easy money induces the entrepreneurs to embark upon businesses which they would not have undertaken at a higher interest rate. With the money borrowed from the banks they enter the market with additional demand and cause a rise in wages and in the prices of the means of production. This boom of course would have to collapse immediately in the absence of further credit expansion, because these price increases would make the new enterprises appear unprofitable again. But if the banks continue with the credit expansion this brake fails to work. The boom continues.

But the boom cannot continue indefinitely. There are two alternatives. Either the banks continue the credit expansion without restriction and thus cause constantly mounting price increases and an ever-growing orgy of speculation, which, as in all other cases of unlimited inflation, ends in a "crack-up boom" and in a collapse of the money and credit system.[2] Or the banks stop before this point is reached, voluntarily renounce further credit expansion and thus bring about the crisis. The depression follows in both instances.

It is obvious that a mere banking process like credit expansion cannot create more goods and wealth. What the credit expansion actually accomplishes is to introduce a source of error in the calculations of the entrepreneurs and thus causes them to misjudge business and investment projects. The entrepreneurs act as if more producers' goods were available than are actually at hand. They plan expansion of production on a scale for which the available quantities of producers' goods are not sufficient. These plans are bound to fail because of the deficiency in the available amount of producers' goods. The result is that there are plants which cannot be used because the complementary facilities are lacking; there are plants which cannot be completed; there are other plants again whose products cannot be sold because consumers desire other products more urgently which cannot be produced in sufficient quantities because the necessary productive facilities are not ready. The boom is not over-investment, it is *misdirected* investment.

It is frequently argued against this conclusion that it would hold true only if at the beginning of the credit expansion there were neither unused capacity nor unemployment. If there were unemployment and idle capac-

---

[2]As explained in this section on "Credit Expansion."

ity, things would be different, they claim. But these assumptions do not affect the argument.

The fact that a part of the productive capacity which cannot be diverted to other uses is unused is the consequence of errors of the past. Investments were made in the past under assumptions which proved to be incorrect; the market now demands something else than what can be produced by these facilities.[3] The accumulation of inventories is speculation. The owner does not want to sell the goods at the current market price because he hopes to realize a higher price at a future date. Unemployment of workers is also an aspect of speculation. The worker does not want to change his location or occupation, nor does he want to lower his wage demands because he hopes to find the work he prefers at the place he prefers and at higher wages. Both the owners of merchandise and the unemployed refuse to adjust themselves to market conditions because they hope for new data which would change market conditions to their advantage. Because they do not make the necessary adjustments the economic system cannot reach "equilibrium."

In the opinion of the advocates of credit expansion, what is necessary fully to utilize the unused capacity, to sell the supply at prices acceptable to the owners, and to enable the unemployed to find work at wages satisfactory to them is merely additional credit which such expansion could provide. This is the view which underlies all plans for "pump priming." It would be correct for the stocks of goods and for the unemployed under two conditions: (1) if the price rises caused by the additional quantity of money and credit would uniformly and simultaneously affect all other prices and wages, and (2) if the owners of the excessive supplies and the unemployed would not increase their prices and wage demands. This would cause the exchange ratios between these goods and services and other goods and services to change in the same way as they would have to be changed in the absence of credit expansion, by reducing the price and wage demands in order to find buyers and employers.

The course of the boom is not any different because, at its inception, there are unused productive capacity, unsold stocks of goods, and unemployed workers. We might assume, for instance, that we are dealing with copper mines, copper inventories, and copper miners. The price of copper is at a point at which a number of mines cannot profitably continue their

---

[3]In the absence of credit expansion there also may be plants which are not fully utilized. But they do not disturb the market any more than does the unused submarginal land.

production; their workers must remain idle if they do not want to change jobs; and the owners of the copper stocks can only sell part of it if they are unwilling to accept a lower price. What is needed to put the idle mines and miners back to work and to dispose of the copper supply without a price drop is an increase (p) in producers' goods in general, which would permit an expansion of overall production, so that an increase in the price, sales, and production of copper would follow. If this increase (p) does not occur, but the entrepreneurs are induced by credit expansion to act as if it had occurred, the effects on the copper market will first be the same as if p actually had appeared. But everything that has been said before of the effects of credit expansion develops in this case as well. The sole difference is that misdirected capital investment, as far as copper is concerned, does not necessitate the withdrawal of capital and labor from other branches of production, which under existing conditions are considered more important by the consumers. But this is only due to the fact that, as far as copper is concerned, the credit expansion boom impinges upon previously misdirected capital and labor which have not yet been adjusted by the normal corrective processes of the price mechanism.

The true meaning of the argument of unused capacity, unsold — or, as it is said inaccurately, unsalable — inventories, and idle labor, now becomes apparent. The beginning of every credit expansion encounters such remnants of older, misdirected capital investments and apparently "corrects" them. In actuality, it does nothing but disturb the workings of the adjustment process. The existence of unused means of production does not invalidate the conclusions of the monetary theory of the business cycle. The advocates of credit expansion are mistaken when they believe that, in view of unused means of production, the suppression of all possibilities of credit expansion would perpetuate the depression. The measures they propose would not perpetuate real prosperity, but would constantly interfere with the process of readjustment and the return of normal conditions.

It is impossible to explain the cyclical changes of business on any basis other than the theory which commonly is referred to as the monetary theory of the business cycle. Even those economists who refuse to recognize in the monetary theory the proper explanation of the business cycle have never attempted to deny the validity of its conclusions about the effects of credit expansion. In order to defend their theories about the business cycle, which differ from the monetary theory, they still have to admit that the upswing cannot occur without simultaneous credit expansion, and that the end of the credit expansion also marks the turning point of the cycle. The opponents of the monetary theory actually confine themselves to the assertion that the upswing of the cycle is not caused by credit expansion, but by other factors, and that the credit expansion, without which the upswing would be impossible, is not the result of a policy intended to lower the interest rate and to invite the execution of additional business plans, but that it is released somehow by conditions leading to the upswing without intervention by the banks or by the authorities.

It has been asserted that the credit expansion is released by the rise in the rate of interest through the failure of the banks to raise their interest rates in accordance with the rise in the "natural" rate.[4] This argument too misses the main point of the monetary theory of the cycle. Whether the credit expansion gets under way because the banks ease credit terms, or because they fail to stiffen the terms in accordance with changed market conditions, is of minor importance. Decisive only is the fact that there is credit expansion because there exist institutions which consider it their task to influence interest rates by the granting of additional credit.[5] Whoever believes that credit expansion is a necessary factor in the movement which forces the economy into the upswing, which must be followed by a crisis and depression, would have to admit that the surest means to achieve a cycle-proof economic system lies in preventing credit expansion. But despite the general agreement that measures should be taken to smooth the wave-like movements of the cycle, measures to prevent credit expansion do not receive consideration. Business cycle policy is given the task to perpetuate the upswing created by the credit expansion and yet to prevent the breakdown. Proposals to prevent credit expansion are refuted because supposedly they would perpetuate the depression. Nothing could be a more convincing proof of the theory which explains the business cycle as originating from interventions in favor of easy money than the obstinate refusal to abandon credit expansion.

---

[4][Fritz] Machlup, (*The Stock Market, Credit and Capital Formation*, London, 1940), p. 248, speaks of "passive inflationism."

[5]If a bank is unable to expand credit it cannot create an upswing even if it lowers its interest rate below the market rate. It would merely make a gift to its debtors. The conclusion to be drawn from the monetary theory of the cycle with regard to stabilizing measures is not the postulate that the banks should not lower the interest rate, but that they should not expand credit. This [Gottfried] Haberler (*Prosperity and Depression*, League of Nations, Geneva, 1939, pp. 65ff.) misunderstood and therefore his criticisms are untenable.

One would have to ignore all facts of recent economic history were one to deny that measures to lower rates are considered desirable and that credit expansion is regarded as the most reliable means to achieve this aim. The fact that the smooth functioning and the development and steady progress of the economy is over and over again disturbed by artificial booms and ensuing depressions is not a necessary characteristic of the market economy. It is rather the inevitable consequence of repeated interventions which intend to create easy money by credit expansion. ❯

THE CAUSES OF THE ECONOMIC CRISIS AND OTHER ESSAYS BEFORE AND AFTER THE GREAT DEPRESSION[6]

"MONETARY STABILIZATION AND CYCLICAL POLICY"

1. The Banking School Fallacy

If notes are issued by the banks, or if bank deposits subject to check or other claim are opened, in excess of the amount of money kept in the vaults as cover, the effect on prices is similar to that obtained by an increase in the quantity of money. Since these fiduciary media, as notes and bank deposits not backed by metal are called, render the service of money as safe and generally accepted, payable on demand monetary claims, they may be used as money in all transactions. On that account, they are genuine money substitutes. Since they are in excess of the given total quantity of money in the narrower sense, they represent an increase in the quantity of money in the broader sense.

The practical significance of these undisputed and indisputable conclusions in the formation of prices is denied by the Banking School with its contention that the issue of such fiduciary media is strictly limited by the

---

[6][Ludwig von Mises, "Monetary Stabilization and Cyclical Policy," in *The Causes of the Economic Crisis and Other Essays Before and After the Great Depression*, ed. Percy L. Greaves, Jr. (1928; Auburn, Ala.: Mises Institute, 2006), chap. 2: "Circulation Credit Theory," pp. 103–15.]

demand for money in the economy. The Banking School doctrine maintains that if fiduciary media are issued by the banks only to discount short-term commodity bills, then no more would come into circulation than were "needed" to liquidate the transactions. According to this doctrine, bank management could exert no influence on the volume of the commodity transactions activated. Purchases and sales from which short-term commodity bills originate would, by this very transaction, already have brought into existence paper credit which can be used, through further negotiation, for the exchange of goods and services. If the bank discounts the bill and, let us say, issues notes against it, that is, according to the Banking School, a neutral transaction as far as the market is concerned. Nothing more is involved than replacing one instrument which is technically less suitable for circulation, the bill of exchange, with a more suitable one, the note. Thus, according to this School, the effect of the issue of notes need not be to increase the quantity of money in circulation. If the bill of exchange is retired at maturity, then notes would flow back to the bank and new notes could enter circulation again only when new commodity bills came into being once more as a result of new business.

The weak link in this well-known line of reasoning lies in the assertion that the volume of transactions completed, as sales and purchases from which commodity bills can derive, is independent of the behavior of the banks. If the banks discount at a lower, rather than at a higher, interest rate, then more loans are made. Enterprises which are unprofitable at 5 percent, and hence are not undertaken, may be profitable at 4 percent. Therefore, by lowering the interest rate they charge, banks can intensify the demand for credit. Then, by satisfying this demand, they can increase the quantity of fiduciary media in circulation. Once this is recognized, the Banking Theory's only argument, that prices are not influenced by the issue of fiduciary media, collapses.

One must be careful not to speak simply of the effects of credit in general on prices, but to specify clearly the effects of "increased credit" or "credit expansion." A sharp distinction must be made between (1) credit which a bank grants by lending its own funds or funds placed at its disposal by depositors, which we call "commodity credit," and (2) that which is granted by the creation of fiduciary media, i.e., notes and deposits not covered by money, which we call "circulation credit." It is only through the granting of circulation credit that the prices of all commodities and services are directly affected.

If the banks grant circulation credit by discounting a three month bill of exchange, they exchange a future good — a claim payable in three months — for a present good that they produce out of nothing. It is not correct, therefore, to maintain that it is immaterial whether the bill of exchange is discounted by a bank of issue or whether it remains in circulation, passing from hand to hand. Whoever takes the bill of exchange in trade can do so only if he has the resources. But the bank of issue discounts by creating the necessary funds and putting them into circulation. To be sure, the fiduciary media flow back again to the bank at expiration of the note. If the bank does not give the fiduciary media out again, precisely the same consequences appear as those which come from a decrease in the quantity of money in its broader sense.

2. Early Effects of Credit Expansion

The fact that in the regular course of banking operations the banks issue fiduciary media only as loans to producers and merchants means that they are not used directly for purposes of consumption. Rather, these fiduciary media are used first of all for production, that is to buy factors of production and pay wages. The first prices to rise, therefore, as a result of an increase of the quantity of money in the broader sense, caused by the issue of such fiduciary media, are those of raw materials, semimanufactured products, other goods of higher orders, and wage rates. Only later do the prices of goods of the first order [consumers' goods] follow. Changes in the purchasing power of a monetary unit, brought about by the issue of fiduciary media, follow a different path and have different accompanying· social side effects from those produced by a new discovery of precious metals or by the issue of paper money. Still in the last analysis, the effect on prices is similar in both instances.

Changes in the purchasing power of the monetary unit do not directly affect the height of the rate of interest. An indirect influence on the height of the interest rate can take place as a result of the fact that shifts in wealth and income relationships, appearing as a result of the change in the value of the monetary unit, influence savings and, thus, the accumulation of capital. If a depreciation of the monetary unit favors the wealthier members of society at the expense of the poorer, its effect will probably be an increase in capital accumulation since the well-to-do are the more important savers. The more they put aside, the more their incomes and fortunes will grow.

If monetary depreciation is brought about by an issue of fiduciary media, and if wage rates do not promptly follow the increase in commodity prices, then the decline in purchasing power will certainly make this effect much more severe. This is the "forced savings" which is quite properly stressed in recent literature.[7] However, three things should not be forgotten. First, it always depends upon the data of the particular case whether shifts of wealth and income, which lead to increased saving, are actually set in motion. Second, under circumstances which need not be discussed further here, by falsifying economic calculation, based on monetary bookkeeping calculations, a very substantial devaluation can lead to capital consumption (such a situation did take place temporarily during the recent inflationary period). Third, as advocates of inflation through credit expansion should observe, any legislative measure which transfers resources to the "rich" at the expense of the "poor" will also foster capital formation.

Eventually, the issue of fiduciary media in such manner can also lead to increased capital accumulation within narrow limits and, hence, to a further reduction of the interest rate. In the beginning, however, an immediate and direct decrease in the loan rate appears with the issue of fiduciary media, but this immediate decrease in the loan rate is distinct in character and degree from the later reduction. The new funds offered on the money market by the banks must obviously bring pressure to bear on the rate of interest. The supply and demand for loan money were adjusted at the interest rate prevailing before the issue of any additional supply of fiduciary media. Additional loans can be placed only if the interest rate is lowered. Such loans are profitable for the banks because the increase in the supply of fiduciary media calls for no expenditure except for the mechanical costs of banking (i.e., printing the notes and bookkeeping). The banks can, therefore, undercut the interest rates which would otherwise appear on the loan market, in the absence of their intervention. Since competition from them compels other money lenders to lower *their* interest charges, the market interest rate must therefore decline. But can this reduction be maintained? *That* is the problem.

---

[7]Albert Hahn and Joseph Schumpeter have given me credit for the expression "forced savings" or "compulsory savings."

3. Inevitable Effects of Credit Expansion on Interest Rates

In conformity with Wicksell's terminology, we shall use "natural interest rate" to describe that interest rate which would be established by supply and demand if real goods were loaned *in natura* [directly, as in barter] without the intermediary of money. "Money rate of interest" will be used for that interest rate asked on loans made in money or money substitutes. Through continued expansion of fiduciary media, it is possible for the banks to force the money rate down to the actual cost of the banking operations, practically speaking that is almost to zero. As a result, several authors have concluded that interest could be completely abolished in this way. Whole schools of reformers have wanted to use banking policy to make credit gratuitous and thus to solve the "social question." No reasoning person today, however, believes that interest can ever be abolished, nor doubts but what, if the "money interest rate" is depressed by the expansion of fiduciary media, it must sooner or later revert once again to the "natural interest rate." The question is only how this inevitable adjustment takes place. The answer to this will explain at the same time the fluctuations of the business cycle.

The Currency Theory limited the problem too much. It only considered the situation that was of practical significance for the England of its time — that is, when the issue of fiduciary media is increased in one country while remaining unchanged in others. Under these assumptions, the situation is quite clear: General price increases at home; hence an increase in imports, a drop in commodity exports; and with this, as notes can circulate only within the country, an outflow of metallic money. To obtain metallic money for export, holders of notes present them for redemption; the metallic reserves of the banks decline; and consideration for their own solvency then forces them to restrict the credit offered.

That is the instant at which the business upswing, brought about by the availability of easy credit, is demonstrated to be illusory prosperity. An abrupt reaction sets in. The "money rate of interest" shoots up; enterprises from which credit is withdrawn collapse and sweep along with them the banks which are their creditors. A long persisting period of business stagnation now follows. The banks, warned by this experience into observing restraint, not only no longer underbid the "natural interest rate" but exercise extreme caution in granting credit.

4. The Price Premium

In order to complete this interpretation, we must, first of all, consider the price premium. As the banks start to expand the circulation credit, the anticipated upward movement of prices results in the appearance of a positive price premium. Even if the banks do not lower the actual interest rate any more, the gap widens between the "money interest rate" and the "natural interest rate" which would prevail in the absence of their intervention. Since loan money is now cheaper to acquire than circumstances warrant, entrepreneurial ambitions expand.

New businesses are started in the expectation that the necessary capital can be secured by obtaining credit. To be sure, in the face of growing demand, the banks now raise the "money interest rate." Still they do not discontinue granting further credit. They expand the supply of fiduciary media issued, with the result that the purchasing power of the monetary unit must decline still further. Certainly the actual "money interest rate" increases during the boom, but it continues to lag behind the rate which would conform to the market, i.e., the "natural interest rate" augmented by the positive price premium.

So long as this situation prevails, the upswing continues. Inventories of goods are readily sold. Prices and profits rise. Business enterprises are overwhelmed with orders because everyone anticipates further price increases and workers find employment at increasing wage rates. However, this situation cannot last forever!

5. Malinvestment of Available Capital Goods

The "natural interest rate" is established at that height which tends toward equilibrium on the market. The tendency is toward a condition where no capital goods are idle, no opportunities for starting profitable enterprises remain unexploited and the only projects not undertaken are those which no longer yield a profit at the prevailing "natural interest rate." Assume, however, that the equilibrium, toward which the market is moving, is disturbed by the interference of the banks. Money may be obtained below the "natural interest rate." As a result businesses may be started which weren't profitable before, and which become profitable only through the lower than "natural interest rate" which appears with the expansion of circulation credit.

Here again, we see the difference which exists between a drop in purchasing power, caused by the expansion of circulation credit, and a loss of purchasing power, brought about by an increase in the quantity of money. In the latter case [i.e., with an increase in the quantity of money in the narrower sense] the prices first affected are either (1) those of consumers' goods only or (2) the prices of both consumers' and producers' goods. Which it will be depends on whether those first receiving the new quantities of money use this new wealth for consumption or production. However, if the decrease in purchasing power is caused by an increase in bank created fiduciary media, then it is the prices of producers' goods which are first affected. The prices of consumers' goods follow only to the extent that wages and profits rise.

Since it always requires some time for the market to reach full "equilibrium," the "static" or "natural"[8] prices, wage rates and interest rates never actually appear. The process leading to their establishment is never completed before changes occur which once again indicate a new "equilibrium." At times, even on the unhampered market, there are some unemployed workers, unsold consumers' goods and quantities of unused factors of production, which would not exist under "static equilibrium." With the revival of business and productive activity, these reserves are in demand right away. However, once they are gone, the increase in the supply of fiduciary media necessarily leads to disturbances of a special kind.

In a given economic situation, the opportunities for production, which may actually be carried out, are limited by the supply of capital goods available. Roundabout methods of production can be adopted only so far as the means for subsistence exist to maintain the workers during the entire period of the expanded process. All those projects, for the completion of which means are not available, must be left uncompleted, even though they may appear technically feasible — that is, if one disregards the supply of capital. However, such businesses, because of the lower loan rate offered by the banks, appear for the moment to be profitable and are, therefore, initiated. However, the existing resources are insufficient. Sooner or later this must become evident. Then it will become apparent that production has gone astray, that plans were drawn up in excess of the economic means available, that speculation, i.e., activity aimed at the provision of future goods, was misdirected. ❯

---

[8]In the language of Knut Wicksell and the classical economists.

CHAPTER 13

Labor Productivity, Wages, and Unemployment

PLANNING FOR FREEDOM AND SIXTEEN OTHER ESSAYS AND ADDRESSES[1]

"WAGES, UNEMPLOYMENT AND INFLATION"

Our economic system — the market economy or capitalism — is a system of consumers' supremacy. The customer is sovereign; he is, says a popular slogan, "always right." Businessmen are under the necessity of turning out what the consumers ask for and they must sell their wares at prices which the consumers can afford and are prepared to pay. A business operation is a manifest failure if the proceeds from the sales do not reimburse the businessman for all he has expended in producing the article. Thus the consumers in buying at a definite price determine also the height of the wages that are paid to all those engaged in the industries.

---

[1][Ludwig von Mises, *Planning for Freedom and Sixteen Other Essays and Addresses* (1952; South Holland, Ill.: Libertarian Press, 1980), chap. 10, pp. 150–61.]

1. Wages Ultimately Paid By the Consumers

It follows that an employer cannot pay more to an employee than the equivalent of the value the latter's work, *according to the judgment of the buying public*, adds to the merchandise. (This is the reason why the movie star gets much more than the charwoman.) If he were to pay more, he would not recover his outlays from the purchasers; he would suffer losses and would finally go bankrupt. In paying wages, the employer acts as a mandatory of the consumers, as it were. It is upon the consumers that the incidence of the wage payments falls. As the immense majority of the goods produced are bought and consumed by people who are themselves receiving wages and salaries, it is obvious that in spending their earnings the wage earners and employees themselves are foremost in determining the height of the compensation they and those like them will get.

2. What Makes Wages Rise

The buyers do not pay for the toil and trouble the worker took nor for the length of time he spent in working. They pay for the products. The better the tools are which the worker uses in his job, the more he can perform in an hour, the higher is, consequently, his remuneration. What makes wages rise and renders the material conditions of the wage earners more satisfactory is improvement in the technological equipment. American wages are higher than wages in other countries because the capital invested per head of the worker is greater and the plants are thereby in the position to use the most efficient tools and machines. What is called the American way of life is the result of the fact that the United States has put fewer obstacles in the way of saving and capital accumulation than other nations. The economic backwardness of such countries as India consists precisely in the fact that their policies hinder both the accumulation of domestic capital and the investment of foreign capital. As the capital required is lacking, the Indian enterprises are prevented from employing sufficient quantities of modern equipment, are therefore producing much less per man-hour, and can only afford to pay wage rates which, compared with American wage rates, appear as shockingly low.

There is only one way that leads to an improvement of the standard of living for the wage-earning masses, viz., the increase in the amount of capital invested. All other methods, however popular they may be, are not only futile, but are actually detrimental to the well-being of those they allegedly want to benefit.

3. What Causes Unemployment

The fundamental question is: is it possible to raise wage rates *for all those eager to find jobs* above the height they would have attained on an unhampered labor market?

Public opinion believes that the improvement in the conditions of the wage earners is an achievement of the unions and of various legislative measures. It gives to unionism and to legislation credit for the rise in wage rates, the shortening of hours of work, the disappearance of child labor, and many other changes. The prevalence of this belief made unionism popular and is responsible for the trend in labor legislation of the last two decades. As people think that they owe to unionism their high standard of living, they condone violence, coercion, and intimidation on the part of unionized labor and are indifferent to the curtailment of personal freedom inherent in the union-shop and closed-shop clauses. As long as these fallacies prevail upon the minds of the voters, it is vain to expect a resolute departure from the policies that are mistakenly called progressive.

Yet this popular doctrine misconstrues every aspect of economic reality. The height of wage rates at which all those eager to get jobs can be employed depends on the marginal productivity of labor. The more capital — other things being equal — is invested, the higher wages climb on the free labor market, i.e., on the labor market not manipulated by the government and the unions. At these market wage rates all those eager to employ workers can hire as many as they want. At these market wage rates all those who want to be employed can get a job. There prevails on a free labor market a tendency toward full employment. In fact, the policy of letting the free market determine the height of wage rates is the only reasonable and successful full-employment policy. If wage rates, either by union pressure and compulsion or by government decree, are raised above this height, lasting unemployment of a part of the potential labor force develops.

4. Credit Expansion No Substitute for Capital

These opinions are passionately rejected by the union bosses and their followers among politicians and the self-styled intellectuals. The panacea they recommend to fight unemployment is credit expansion and inflation, euphemistically called "an easy money policy."

As has been pointed out above, an addition to the available stock of capital previously accumulated makes a further improvement of the industries' technological equipment possible, thus raises the marginal productivity of labor and consequently also wage rates. But credit expansion, whether it is effected by issuing additional banknotes or by granting additional credits on bank accounts subject to check, does not add anything to the nation's wealth of capital goods. It merely creates the illusion of an increase in the amount of funds available for an expansion of production. Because they can obtain cheaper credit, people erroneously believe that the country's wealth has thereby been increased and that therefore certain projects that could not be executed before are now feasible. The inauguration of these projects enhances the demand for labor and for raw materials and makes wage rates and commodity prices rise. An artificial boom is kindled.

Under the conditions of this boom, nominal wage rates which before the credit expansion were too high for the state of the market and therefore created unemployment of a part of the potential labor force are no longer too high and the unemployed can get jobs again. However, this happens only because under the changed monetary and credit conditions prices are rising or, what is the same expressed in other words, the purchasing power of the monetary unit drops. Then the same amount of nominal wages, i.e., wage rates expressed in terms of money, means less in real wages, i.e., in terms of commodities that can be bought by the monetary unit. Inflation can cure unemployment only by curtailing the wage earner's *real* wages. But then the unions ask for a new increase in wages in order to keep pace with the rising cost of living and we are back where we were before, i.e., in a situation in which large-scale unemployment can only be prevented by a further expansion of credit.

This is what happened in this country as well as in many other countries in the last years. The unions, supported by the government, forced the enterprises to agree to wage rates that went beyond the potential market rates, i.e., the rates which the public was prepared to refund to the employers in purchasing their products. This would have inevitably resulted in rising unemployment figures. But the government policies tried to prevent the emergence of serious unemployment by credit expansion, i.e., inflation. The outcome was rising prices, renewed demands for higher wages and reiterated credit expansion; in short, protracted inflation. ❱

HUMAN ACTION[2]

4. Catallactic Unemployment

If a job-seeker cannot obtain the position he prefers, he must look for another kind of job. If he cannot find an employer ready to pay him as much as he would like to earn, he must abate his pretensions. If he refuses, he will not get any job. He remains unemployed.

What causes unemployment is the fact that — contrary to the above-mentioned doctrine of the worker's inability to wait — those eager to earn wages can and do wait. A job-seeker who does not want to wait will always get a job in the unhampered market economy in which there is always unused capacity of natural resources and very often also unused capacity of produced factors of production. It is only necessary for him either to reduce the amount of pay he is asking for or to alter his occupation or his place of work.

There were and still are people who work only for some time and then live for another period from the savings they have accumulated by working. In countries in which the cultural state of the masses is low, it is often difficult to recruit workers who are ready to stay on the job. The average man there is so callous and inert that he knows of no other use for his earnings than to buy some leisure time. He works only in order to remain unemployed for some time.

It is different in the civilized countries. Here the worker looks upon unemployment as an evil. He would like to avoid it provided the sacrifice required is not too grievous. He chooses between employment and unemployment in the same way in which he proceeds in all other actions and choices: he weighs the pros and cons. If he chooses unemployment, this unemployment is a market phenomenon whose nature is not different from other market phenomena as they appear in a changing market economy. We may call this kind of unemployment market-generated or *catallactic unemployment*.

The various considerations which may induce a man to decide for unemployment can be classified in this way:

---

[2][Ludwig von Mises, *Human Action* (1949; Auburn, Ala.: Mises Institute, 1998), chap. 21: "Work and Wages," pp. 595–98.]

1. The individual believes that he will find at a later date a remunerative job in his dwelling place and in an occupation which he likes better and for which he has been trained. He seeks to avoid the expenditure and other disadvantages involved in shifting from one occupation to another and from one geographical point to another. There may be special conditions increasing these costs. A worker who owns a homestead is more firmly linked with the place of his residence than people living in rented apartments. A married woman is less mobile than an unmarried girl. Then there are occupations which impair the worker's ability to resume his previous job at a later date. A watchmaker who works for some time as a lumberman may lose the dexterity required for his previous job. In all these cases the individual chooses temporary unemployment because he believes that this choice pays better in the long run.

2. There are occupations the demand for which is subject to considerable seasonal variations. In some months of the year the demand is very intense, in other months it dwindles or disappears altogether. The structure of wage rates discounts these seasonal fluctuations. The branches of industry subject to them can compete on the labor market only if the wages they pay in the good season are high enough to indemnify the wage earners for the disadvantages resulting from the seasonal irregularity in demand. Then many of the workers, having saved a part of their ample earnings in the good season, remain unemployed in the bad season.

3. The individual chooses temporary unemployment for considerations which in popular speech are called noneconomic or even irrational. He does not take jobs which are incompatible with his religious, moral, and political convictions. He shuns occupations the exercise of which would impair his social prestige. He lets himself be guided by traditional standards of what is proper for a gentleman and what is unworthy. He does not want to lose face or caste.

Unemployment in the unhampered market is always voluntary. In the eyes of the unemployed man, unemployment is the minor of two evils between which he has to choose. The structure of the market may sometimes cause wage rates to drop. But, on the unhampered market, there is always for each type of labor a rate at which all those eager to work can get a job. The final wage rate is that rate at which all job-seekers get jobs and all employers as many workers as they want to hire. Its height is determined by the marginal productivity of each type of work.

Wage rate fluctuations are the device by means of which the sovereignty of the consumers manifests itself on the labor market. They are the measure adopted for the allocation of labor to the various branches of production. They penalize disobedience by cutting wage rates in the comparatively overmanned branches and recompense obedience by raising wage rates in the comparatively undermanned branches. They thus submit the individual to a harsh social pressure. It is obvious that they indirectly limit the individual's freedom to choose his occupation. But this coercion is not rigid. It leaves to the individual a margin in the limits of which he can choose between what suits him better and what less. Within this orbit he is free to act of his own accord. This amount of freedom is the maximum of freedom that an individual can enjoy in the framework of the social division of labor, and this amount of coercion is the minimum of coercion that is indispensable for the preservation of the system of social cooperation. There is only one alternative left to the catallactic pressure exercised by the wages system: the assignment of occupations and jobs to each individual by the peremptory decrees of an authority, a central board planning all production activities. This is tantamount to the suppression of all freedom.

It is true that under the wages system the individual is not free to choose permanent unemployment. But no other imaginable social system could grant him a right to unlimited leisure. That man cannot avoid submitting to the disutility of labor is not an outgrowth of any social institution. It is an inescapable natural condition of human life and conduct.

It is not expedient to call catallactic unemployment in a metaphor borrowed from mechanics "frictional" unemployment. In the imaginary construction of the evenly rotating economy there is no unemployment because we have based this construction on such an assumption. Unemployment is a phenomenon of a changing economy. The fact that a worker discharged on account of changes occurring in the arrangement of production processes does not instantly take advantage of every opportunity to get another job but waits for a more propitious opportunity is not a consequence of the tardiness of the adjustment to the change in conditions, but is one of the factors slowing down the pace of this adjustment. It is not an automatic reaction to the changes which have occurred, independent of the will and the choices of the job-seekers concerned, but the effect of their intentional actions. It is speculative, not frictional.

Catallactic unemployment must not be confused with *institutional unemployment*. Institutional unemployment is not the outcome of the decisions of the individual job-seekers. It is the effect of interference with the market phenomena intent upon enforcing by coercion and compulsion wage rates higher than those the unhampered market would have determined. The treatment of institutional unemployment belongs to the analysis of the problems of interventionism. ❯

CHAPTER 14

The Hampered Market Economy

PLANNING FOR FREEDOM AND SIXTEEN OTHER ESSAYS AND ADDRESSES[1]

"MIDDLE-OF-THE-ROAD POLICY LEADS TO SOCIALISM"

The fundamental dogma of all brands of socialism and communism is that the market economy or capitalism is a system that hurts the vital interests of the immense majority of people for the sole benefit of a small minority of rugged individualists. It condemns the masses to progressing impoverishment. It brings about misery, slavery, oppression, degradation and exploitation of the working men, while it enriches a class of idle and useless parasites.

This doctrine was not the work of Karl Marx. It had been developed long before Marx entered the scene. Its most successful propagators were not the Marxian authors, but such men as Carlyle and Ruskin, the British Fabians, the German professors and the American Institutionalists. And it

---

[1] [Ludwig von Mises, *Planning for Freedom and Sixteen Other Essays and Addresses* (1952; South Holland, Ill.: Libertarian Press, 1980), chap. 2, pp. 18–35.]

is a very significant fact that the correctness of this dogma was contested only by a few economists who were very soon silenced and barred from access to the universities, the press, the leadership of political parties and, first of all, public office. Public opinion by and large accepted the condemnation of capitalism without any reservation.

1. Socialism

But, of course, the practical political conclusions which people drew from this dogma were not uniform. One group declared that there is but one way to wipe out these evils, namely to abolish capitalism entirely. They advocate the substitution of public control of the means of production for private control. They aim at the establishment of what is called socialism, communism, planning, or state capitalism. All these terms signify the same thing. No longer should the consumers, by their buying and abstention from buying, determine what should be produced, in what quantity and of what quality. Henceforth a central authority alone should direct all production activities.

2. Interventionism, Allegedly a Middle-of-the-Road Policy

A second group seems to be less radical. They reject socialism no less than capitalism. They recommend a third system, which, as they say, is as far from capitalism as it is from socialism, which as a third system of society's economic organization, stands midway between the two other systems, and while retaining the advantages of both, avoids the disadvantages inherent in each. This third system is known as the system of interventionism. In the terminology of American politics it is often referred to as the middle-of-the-road policy.

What makes this third system popular with many people is the particular way they choose to look upon the problems involved. As they see it, two classes, the capitalists and entrepreneurs on the one hand and the wage earners on the other hand, are arguing about the distribution of the yield of capital and entrepreneurial activities. Both parties are claiming the whole cake for themselves. Now, suggest these mediators, let us make peace by splitting the disputed value equally between the two classes. The State as an impartial arbiter should interfere, and should curb the greed of the capitalists and assign a part of the profits to the working classes. Thus it will be possible to dethrone the moloch capitalism without enthroning the moloch of totalitarian socialism.

Yet this mode of judging the issue is entirely fallacious. The antagonism between capitalism and socialism is not a dispute about the distribution of booty. It is a controversy about which two schemes for society's economic organization, capitalism or socialism, is conducive to the better attainment of those ends which all people consider as the ultimate aim of activities commonly called economic, viz., the best possible supply of useful commodities and services. Capitalism wants to attain these ends by private enterprise and initiative, subject to the supremacy of the public's buying and abstention from buying on the market. The socialists want to substitute the unique plan of a central authority for the plans of the various individuals. They want to put in place of what Marx called the "anarchy of production" the exclusive monopoly of the government. The antagonism does not refer to the mode of distributing a fixed amount of amenities. It refers to the mode of producing all those goods which people want to enjoy.

The conflict of the two principles is irreconcilable and does not allow for any compromise. Control is indivisible. Either the consumers' demand as manifested on the market decides for what purposes and how the factors of production should be employed, or the government takes care of these matters. There is nothing that could mitigate the opposition between these two contradictory principles. They preclude each other. Interventionism is not a golden mean between capitalism and socialism. It is the design of a third system of society's economic organization and must be appreciated as such.

3. How Interventionism Works

It is not the task of today's discussion to raise any questions about the merits either of capitalism or of socialism. I am dealing today with interventionism alone. And I do not intend to enter into an arbitrary evaluation of interventionism from any preconceived point of view. My only concern is to show how interventionism works and whether or not it can be considered as a pattern of a permanent system for society's economic organization.

The interventionists emphasize that they plan to retain private ownership of the means of production, entrepreneurship and market exchange. But, they go on to say, it is peremptory to prevent these capitalist institutions from spreading havoc and unfairly exploiting the majority of people. It is the duty of government to restrain, by orders and prohibitions, the greed of the propertied classes lest their acquisitiveness harm the poorer classes. Unhampered or laissez-faire capitalism is an evil. But in order to eliminate its evils, there is no need to abolish capitalism entirely. It is possible to improve the capitalist system by government interference with the actions of the capitalists and entrepreneurs. Such government regulation and regimentation of business is the only method to keep off totalitarian socialism and to salvage those features of capitalism which are worth preserving. On the ground of this philosophy, the interventionists advocate a galaxy of various measures. Let us pick out one of them, the very popular scheme of price control.

4. How Price Control Leads to Socialism

The government believes that the price of a definite commodity, e.g., milk, is too high. It wants to make it possible for the poor to give their children more milk. Thus it resorts to a price ceiling and fixes the price of milk at a lower rate than that prevailing on the free market. The result is that the marginal producers of milk, those producing at the highest cost, now incur losses. As no individual farmer or businessman can go on producing at a loss, these marginal producers stop producing and selling milk on the market. They will use their cows and their skill for other more profitable purposes. They will, for example, produce butter, cheese or meat. There will be less milk available for the consumers, not more. This, or course, is contrary to the intentions of the government. It wanted to make it easier for some people to buy more milk. But, as an outcome of its interference, the supply available drops. The measure proves abortive from the very point of view of the government and the groups it was eager to favor. It brings about a state of affairs, which — again from the point of view of the government — is even less desirable than the previous state of affairs which it was designed to improve.

Now, the government is faced with an alternative. It can abrogate its decree and refrain from any further endeavors to control the price of milk. But if it insists upon its intention to keep the price of milk below the rate the unhampered market would have determined and wants nonetheless to avoid a drop in the supply of milk, it must try to eliminate the causes that render the marginal producers' business unremunerative. It must add to the first decree concerning only the price of milk a second decree fixing the prices of the factors of production necessary for the production of milk at such a low rate that the marginal producers of milk will no longer suffer losses and will therefore abstain from restricting output. But then the same story repeats itself on a remoter plane. The supply of the factors of production required for the production of milk drops, and again the government is back where it started. If it does not want to admit defeat and to abstain from any meddling with prices, it must push further and fix the prices of those factors of production which are needed for the production of the factors necessary for the production of milk. Thus the government is forced to go further and further, fixing step by step the prices of all consumers' goods and of all factors of production — both human, i.e., labor, and material — and to order every entrepreneur and every worker to continue work at these prices and wages. No branch of industry can be omitted from this all-around fixing of prices and wages and from this obligation to produce those quantities which the government wants to see produced. If some branches were to be left free out of regard for the fact that they produce only goods qualified as non-vital or even as luxuries, capital and labor would tend to flow into them and the result would be a drop in the supply of those goods, the prices of which government has fixed precisely because it considers them as indispensable for the satisfaction of the needs of the masses.

But when this state of all-around control of business is attained, there can no longer be any question of a market economy. No longer do the citizens by their buying and abstention from buying determine what should be produced and how. The power to decide these matters has devolved upon the government. This is no longer capitalism; it is all-around planning by the government, it is socialism.

5. *The Zwangswirtschaft Type of Socialism*

It is, of course, true that this type of socialism preserves some of the labels and the outward appearance of capitalism. It maintains, seemingly and nominally, private ownership of the means of production, prices, wages, interest rates and profits. In fact, however, nothing counts but the government's unrestricted autocracy. The government tells the entrepreneurs and capitalists what to produce and in what quantity and quality, at what prices to buy and from whom, at what prices to sell and to whom. It decrees at what wages and where the workers must work. Market exchange is but a sham. All the prices, wages, and interest rates are determined by the authority. They are prices, wages, and interest rates in appearance only; in fact they are merely quantity relations in the government's orders. The government, not the consumers, directs production. The government determines, directs production. The government determines each citizen's income, it assigns to everybody the position in which he has to work. This is socialism in the outward guise of capitalism. It is the Zwangswirtschaft of Hitler's German Reich and the planned economy of Great Britain.

6. German and British Experience

For the scheme of social transformation which I have depicted is not merely a theoretical construction. It is a realistic portrayal of the succession of events that brought about socialism in Germany, in Great Britain and in some other countries.

The Germans, in the first World War, began with price ceilings for a small group of consumers' goods considered as vital necessities. It was the inevitable failure of these measures that impelled them to go further and further until, in the second period of the war, they designed the *Hindenburg plan*. In the context of the Hindenburg plan no room whatever was left for a free choice on the part of the consumers and for initiative action on the part of business. All economic activities were unconditionally subordinated to the exclusive jurisdiction of the authorities. The total defeat of the Kaiser swept the whole imperial apparatus of administration away and with it went also the grandiose plan. But when in 1931 Chancellor Brüning embarked anew on a policy of price control and his successors, first of all Hitler, obstinately clung to it, the same story repeated itself.

Great Britain and all the other countries which in the first World War adopted measures of price control, had to experience the same failure. They too were pushed further and further in their attempts to make the initial decrees work. But they were still at a rudimentary stage of this development when the victory and the opposition of the public brushed away all schemes for controlling prices.

It was different in the second World War. Then Great Britain again resorted to price ceilings for a few vital commodities and had to run the whole gamut proceeding further and further until it had substituted all-around planning of the country's whole economy for economic freedom. When the war came to an end, Great Britain was a socialist commonwealth.

It is noteworthy to remember that British socialism was not an achievement of Mr. Attlee's Labor Government, but of the war cabinet of Mr. Winston Churchill. What the Labor Party did was not the establishment of socialism in a free country, but retaining socialism as it had developed during the war and in the post-war period. The fact has been obscured by the great sensation made about the nationalization of the Bank of England, the coal mines and other branches of business. However, Great Britain is to be called a socialist country not because certain enterprises have been formally expropriated and nationalized, but because all the economic activities of all citizens are subject to full control of the government and its agencies. The authorities direct the allocation of capital and of manpower to the various branches of business. They determine what should be produced. Supremacy in all business activities is exclusively vested in the government. The people are reduced to the status of wards, unconditionally bound to obey orders. To the businessmen, the former entrepreneurs, merely ancillary functions are left. All that they are free to do is to carry into effect, within a nearly circumscribed narrow field, the decisions of the government departments.

What we have to realize is that price ceilings affecting only a few commodities fail to attain the ends sought. On the contrary. They produce effects which from the point of view of the government are even worse than the previous state of affairs which the government wanted to alter. If the government, in order to eliminate these inevitable but unwelcome consequences, pursues its course further and further, it finally transforms the system of capitalism and free enterprise into socialism of the Hindenburg pattern.

7. Crises and Unemployment

The same is true of all other types of meddling with the market phenomena. Minimum wage rates, whether decreed and enforced by the government or by labor union pressure and violence, result in mass unemployment prolonged year after year as soon as they try to raise wage rates above the height of the unhampered market. The attempts to lower interest rates by credit expansion generate, it is true, a period of booming business. But the prosperity thus created is only an artificial hot-house product and must inexorably lead to the slump and to the depression. People must pay heavily for the easy-money orgy of a few years of credit expansion and inflation.

The recurrence of periods of depression and mass unemployment has discredited capitalism in the opinion of injudicious people. Yet these events are not the outcome of the operation of the free market. They are on the contrary the result of well-intentioned but ill-advised government interference with the market. There are no means by which the height of wage rates and the general standard of living can be raised other than by accelerating the increase of capital as compared with population. The only means to raise wage rates permanently for all those seeking jobs and eager to earn wages is to raise the productivity of the industrial effort by increasing the per-head quota of capital invested. What makes American wage rates by far exceed the wage rates of Europe and Asia is the fact that the American worker's toil and trouble is aided by more and better tools. All that good government can do to improve the material well-being of the people is to establish and to preserve an institutional order in which there are no obstacles to the progressing accumulation of new capital required for the improvement of technological methods of production. This is what capitalism did achieve in the past and will achieve in the future too if not sabotaged by a bad policy.

8. *Two Roads to Socialism*

Interventionism cannot be considered as an economic system destined to stay. It is a method for the transformation of capitalism into socialism by a series of successive steps. It is as such different from the endeavors of the communists to bring about socialism at one stroke. The difference does not refer to the ultimate end of the political movement; it refers mainly to the tactics to be resorted to for the attainment of an end that both groups are aiming at.

Karl Marx and Friedrich Engels recommended successively each of these two ways for the realization of socialism. In 1848, in the *Communist Manifesto*, they outlined a plan for the step-by-step transformation of capitalism into socialism. The proletariat should be raised to the position of the ruling class and use its political supremacy "to wrest, by degrees, all capital from the bourgeoisie." This, they declare, "cannot be effected except by means of despotic inroads on the rights of property and on the conditions of bourgeois production; by means of measures, therefore, which appear economically insufficient and untenable, but which in the course of the movement outstrip themselves, necessitate further inroads upon the old social order, and are unavoidable as a means of entirely revolutionizing the mode of production." In this vein they enumerate by way of example ten measures.

In later years Marx and Engels changed their minds. In his main treatise, *Das Capital*, first published in 1867, Marx saw things in a different way. Socialism is bound to come "with the inexorability of a law of nature." But it cannot appear before capitalism has reached its full maturity. There is but *one* road to the collapse of capitalism, namely the progressive evolution of capitalism itself. Then only will the great final revolt of the working class give it the finishing stroke and inaugurate the everlasting age of abundance.

From the point of view of this later doctrine Marx and the school of orthodox Marxism reject all policies that pretend to restrain, to regulate and to improve capitalism. Such policies, they declare, are not only futile, but outright harmful. For they rather delay the coming of age of capitalism, its maturity, and thereby also its collapse. They are therefore not progressive, but reactionary. It was this idea that led the German Social Democratic party to vote against Bismarck's social security legislation and to frustrate Bismarck's plan to nationalize the German tobacco industry. From the point of view of the same doctrine, the communists branded the American New Deal as a reactionary plot extremely detrimental to the true interests of the working people.

What we must realize is that the antagonism between the interventionists and the communists is a manifestation of the conflict between the two doctrines of the early Marxism and of the late Marxism. It is the conflict between the Marx of 1848, the author of the *Communist Manifesto*, and the Marx of 1867, the author of *Das Capital*. And it is paradoxical indeed that the document in which Marx endorsed the policies of the present-day self-styled anti-communists is called the *Communist Manifesto*.

There are two methods available for the transformation of capitalism into socialism. One is to expropriate all farms, plants, and shops and to operate them by a bureaucratic apparatus as departments of the government. The whole of society, says Lenin, becomes "one office and one factory, with equal work and equal pay,"[2] the whole economy will be organized "like the postal system."[3] The second method is the method of the Hindenburg plan, the originally German pattern of the welfare state and of planning. It forces every firm and every individual to comply strictly with the orders issued by the government's central board of production management. Such was the intention of the National Industrial Recovery Act of 1993 which the resistance of business frustrated and the Supreme Court declared unconstitutional. Such is the idea implied in the endeavors to substitute planning for private enterprise.

---

[2]Cf. [V.I.] Lenin, *State and Revolution* (Little Lenin Library No. 14, New York, 1932) p. 84.
[3]Ibid., p. 44.

9. Foreign Exchange Control

The foremost vehicle for the realization of this second type of socialism in industrial countries like Germany and Great Britain is foreign exchange control. These countries cannot feed and clothe their people out of domestic resources. They must import large quantities of food and raw materials. In order to pay for these badly needed imports, they must export manufactures, most of them produced out of imported raw material. In such countries almost every business transaction directly or indirectly is conditioned either by exporting or importing or by both exporting and importing. Hence the government's monopoly of buying and selling foreign exchange makes every kind of business activity depend on the discretion of the agency entrusted with foreign exchange control. In this country matters are different. The volume of foreign trade is rather small when compared with the total volume of the nation's trade. Foreign exchange control would only slightly affect the much greater part of American business. This is the reason why in the schemes of our planners there is hardly any question of foreign exchange control. Their pursuits are directed toward the control of prices, wages, and interest rates, toward the control of investment and the limitation of profits and incomes.

10. Progressive Taxation

Looking backward on the evolution of income tax rates from the beginning of the Federal income tax in 1913 until the present day, one can hardly expect that the tax will not one day absorb 100 percent of all surplus above the income of the average voter. It is this that Marx and Engels had in mind when in the *Communist Manifesto* they recommended "a heavy progressive or graduated income tax."

Another of the suggestions of the *Communist Manifesto* was "abolition of all right of inheritance." Now, neither in Great Britain nor in this country have the laws gone up to this point. But again, looking backward upon the past history of the estate taxes, we have to realize that they more and more have approached the goal set by Marx. Estate taxes of the height they have already attained for the upper brackets are no longer to be qualified as taxes. They are measures of expropriation.

The philosophy underlying the system of progressive taxation is that the income and the wealth of the well-to-do classes can be freely tapped. What the advocates of these tax rates fail to realize is that the greater part of the income taxed away would not have been consumed but saved and invested. In fact, this fiscal policy does not only prevent the further accumulation of new capital. It brings about capital decumulation. This is certainly today the state of affairs in Great Britain.

11. The Trend Toward Socialism

The course of events in the past thirty years shows a continuous, although sometimes interrupted progress toward the establishment in this country of socialism of the British and German pattern. The United States embarked later than these two other countries upon this decline and is today still farther away from its end. But if the trend of this policy will not change, the final result will only in accidental and negligible points differ from what happened in the England of Attlee and in the Germany of Hitler. The middle-of-the-road policy is not an economic system that can last. It is a method for the realization of socialism by installments.

12. Loopholes Capitalism

Many people object. They stress the fact that most of the laws which aim at planning or at expropriation by means of progressive taxation have left some loopholes which offer to private enterprise a margin within which it can go on. That such loopholes still exist and that thanks to them this country is still a free country is certainly true. But this "loopholes capitalism" is not a lasting system. It is a respite. Powerful forces are at work to close these loopholes. From day to day the field in which private enterprise is free to operate is narrowed down.

13. The Coming of Socialism is Not Inevitable

Of course, this outcome is not inevitable. The trend can be reversed as was the case with many other trends in history. The Marxian dogma according to which socialism is bound to come "with the inexorability of a law of nature" is just an arbitrary surmise devoid of any proof.

But the prestige which this vain prognostic enjoys not only with the Marxians, but with many self-styled non-Marxians, is the main instrument of the progress of socialism. It spreads defeatism among those who otherwise would gallantly fight the socialist menace. The most powerful ally of Soviet Russia is the doctrine that the "wave of the future" carries us toward socialism and that it is therefore "progressive" to sympathize with all measures that restrict more and more the operation of the market economy.

Even in this country which owes to a century of "rugged individualism" the highest standard of living ever attained by any nation, public opinion condemns laissez-faire. In the last fifty years, thousands of books have been published to indict capitalism and to advocate radical interventionism, the welfare state, and socialism. The few books which tried to explain adequately the working of the free-market economy were hardly noticed by the public. Their authors remained obscure, while such authors as Veblen, Commons, John Dewey, and Laski were exuberantly praised. It is a well-known fact that the legitimate stage as well as the Hollywood industry are no less radically critical of free enterprise than are many novels. There are in this country many periodicals which in every issue furiously attack economic freedom. There is hardly any magazine of opinion that would plead for the system that supplied the immense majority of the people with good food and shelter, with cars, refrigerators, radio sets, and other things which the subjects of other countries call luxuries.

The impact of this state of affairs is that practically very little is done to preserve the system of private enterprise. There are only middle-of-the-roaders who think they have been successful when they have delayed for some time an especially ruinous measure. They are always in retreat. They put up today with measures which only ten or twenty years ago they would have considered as undiscussable. They will in a few years acquiesce in other measures which they today consider as simply out of the question. What can prevent the coming of totalitarian socialism is only a thorough change in ideologies.

What we need is neither anti-socialism nor anti-communism but an open positive endorsement of that system to which we owe all the wealth that distinguishes our age from the comparatively straitened conditions of ages gone by. ◗

CHAPTER 15

Price Controls

ECONOMIC POLICY:
THOUGHTS FOR TOMORROW AND TODAY[1]

"INTERVENTIONISM"

A famous, very often quoted phrase says: "That government is best, which governs least." I do not believe this to be a correct description of the functions of a good government. Government ought to do all the things for which it is needed and for which it was established. Government ought to protect the individuals within the country against the violent and fraudulent attacks of gangsters, and it should defend the country against foreign enemies. These are the functions of government within a free system, within the system of the market economy.

Under socialism, of course, the government is totalitarian, and there is nothing outside its sphere and its jurisdiction. But in the market economy the main task of the government is to protect the smooth functioning of

---

[1][Ludwig von Mises, *Economic Policy: Thoughts for Tomorrow and Today* (1979; Washington, D.C.: Regnery Gateway, 2006), Lecture 3, pp. 37–54.]

the market economy against fraud or violence from within and from outside the country.

People who do not agree with this definition of the functions of government may say: "This man hates the government." Nothing could be farther from the truth. If I should say that gasoline is a very useful liquid, useful for many purposes, but that I would nevertheless not drink gasoline because I think that would not be the right use for it, I am not an enemy of gasoline, and I do not hate gasoline. I only say that gasoline is very useful for certain purposes, but not fit for other purposes. If I say it is the government's duty to arrest murderers and other criminals, but not its duty to run the railroads or to spend money for useless things, then I do not hate the government by declaring that it is fit to do certain things but not fit to do other things.

It has been said that under present-day conditions we no longer have a free market economy. Under present-day conditions we have something called the "mixed economy." And for evidence of our "mixed economy," people point to the many enterprises which are operated and owned by the government. The economy is mixed, people say, because there are, in many countries, certain institutions — like the telephone, telegraph, and railroads — which are owned and operated by the government.

That some of these institutions and enterprises are operated by the government is certainly true. But this fact alone does *not* change the character of our economic system. It does not even mean there is a "little socialism" within the otherwise nonsocialist, free market economy. For the government, in operating these enterprises, is subject to the supremacy of the market, which means it is subject to the supremacy of the consumers. The government — if it operates, let us say, post offices or railroads — has to hire people who have to work in these enterprises. It also has to buy the raw materials and other things that are needed for the conduct of these enterprises. And on the other hand, it "sells" these services or commodities to the public. Yet, even though it operates these institutions using the methods of the free economic system, the result, as a rule, is a deficit. The government, however, is in a position to finance such a deficit — at least the members of the government and of the ruling party believe so.

It is certainly different for an individual. The individual's power to operate something with a deficit is very limited. If the deficit is not very soon eliminated, and if the enterprise does not become profitable (or at least show that no further deficit losses are being incurred), the individual goes bankrupt and the enterprise must come to an end.

But for the government, conditions are different. The government can run at a deficit, because it has the power to *tax* people. And if the taxpayers are prepared to pay higher taxes in order to make it possible for the government to operate an enterprise at a loss — that is, in a less efficient way than it would be done by a private institution — and if the public will accept this loss, then of course the enterprise will continue.

In recent years, governments have increased the number of nationalized institutions and enterprises in most countries to such an extent that the deficits have grown far beyond the amount that could be collected in taxes from the citizens. What happens then is not the subject of today's lecture. It is inflation, and I shall deal with that tomorrow. I mentioned this only because the mixed economy must not be confused with the problem of *interventionism*, about which I want to talk tonight.

What is interventionism? Interventionism means that the government does not restrict its activity to the preservation of order, or — as people used to say a hundred years ago — to "the production of security." Interventionism means that the government wants to do more. It wants to interfere with market phenomena.

If one objects and says the government should not interfere with business, people very often answer: "But the government necessarily always interferes. If there are policemen on the street, the government interferes. It interferes with a robber looting a shop or it prevents a man from stealing a car." But when dealing with interventionism and defining what is meant by interventionism, we are speaking about government interference with the market. (That the government and the police are expected to protect the citizens, which includes businessmen, and of course their employees, against attacks on the part of domestic or foreign gangsters, is in fact a normal, necessary expectation of any government. Such protection is not an intervention, for the government's only legitimate function is, precisely, to produce security.)

What we have in mind when we talk about interventionism is the government's desire to do *more* than prevent assaults and fraud. Interventionism means that the government not only fails to protect the smooth functioning of the market economy, but that it interferes with the various market phenomena; it interferes with prices, with wage rates, interest rates, and profits.

The government wants to interfere in order to force businessmen to conduct their affairs in a different way than they would have chosen if they had obeyed only the consumers. Thus, all the measures of interventionism by the government are directed toward restricting the supremacy of consumers. The government wants to arrogate to itself the power, or at least a part of the power, which, in the free market economy, is in the hands of the consumers.

Let us consider one example of interventionism, very popular in many countries and tried again and again by many governments, especially in times of inflation. I refer to price control.

Governments usually resort to price control when they have inflated the money supply and people have begun to complain about the resulting rise in prices. There are many famous historical examples of price control methods that failed, but I shall refer to only two of them because, in both these cases, the governments were really very energetic in enforcing or trying to enforce their price controls.

The first famous example is the case of the Roman Emperor Diocletian, very well-known as the last of those Roman emperors who persecuted the Christians. The Roman emperor in the second part of the third century had only one financial method, and this was currency debasement. In those primitive ages, before the invention of the printing press, even inflation was, let us say, primitive. It involved debasement of the coinage, especially the silver. The government mixed more and more copper into the silver until the color of the silver coins was changed and the weight was reduced considerably. The result of this coinage debasement and the associated increase in the quantity of money was an increase in prices, followed by an edict to control prices. And Roman emperors were not very mild when they enforced a law; they did not consider death too mild a punishment for a man who had asked for a higher price. They enforced price control, but they failed to maintain the society. The result was the disintegration of the Roman Empire and the system of the division of labor.

Then, 1500 years later, the same currency debasement took place during the French Revolution. But this time a different method was used. The technology for producing money was considerably improved. It was no longer necessary for the French to resort to debasement of the coinage: they had the printing press. And the printing press was very efficient. Again, the result was an unprecedented rise in prices. But in the French Revolution maximum prices were not enforced by the same method of capital punishment which the Emperor Diocletian had used. There had also been an improvement in the technique of killing citizens. You all remember the famous Doctor J.I. Guillotin (1738–1814), who advocated the use of the guillotine. Despite the guillotine the French also failed with their laws of maximum prices. When Robespierre himself was carted off to the guillotine the people shouted, "There goes the dirty Maximum."

I wanted to mention this, because people often say: "What is needed in order to make price control effective and efficient is merely more brutality and more energy." Now certainly, Diocletian was very brutal, and so was the French Revolution. Nevertheless, price control measures in both ages failed entirely.

Now let us analyze the reasons for this failure. The government hears people complain that the price of milk has gone up. And milk is certainly very important, especially for the rising generation, for children. Consequently, the government declares a maximum price for milk, a maximum price that is lower than the potential market price would be. Now the government says: "Certainly we have done everything needed in order to make it possible for poor parents to buy as much milk as they need to feed their children."

But what happens? On the one hand, the lower price of milk increases the demand for milk; people who could not afford to buy milk at a higher price are now able to buy it at the lower price which the government has decreed. And on the other hand some of the producers, those producers of milk who are producing at the highest cost — that is, the marginal producers — are now suffering losses, because the price which the government has decreed is lower than their costs. This is the important point in the market economy. The private entrepreneur, the private producer, cannot take losses in the long run. And as he cannot take losses in milk, he restricts the production of milk for the market. He may sell some of his cows for the slaughter house, or instead of milk he may sell some products made out of milk, for instance sour cream, butter, or cheese.

Thus the government's interference with the price of milk will result in less milk than there was before, and at the same time there will be a greater demand. Some people who are prepared to pay the government-decreed price cannot buy it. Another result will be that anxious people will hurry to be first at the shops. They have to wait outside. The long lines of people waiting at shops always appear as a familiar phenomenon in a city in which the government has decreed maximum prices for commodities that the government considers as important. This has happened everywhere when the price of milk was controlled. This was always prognosticated by economists. Of course, only by sound economists, and their number is not very great.

But what is the result of the government's price control? The government is disappointed. It wanted to increase the satisfaction of the milk drinkers. But actually it has dissatisfied them. Before the government interfered, milk was expensive, but people could buy it. Now there is only an insufficient quantity of milk available. Therefore, the total consumption of milk drops. The children are getting less milk, not more. The next measure to which the government now resorts, is rationing. But rationing only means that certain people are privileged and are getting milk while other people are *not* getting any at all. Who gets milk and who does not, of course, is always very arbitrarily determined. One order may determine, for example, that children under four years old should get milk, and that children over four years, or between the age of four and six should get only half the ration which children under four years receive.

Whatever the government does, the fact remains, there is only a smaller amount of milk available. Thus people are still more dissatisfied than they were before. Now the government asks the milk producers (because the government does not have enough imagination to find out for itself): "Why do you not produce the same amount of milk you produced before?" The government gets the answer: "We cannot do it, since the costs of production are higher than the maximum price which the government has established." Now the government studies the costs of the various items of production, and it discovers one of the items is fodder.

"Oh," says the government, "the same control we applied to milk we will now apply to fodder. We will determine a maximum price for fodder, and then you will be able to feed your cows at a lower price, at a lower expenditure. Then everything will be all right; you will be able to produce more milk and you will sell more milk."

But what happens now? The same story repeats itself with fodder, and as you can understand, for the same reasons. The production of fodder drops and the government is again faced with a dilemma. So the government arranges new hearings, to find out what is wrong with fodder production. And it gets an explanation from the producers of fodder precisely like the one it got from the milk producers. So the government must go a step farther, since it does not want to abandon the principle of price control. It determines maximum prices for producers' goods which are necessary for the production of fodder. And the same story happens again.

The government at the same time starts controlling not only milk, but also eggs, meat, and other necessities. And every time the government gets the same result, everywhere the consequence is the same. Once the government fixes a maximum price for consumer goods, it has to go farther back to producers' goods, and limit the prices of the producers' goods required for the production of the price-controlled consumer goods. And so the government, having started with only a few price controls, goes farther and farther back in the process of production, fixing maximum prices for all kinds of producers' goods, including of course the price of labor, because without wage control, the government's "cost control" would be meaningless.

Moreover, the government cannot limit its interference into the market to only those things which it views as vital necessities, like milk, butter, eggs, and meat. It must necessarily include luxury goods, because if it did not limit *their* prices, capital and labor would abandon the production of vital necessities and would turn to producing those things which the government considers unnecessary luxury goods. Thus, the isolated interference with one or a few prices of consumer goods always brings about effects — and this is important to realize — which are even *less* satisfactory than the conditions that prevailed before.

Before the government interfered, milk and eggs were expensive; after the government interfered they began to disappear from the market. The government considered those items to be so important that it interfered; it wanted to increase the quantity and improve the supply. The result was the opposite: the isolated interference brought about a condition which — from the point of view of the government — is even *more* undesirable than the previous state of affairs which the government wanted to alter. And as the government goes farther and farther, it will finally arrive at a point where all prices, all wage rates, all interest rates, in short everything in the whole economic system, is determined by the government. And this, clearly, is *socialism*.

What I have told you here, this schematic and theoretical explanation, is precisely what happened in those countries which tried to enforce a maximum price control, where governments were stubborn enough to go step by step until they came to the end. This happened in the First World War in Germany and England.

Let us analyze the situation in both countries. Both countries experienced inflation. Prices went up, and the two governments imposed price controls. Starting with a few prices, starting with only milk and eggs, they had to go farther and farther. The longer the war went on, the more inflation was generated. And after three years of war, the Germans — systematically as always — elaborated a great plan. They called it the *Hindenburg*

Plan: everything in Germany considered to be good by the government at that time was named after Hindenburg.

The Hindenburg Plan meant that the whole German economic system should be controlled by the government: prices, wages, profits ... everything. And the bureaucracy immediately began to put this into effect. But before they had finished, the debacle came: the German empire broke down, the entire bureaucratic apparatus disappeared, the revolution brought its bloody results — things came to an end.

In England they started in the same way, but after a time, in the spring of 1917, the United States entered the war and supplied the British with sufficient quantities of everything. Therefore the road to socialism, the road to serfdom, was interrupted.

Before Hitler came to power, Chancellor Brüning again introduced price control in Germany for the usual reasons. Hitler enforced it, even before the war started. For in Hitler's Germany there was no private enterprise or private initiative. In Hitler's Germany there was a system of socialism which differed from the Russian system only to the extent that the *terminology* and *labels* of the free economic system were still retained. There still existed "private enterprises," as they were called. But the owner was no longer an entrepreneur, the owner was called a "shop manager" (*Betriebsführer*).

The whole of Germany was organized in a hierarchy of führers; there was the Highest Führer, Hitler of course, and then there were führers down to the many hierarchies of smaller führers. And the head of an enterprise was the *Betriebsführer*. And the workers of the enterprise were named by a word that, in the Middle Ages, had signified the retinue of a feudal lord: the *Gefolgschaft*. And all of these people had to obey the orders issued by an institution which had a terribly long name: *Reichsführerwirtschaftsmin isterium*,[2] at the head of which was the well-known fat man, named Goering, adorned with jewelry and medals.

And from this body of ministers with the long name came all the orders to every enterprise: what to produce, in what quantity, where to get the raw materials and what to pay for them, to whom to sell the products and at what prices to sell them. The workers got the order to work in a definite factory, and they received wages which the government decreed.

---

[2]Führer of the Reich's, i.e., the empire's, Ministry of Economics.

The whole economic system was now regulated in every detail by the government.

The *Betriebsführer* did not have the right to take the profits for himself; he received what amounted to a salary, and if he wanted to get more he would, for example, say: "I am very sick, I need an operation immediately, and the operation will cost 500 Marks," then he had to ask the führer of the district (the *Gauführer* or *Gauleiter*) whether he had the right to take out more than the salary which was given to him. The prices were no longer prices, the wages were no longer wages, they were all quantitative *terms* in a system of socialism.

Now let me tell you how that system broke down. One day, after years of fighting, the foreign armies arrived in Germany. They tried to preserve this government-directed economic system, but the brutality of Hitler would have been necessary to preserve it and, without this, it did not work.

And while this was going on in Germany, Great Britain — during the Second World War — did precisely what Germany did. Starting with the price control of some commodities only, the British government began step by step (in the same way Hitler had done in peacetime, even before the start of the war) to control more and more of the economy until, by the time the war ended, they had reached something that was almost pure socialism.

Great Britain was not brought to socialism by the Labour government which was established in 1945. Great Britain became socialist *during* the war, through the government of which Sir Winston Churchill was the prime minister. The Labour government simply retained the system of socialism which the government of Sir Winston Churchill had already introduced. And this in spite of great resistance by the people.

The nationalizations in Great Britain did not mean very much; the nationalization of the Bank of England was merely nominal, because the Bank of England was already under the complete control of the government. And it was the same with the nationalization of the railroads and the steel industry. The "war socialism," as it was called — meaning the system of interventionism proceeding step by step — had already virtually nationalized the system.

The difference between the German and British systems was not important since the people who operated them had been appointed by the government and in both cases they had to obey the government's orders in every respect. As I said before, the system of the German Nazis retained the labels and terms of the capitalistic free market economy. But they meant something very different: there were now only government decrees.

This was also true for the British system. When the Conservative party in Britain was returned to power, some of those controls were removed. In Great Britain we now have attempts from one side to retain controls and from the other side to abolish them. (But one must not forget that, in England, conditions are very different from conditions in Russia.) The same is true for other countries which depend on the importation of food and raw materials and therefore have to export manufactured goods. For countries depending heavily on export trade, a system of government control simply does not work.

Thus, as far as there is economic freedom left (and there is still substantial freedom in some countries, such as Norway, England, Sweden), it exists because of the *necessity to retain export trade*. Earlier, I chose the example of milk, not because I have a special preference for milk, but because practically all governments — or most of them — in recent decades, have regulated milk, egg or butter prices.

I want to refer, in a few words, to another example, and that is rent control. If the government controls rents, one result is that people who would otherwise have moved from bigger apartments to smaller ones when their family conditions changed, will no longer do so. For example, consider parents whose children left home when they came into their twenties, married or went into other cities to work. Such parents used to change their apartments and take smaller and cheaper ones. This necessity disappeared when rent controls were imposed.

In Vienna, Austria, in the early twenties, where rent control was well-established, the amount of money that the landlord received for an average apartment under rent control was not more than twice the price of a ticket for a ride on the city-owned street cars. You can imagine that people did not have any incentive to change their apartments. And, on the other hand, there was no construction of new houses. Similar conditions prevailed in the United States after the Second World War and are continuing in many cities to this day.

One of the main reasons why many cities in the United States are in such great financial difficulty is that they have rent control and a resulting shortage of housing. So the government has spent billions for the building of new houses. But why was there such a housing shortage? The housing shortage developed for the same reasons that brought milk shortages when there was milk price control. That means: *when the government interferes with the market, it is more and more driven towards socialism.*

And this is the answer to those people who say: "We are not socialists, we do not want the government to control everything. We realize this is bad. But why should not the government interfere a little bit with the market? Why shouldn't the government do away with some things which we do not like?"

These people talk of a "middle-of-the-road" policy. What they do not see is that the *isolated* interference, which means the interference with only one small part of the economic system, brings about a situation which the government itself — and the people who are asking for government interference — find worse than the conditions they wanted to abolish: the people who are asking for rent control are very angry when they discover there is a shortage of apartments and a shortage of housing.

But this shortage of housing was created precisely by government interference, by the establishment of rents below the level people would have had to pay in a free market.

The idea that there is a *third* system — between socialism and capitalism, as its supporters say — a system as far away from socialism as it is from capitalism but that retains the advantages and avoids the disadvantages of each — is pure nonsense. People who believe there is such a mythical system can become really poetic when they praise the glories of interventionism. One can only say they are mistaken. The government interference which they praise brings about conditions which they themselves do not like.

One of the problems I will deal with later is *protectionism.* The government tries to isolate the domestic market from the world market. It introduces tariffs which raise the domestic price of a commodity above the world market price, making it possible for domestic producers to form cartels. The cartels are then attacked by the government declaring: "Under these conditions, anti-cartel legislation is necessary."

This is precisely the situation with most of the European governments. In the United States, there are yet other reasons for antitrust legislation and the government's campaign against the specter of monopoly.

It is absurd to see the government — which creates by its own intervention the conditions making possible the emergence of domestic cartels — point its finger at business, saying: "There are cartels, therefore government interference with business is necessary." It would be much simpler to avoid cartels by ending the government's interference with the market — an interference which makes these cartels possible.

The idea of government interference as a "solution" to economic problems leads, in every country, to conditions which, at the least, are very unsatisfactory and often quite chaotic. If the government does not stop in time, it will bring on socialism.

Nevertheless, government interference with business is still very popular. As soon as someone does not like something that happens in the world, he says: "The government ought to do something about it. What do we have a government for? The government should do it." And this is a characteristic remnant of thought from past ages, of ages *preceding* modern freedom, modern constitutional government, before representative government or modern republicanism.

For centuries there was the doctrine — maintained and accepted by everyone — that a king, an anointed king, was the messenger of God; he had more wisdom than his subjects, and he had supernatural powers. As recently as the beginning of the nineteenth century, people suffering from certain diseases expected to be cured by the royal touch, by the hand of the king. Doctors were usually better; nevertheless, they had their patients try the king.

This doctrine of the superiority of a paternal government, of the supernatural and superhuman powers of the hereditary kings gradually disappeared — or at least we thought so. But it came back again. There was a German professor named Werner Sombart (I knew him very well), who was known the world over, who was an honorary doctor of many universities and an honorary member of the American Economic Association. That professor wrote a book, which is available in an English translation, published by the Princeton University Press. It is available also in a French translation, and probably also in Spanish — at least I hope it is available, because then you can check what I am saying. In this book, published in our century, not in the Dark Ages, Werner Sombart, a professor of economics, simply says: "The Führer, our Führer" — he means, of course, Hitler — "gets his orders directly from God, the Führer of the Universe."

I spoke of this hierarchy of the führers earlier, and in this hierarchy. I mentioned Hitler as the "Supreme Führer." ... But there is, according to Werner Sombart, a still higher Führer, God, the Führer of the universe. And God, he wrote, gives His orders directly to Hitler. Of course, Professor Sombart said very modestly: "We do not know how God communicates with the Führer. But the fact cannot be denied."

Now, if you hear that such a book can be published in the German language, the language of a nation which was once hailed as "the nation of philosophers and poets," and if you see it translated into English and French, then you will not be astonished at the fact that even a little bureaucrat considers himself wiser and better than the citizens and wants to interfere with everything, even though he is only a poor little bureaucrat, and not the famous Professor Werner Sombart, honorary member of everything.

Is there a remedy against such happenings? I would say, yes, there is a remedy. And this remedy is the power of the citizens; they have to prevent the establishment of such an autocratic regime that arrogates to itself a higher wisdom than that of the average citizen. This is the fundamental difference between freedom and serfdom.

The socialist nations have arrogated to themselves the term *democracy*. The Russians call their own system a People's Democracy; they probably maintain that the people are represented in the person of the dictator. I think that *one* dictator, Juan Perón here in Argentina, was given a good answer when he was forced into exile in 1955. Let us hope that all other dictators, in other nations, will be accorded a similar response. ◗

CHAPTER 16

Keynes and Keynesianism

PLANNING FOR FREEDOM
AND SIXTEEN OTHER ESSAYS AND ADDRESSES[1]

"STONES INTO BREAD, THE KEYNESIAN MIRACLE"

I

The stock-in-trade of all Socialist authors is the idea that there is potential plenty and that the substitution of socialism for capitalism would make it possible to give to everybody "according to his needs." Other authors want to bring about this paradise by a reform of the monetary and credit system. As they see it, all that is lacking is more money and credit. They consider that the rate of interest is a phenomenon artificially created by the man-made scarcity of the "means of payment." In hundreds, even thousands, of books and pamphlets they passionately blame the "orthodox" economists for their reluctance to admit that inflationist and expansionist doctrines are sound. All evils, they repeat again and again, are caused by the erroneous teachings of the "dismal science"

---

[1][Ludwig von Mises, *Planning for Freedom and Sixteen Other Essays and Addresses* (1952; South Holland, Ill.: Libertarian Press, 1980), chap. 6, pp. 50–63.]

of economics and the "credit monopoly" of the bankers and usurers. To unchain money from the fetters of "restrictionism," to create free money (*Freigeld*, in the terminology of Silvio Gesell) and to grant cheap or even gratuitous credit, is the main plank in their political platform.

Such ideas appeal to the uninformed masses. And they are very popular with governments committed to a policy of increasing the quantity both of money in circulation and of deposits subject to check. However, the inflationist governments and parties have not been ready to admit openly their endorsement of the tenets of the inflationists. While most countries embarked upon inflation and on a policy of easy money, the literary champions of inflationism were still spurned as "monetary cranks." Their doctrines were not taught at the universities.

John Maynard Keynes, late economic adviser to the British government, is the new prophet of inflationism. The "Keynesian Revolution" consisted in the fact that he openly espoused the doctrines of Silvio Gesell. As the foremost of the British Gesellians, Lord Keynes adopted also the peculiar messianic jargon of inflationist literature and introduced it into official documents. Credit expansion, says the *Paper of the British Experts* of April 8, 1943, performs the "miracle ... of turning a stone into bread." The author of this document was, of course, Keynes. Great Britain has indeed traveled a long way to this statement from Hume's and Mill's views on miracles.

II

Keynes entered the political scene in 1920 with his book, *The Economic Consequences of the Peace.* He tried to prove that the sums demanded for reparations were far in excess of what Germany could afford to pay and to "transfer." The success of the book was overwhelming. The propaganda machine of the German nationalists, well entrenched in every country, was busily representing Keynes as the world's most eminent economist and Great Britain's wisest statesman.

Yet it would be a mistake to blame Keynes for the suicidal foreign policy that Great Britain followed in the interwar period. Other forces, especially the adoption of the Marxian doctrine of imperialism and "capitalist warmongering," were of incomparably greater importance in the rise of appeasement. With the exception of a small number of keen-sighted men, all Britons supported the policy which finally made it possible for the Nazis to start the Second World War.

A highly gifted French economist, Étienne Mantoux, has analyzed Keynes's famous book point for point. The result of his very careful and conscientious study is devastating for Keynes the economist and statistician, as well as Keynes the statesman. The friends of Keynes are at a loss to find any substantial rejoinder. The only argument that his friend and biographer, Professor E.A.G. Robinson, could advance is that this powerful indictment of Keynes's position came "as might have been expected, from a Frenchman."[2] As if the disastrous effects of appeasement and defeatism had not affected Great Britain also!

Étienne Mantoux, son of the famous historian Paul Mantoux, was the most distinguished of the younger French economists. He had already made valuable contributions to economic theory — among them a keen critique of Keynes's *General Theory,* published in 1937 in the *Revue d'Économie Politique* — before he began his *The Carthaginian Peace or the Economic Consequences of Mr. Keynes.*[3] He did not live to see his book published. As an officer in the French forces he was killed on active service during the last days of the war. His premature death was a heavy blow to France, which is today badly in need of sound and courageous economists.

III

It would be a mistake, also, to blame Keynes for the faults and failures of contemporary British economic and financial policies. When he began to write, Britain had long since abandoned the principle of *laissez-faire.* That was the achievement of such men as Thomas Carlyle and John Ruskin and, especially, of the Fabians. Those born in the eighties of the nineteenth century and later were merely epigones of the university and parlor Socialists of the late Victorian period. They were no critics of the ruling system, as their predecessors had been, but apologists of government and pressure group policies whose inadequacy, futility and perniciousness became more and more evident.

Professor Seymour E. Harris has just published a stout volume of collected essays by various academic and bureaucratic authors dealing with Keynes's doctrines as developed in his *General Theory of Employment, Interest and Money,* published in 1936. The title of the volume is *The New Economics, Keynes' Influence on Theory and Public Policy.*[4] Whether

---

[2] *Economic Journal*, vol. 57, p. 23.

[3] Oxford University Press, 1946.

[4] Alfred A. Knopf, New York, 1947.

Keynesianism has a fair claim to the appellation *"new* economics" or whether it is not, rather, a rehash of often-refuted Mercantilist fallacies and of the syllogisms of the innumerable authors who wanted to make everybody prosperous by fiat money, is unimportant. What matters is not whether a doctrine is new, but whether it is sound.

The remarkable thing about this symposium is that it does not even attempt to refute the *substantiated* objections raised against Keynes by serious economists. The editor seems to be unable to conceive that any honest and uncorrupted man could disagree with Keynes. As he sees it, opposition to Keynes comes from "the vested interests of scholars in the older theory" and "the preponderant influence of press, radio, finance and subsidized research." In his eyes, non-Keynesians are just a bunch of bribed sycophants, unworthy of attention. Professor Harris thus adopts the methods of the Marxians and the Nazis, who preferred to smear their critics and to question their motives instead of refuting their theses.

A few of the contributions are written in dignified language and are reserved, even critical, in their appraisal of Keynes's achievements. Others are simply dithyrambic outbursts. Thus Professor Paul A. Samuelson tells us: "To have been born as an economist before 1936 was a boon — yes. But not to have been born too long before!" And he proceeds to quote Wordsworth:

Bliss was it in that dawn to be alive,
But to be young was very heaven!

Descending from the lofty heights of Parnassus into the prosaic valleys of quantitative science, Professor Samuelson provides us with exact information about the susceptibility of economists to the Keynesian gospel of 1936. Those under the age of 35 fully grasped its meaning after some time; those beyond 50 turned out to be quite immune, while economists in-between were divided. After thus serving us a warmed-over version of Mussolini's *giovanezza* theme, he offers more of the outworn slogans of fascism, e.g., the "wave of the future." However, on this point another contributor, Mr. Paul M. Sweezy, disagrees. In his eyes Keynes, tainted by "the shortcomings of bourgeois thought" as he was, is not the savior of mankind, but only the forerunner whose historical mission it is to prepare the British mind for the acceptance of pure Marxism and to make Great Britain ideologically ripe for full socialism.

IV

In resorting to the method of innuendo and trying to make their adversaries suspect by referring to them in ambiguous terms allowing of various interpretations, the camp-followers of Lord Keynes are imitating their idol's own procedures. For what many people have admiringly called Keynes's "brilliance of style" and "mastery of language" were, in fact, cheap rhetorical tricks.

Ricardo, says Keynes, "conquered England as completely as the Holy Inquisition conquered Spain." This is as vicious as any comparison could be. The Inquisition, aided by armed constables and executioners, beat the Spanish people into submission. Ricardo's theories were accepted as correct by British intellectuals without any pressure or compulsion being exercised in their favor. But in comparing the two entirely different things, Keynes obliquely hints that there was something shameful in the success of Ricardo's teachings and that those who disapprove of them are as heroic, noble and fearless champions of freedom as were those who fought the horrors of the Inquisition.

The most famous of Keynes's *aperçus* is: "Two pyramids, two masses for the dead, are twice as good as one; but not so two railways from London to York." It is obvious that this sally, worthy of a character in a play by Oscar Wilde or Bernard Shaw, does not in any way prove the thesis that digging holes in the ground and paying for them out of savings "will increase the real national dividend of useful goods and services." But it puts the adversary in the awkward position of either leaving an apparent argument unanswered or of employing the tools of logic and discursive reasoning against sparkling wit.

Another instance of Keynes's technique is provided by his malicious description of the Paris Peace Conference. Keynes disagreed with Clemenceau's ideas. Thus, he tried to ridicule his adversary by broadly expatiating upon his clothing and appearance which, it seems, did not meet with the standard set by London outfitters. It is hard to discover any connection with the German reparations problem in the fact that Clemenceau's boots "were of thick black leather, very good, but of a country style, and sometimes fastened in front, curiously, by a buckle instead of laces." After 15 million human beings had perished in the war, the foremost statesmen of the world were assembled to give mankind a new international order and lasting peace — and the British Empire's financial expert was amused by the rustic style of the French prime minister's footwear.

Fourteen years later there was another international conference. This time Keynes was not a subordinate adviser, as in 1919, but one of the main figures. Concerning this London World Economic Conference of 1933, Professor Robinson observes: "Many economists the world over will remember ... the performance in 1933 at Covent Garden in honour of the Delegates of the World Economic Conference, which owed its conception and organization very much to Maynard Keynes."

Those economists who were not in the service of one of the lamentably inept governments of 1933 and therefore were not delegates and did not attend the delightful ballet evening will remember the London Conference for other reasons. It marked the most spectacular failure in the history of international affairs of those policies of neo-Mercantilism which Keynes backed. Compared with this fiasco of 1933, the Paris Conference of 1919 appears to have been a highly successful affair. But Keynes did not publish any sarcastic comments on the coats, boots and gloves of the delegates of 1933.

V

Although Keynes looked upon "the strange, unduly neglected prophet Silvio Gesell" as a forerunner, his own teachings differ considerably from those of Gesell. What Keynes borrowed from Gesell as well as from the host of other pro-inflation propagandists was not the content of their doctrine, but their practical conclusions and the tactics they applied to undermine their opponents' prestige. These stratagems are:

(a) All adversaries, that is, all those who do not consider credit expansion as the panacea, are lumped together and called *orthodox*. It is implied that there are no differences between them.

(b) It is assumed that the evolution of economic science culminated in Alfred Marshall and ended with him. The findings of modern subjective economics are disregarded.

(c) All that economists from David Hume on down to our time have done to clarify the results of changes in the quantity of money and money substitutes is simply ignored. Keynes never embarked upon the hopeless task of refuting these teachings by ratiocination.

In all these respects the contributors to the symposium adopt their master's technique. Their critique aims at a body of doctrine created by their own illusions, which has no resemblance to the theories expounded by serious economists. They pass over in silence all that economists have said about the inevitable outcome of credit expansion. It seems as if they have never heard anything about the monetary theory of the trade cycle.

For a correct appraisal of the success which Keynes's *General Theory* found in academic circles, one must consider the conditions prevailing in university economics during the period between the two world wars.

Among the men who occupied chairs of economics in the last few decades, there have been only a few genuine economists, i.e., men fully conversant with the theories developed by modern subjective economics. The ideas of the old classical economists, as well as those of the modern economists, were caricatured in the textbooks and in the classrooms; they were called such names as old-fashioned, orthodox, reactionary, bourgeois or Wall Street economics. The teachers prided themselves on having refuted for all time the abstract doctrines of Manchesterism and *laissez-faire.*

The antagonism between the two schools of thought had its practical focus in the treatment of the labor union problem. Those economists disparaged as orthodox taught that a permanent rise in wage rates for all people eager to earn wages is possible only to the extent that the per capita quota of capital invested and the productivity of labor increases. If — whether by government decree or by labor union pressure — minimum wage rates are fixed at a higher level than that at which the unhampered market would have fixed them, unemployment results as a permanent mass phenomenon.

Almost all professors of the fashionable universities sharply attacked this theory. As these self-styled "unorthodox" doctrinaires interpreted the economic history of the last two hundred years, the unprecedented rise in real wage rates and standards of living was caused by labor unionism and government pro-labor legislation. Labor unionism was, in their opinion, highly beneficial to the true interests of all wage-earners and of the whole nation. Only dishonest apologists of the manifestly unfair interests of callous exploiters could find fault with the violent acts of the unions, they maintained. The foremost concern of popular government, they said, should be to encourage the unions as much as possible and to give them all the assistance they needed to combat the intrigues of the employers and to fix wage rates higher and higher.

But as soon as the governments and legislatures had vested the unions with all the powers they needed to enforce their minimum wage rates, the consequences appeared which the "orthodox" economists had predicted; unemployment of a considerable part of the potential labor force was prolonged year after year.

The "unorthodox" doctrinaires were perplexed. The only argument they had advanced against the "orthodox" theory was the appeal to their own fallacious interpretation of experience. But now events developed precisely as the "abstract school" had predicted. There was confusion among the "unorthodox."

It was at this moment that Keynes published his *General Theory*. What a comfort for the embarrassed "progressives"! Here, at last, they had something to oppose to the "orthodox" view. The cause of unemployment was not the inappropriate labor policies, but the shortcomings of the monetary and credit system. No need to worry any longer about the insufficiency of savings and capital accumulation and about deficits in the public household. On the contrary. The only method to do away with unemployment was to increase "effective demand" through public spending financed by credit expansion and inflation.

The policies which the *General Theory* recommended were precisely those which the "monetary cranks" had advanced long before and which most governments had espoused in the depression of 1929 and the following years. Some people believe that Keynes's earlier writings played an important part in the process which converted the world's most powerful governments to the doctrines of reckless spending, credit expansion and inflation. We may leave this minor issue undecided. At any rate it cannot be denied that the governments and peoples did not wait for the *General Theory* to embark upon these "Keynesian" — or more correctly, Gesellian policies.

VI

Keynes's *General Theory* of 1936 did not inaugurate a new age of economic policies; rather, it marked the end of a period. The policies which Keynes recommended were already then very close to the time when their inevitable consequences would be apparent and their continuation would be impossible. Even the most fanatical Keynesians do not dare to say that present-day England's distress is an effect of too much saving and insufficient spending. The essence of the much glorified "progressive" economic policies of the last decades was to expropriate ever-increasing parts of the higher incomes and to employ the funds thus raised for financing public waste and for subsidizing the members of the most powerful pressure groups. In the eyes of the "unorthodox," every kind of policy, however manifest its inadequacy may have been, was justified as a means of bringing about more equality. Now this process has reached its end. With the present tax rates and the methods applied in the control of prices, profits and interest rates, the system has liquidated itself. Even the confiscation of every penny earned above 1,000 pounds a year will not provide any perceptible increase to Great Britain's public revenue. The most bigoted

Fabians cannot fail to realize that henceforth funds for public spending must be taken from the same people who are supposed to profit from it. Great Britain has reached the limit both of monetary expansionism and of spending.

Conditions in this country are not essentially different. The Keynesian recipe to make wage rates soar no longer works. Credit expansion, on an unprecedented scale engineered by the New Deal, for a short time delayed the consequences of inappropriate labor policies. During this interval the Administration and the union bosses could boast of the "social gains" they had secured for the "common man." But now the inevitable consequences of the increase in the quantity of money and deposits has become visible; prices are rising higher and higher. What is going on today in the United States is the final failure of Keynesianism.

There is no doubt that the American public is moving away from the Keynesian notions and slogans. Their prestige is dwindling. Only a few years ago politicians were naively discussing the extent of national income in dollars without taking into account the changes which government-made inflation had brought about in the dollar's purchasing power. Demagogues specified the level to which they wanted to bring the national (dollar) income. Today this form of reasoning is no longer popular. At last the "common man" has learned that increasing the quantity of dollars does not make America richer. Professor Harris still praises the Roosevelt Administration for having raised dollar incomes. But such Keynesian consistency is found today only in classrooms.

There are still teachers who tell their students that "an economy can lift itself by its own bootstraps" and that "we can spend our way into prosperity."[5] But the Keynesian miracle fails to materialize; the stones do not turn into bread. The panegyrics of the learned authors who cooperated in the production of the present volume merely confirm the editor's introductory statement that "Keynes could awaken in his disciples an almost religious fervor for his economics, which could be effectively harnessed for the dissemination of the new economics." And Professor Harris goes on to say, "Keynes indeed had the Revelation."

There is no use in arguing with people who are driven by "an almost religious fervor" and believe that their master "had the Revelation." It is one of the tasks of economics to analyze carefully each of the inflationist

---

[5]Cf. Lorie Tarshis, *The Elements of Economics* (New York 1947), p. 565.

plans, those of Keynes and Gesell no less than those of their innumerable predecessors from John Law down to Major Douglas. Yet no one should expect that any logical argument or any experience could ever shake the almost religious fervor of those who believe in salvation through spending and credit expansion. ▶

HUMAN ACTION[6]

The Chimera of Contracyclical Policies

An essential element of the "unorthodox" doctrines, advanced both by all socialists and by all interventionists, is that the recurrence of depressions is a phenomenon inherent in the very operation, of the market economy. But while the socialists contend that only the substitution of socialism for capitalism can eradicate the evil, the interventionists ascribe to the government the power to correct the operation of the market economy in such a way as to bring about what they call "economic stability." These interventionists would be right if their antidepression plans were to aim at a radical abandonment of credit expansion policies. However, they reject this idea in advance. What they want is to expand credit more and more and to prevent depressions by the adoption of special "contracyclical" measures.

In the context of these plans the government appears as a deity that stands and works outside the orbit of human affairs, that is independent of the actions of its subjects, and has the power to interfere with these actions from without. It has at its disposal means and funds that are not provided by the people and can be freely used for whatever purposes the rulers are prepared to employ them for. What is needed to make the most beneficent use of this power is merely to follow the advice given by the experts.

The most advertised among these suggested remedies is contracyclical timing of public works and expenditure on public enterprises. The idea is not so new as its champions would have us believe. When depression came, in the past, public opinion always asked the government to embark upon public works in order to create jobs and to stop the drop in prices. But the

---

6[Ludwig von Mises, *Human Action* (1949; Auburn, Ala.: Mises Institute, 1998), chap. 31: "Currency and Credit Manipulation," pp. 792–94.]

problem is how to finance these public works. If the government taxes the citizens or borrows from them, it does not add anything to what the Keynesians call the aggregate amount of spending. It restricts the private citizen's power to consume or to invest to the same extent that it increases its own. If, however, the government resorts to the cherished inflationary methods of financing, it makes things worse, not better. It may thus delay for a short time the outbreak of the slump. But when the unavoidable payoff does come, the crisis is the heavier the longer the government has postponed it.

The interventionist experts are at a loss to grasp the real problems involved. As they see it, the main thing is "to plan public capital expenditure well in advance and to accumulate a shelf of fully worked out capital projects which can be put into operation at short notice." This, they say, "is the right policy and one which we recommend all countries should adopt."[7] However, the problem is not to elaborate projects, but to provide the material means for their execution. The interventionists believe that this could be easily achieved by holding back government expenditure in the boom and increasing it when the depression comes.

Now, restriction of government expenditure may certainly be a good thing. But it does not provide the funds a government needs for a later expansion of its expenditure. An individual may conduct his affairs in this way. He may accumulate savings when his income is high and spend them later when his income drops. But it is different with a nation or all nations together. The treasury may hoard a considerable part of the lavish revenue from taxes which flows into the public exchequer as a result of the boom. As far and as long as it withholds these funds from circulation, its policy is really deflationary and contracyclical and may to this extent weaken the boom created by credit expansion. But when these funds are spent again, they alter the money relation and create a cash-induced tendency toward a drop in the monetary unit's purchasing power. By no means can these funds provide the capital goods required for the execution of the shelved public works.

The fundamental error of the interventionists consists in the fact that they ignore the shortage of capital goods. In their eyes the depression is merely caused by a mysterious lack of the people's propensity both to consume and to invest. While the only real problem is to produce more and to

---

consume less in order to increase the stock of capital goods available, the interventionists want to increase both consumption and investment. They want the government to embark upon projects which are unprofitable precisely because the factors of production needed for their execution must be withdrawn from other lines of employment in which they would fulfill wants the satisfaction of which the consumers consider more urgent. They do not realize that such public works must considerably intensify the real evil, the shortage of capital goods.

One could, of course, think of another mode for the employment of the savings the government makes in the boom period. The treasury could invest its surplus in buying large stocks of all those materials which it will later, when the depression comes, need for the execution of the public works planned and of the consumers' goods which those occupied in these public works will ask for. But if the authorities were to act in this way, they would considerably intensify the boom, accelerate the outbreak of the crisis, and make its consequences more serious.[8]

All this talk about contracyclical government activities aims at one goal only, namely, to divert the public's attention from cognizance of the real cause of the cyclical fluctuations of business. All governments are firmly committed to the policy of low interest rates, credit expansion, and inflation. When the unavoidable aftermath of these short-term policies appears, they know only of one remedy — to go on in inflationary ventures. ◗

---

[8]In dealing with the contracyclical policies the interventionists always refer to the alleged success of these policies in Sweden. It is true that public capital expenditure in Sweden was actually doubled between 1932 and 1939. But this was not the cause, but an effect, of Sweden's prosperity in the thirties. This prosperity was entirely due to the rearmament of Germany. This Nazi policy increased the German demand for Swedish products on the one hand and restricted, on the other hand, German competition on the world market for those products which Sweden could supply. Thus Swedish exports increased from 1932 to 1938 (in thousands of tons): iron ore from 2,219 to 12,485; pig iron from 31,047 to 92,980; ferro-alloys from 15,453 to 28,605; other kinds of iron and steel from 134,237 to 256,146; machinery from 46,230 to 70,605. The number of unemployed applying for relief was 114,000 in 1932 and 165,000 in 1933. It dropped, as soon as German rearmament came into full swing, to 115,000 in 1934, to 62,000 in 1935, and was 16,000 in 1938. The author of this "miracle" was not Keynes, but Hitler.

CHAPTER 17

Economic Progress

ECONOMIC POLICY:
THOUGHTS FOR TOMORROW AND TODAY[1]

"FOREIGN INVESTMENT"

Some people call the programs of economic freedom a negative program. They say: "What do you liberals really want? You are against socialism, government intervention, inflation, labor union violence, protective tariffs. ... You say 'no' to everything."

I would call this statement a one-sided and shallow formulation of the problem. For it is possible to formulate a liberal program in a *positive* way. If a man says: "I am against censorship," he is not negative; he is *in favor* of authors having the right to determine what they want to publish without the interference of government. This is not negativism, this is precisely freedom. (Of course, when I use the term "liberal" with respect to the conditions of the economic system, I mean liberal in the old *classical* sense of the word.)

---

[1][Ludwig von Mises, *Economic Policy: Thoughts for Tomorrow and Today* (1979; Washington, D.C.: Regnery Gateway, 2006), Lecture 5, pp. 75–91.]

Today, most people regard the considerable differences in the standard of living between many countries as unsatisfactory. Two hundred years ago, conditions in Great Britain were much worse than they are today in India. But the British in 1750 did not call themselves "undeveloped" or "backward," because they were not in a position to compare the conditions of their country with those of countries in which economic conditions were more satisfactory. Today all people who have not attained the average standard of living of the United States believe that there is something wrong with their own economic situation. Many of these countries call themselves "developing countries" and, as such, are asking for aid from the so-called developed or even overdeveloped countries.

Let me explain the reality of this situation. The standard of living is lower in the so-called developing countries because the average earnings for the same type of labor is lower in those countries than it is in some countries of Western Europe, Canada, Japan, and especially in the United States. If we try to find the reasons for this difference, we must realize that it is not due to an inferiority of the workers or other employees. There prevails among some groups of North American workers a tendency to believe that they themselves are better than other people — that it is through their own merit that they are getting higher wages than other people.

It would only be necessary for an American worker to visit another country — let us say, Italy, where many American workers came from — in order to discover that it is *not* his personal qualities but the conditions in the country that make it possible for him to earn higher wages. If a man from Sicily immigrates to the United States, he can very soon earn the wage rates that are customary in the United States. And if the same man returns to Sicily, he will discover that his visit to the United States did not give him qualities which would permit him to earn higher wages in Sicily than his fellow countrymen.

Nor can one explain this economic situation by assuming any inferiority on the part of the entrepreneurs outside the United States. It is a fact that outside of the United States, Canada, Western Europe, and certain parts of Asia the equipment of the factories and the technological methods employed are, by and large, inferior to those within the United States. But this is not due to the ignorance of the entrepreneurs in those "undeveloped" countries. They know very well that the factories in the United States and Canada are much better equipped. They themselves know everything they must know about technology, and if they do not, they have the opportunity to learn what they must know from textbooks and technical magazines which disseminate this knowledge.

Once again: the difference is not personal inferiority or ignorance. The difference is the supply of capital, the quantity of capital goods available. In other words, the amount of capital invested per unit of the population is greater in the so-called advanced nations than in the developing nations.

A businessman cannot pay a worker more than the amount added by the work of this employee to the value of the product. He cannot pay him more than the customers are prepared to pay for the *additional* work of this individual worker. If he pays him more, he will not recover his expenditures from the customers. He incurs losses and, as I have pointed out again and again, and as everybody knows, a businessman who suffers losses must change his methods of business, or go bankrupt.

The economists describe this state of affairs by saying "wages are determined by the marginal productivity of labor." This is only another expression for what I have just said before. It is a fact that the scale of wages is determined by the amount a man's work increases the value of the product. If a man works with better and more efficient tools, then he can perform in one hour much more than a man who works one hour with less efficient instruments. It is obvious that 100 men working in an American shoe factory, equipped with the most modern tools and machines, produce much more in the same length of time than 100 shoemakers in India, who have to work with old-fashioned tools in a less sophisticated way.

The employers in all of these developing nations know very well that better tools would make their own enterprises more profitable. They would like to build more and better factories. The only thing that prevents them from doing it is the shortage of capital. The difference between the less developed and the more developed nations is a function of time: the British started to save sooner than all other nations: they also started sooner to accumulate capital and to invest it in business. Because they started sooner, there was a higher standard of living in Great Britain when, in all other European countries, there was still a lower standard of living. Gradually, all the other nations began to study British conditions, and it was not difficult for them to discover the reason for Great Britain's wealth. So they began to imitate the methods of British business.

Since other nations started later, and since the British did not stop investing capital, there remained a large difference between conditions in England and conditions in those other countries. But something happened which caused the headstart of Great Britain to disappear.

What happened was the greatest event in the history of the nineteenth century, and this means not only in the history of an individual country. This great event was the development, in the nineteenth century, of *foreign investment*. In 1817, the great British economist Ricardo still took it for granted that capital could be invested only within the borders of a country. He took it for granted that capitalists would not try to invest abroad. But a few decades later, capital investment abroad began to play a most important role in world affairs.

Without capital investment it would have been necessary for nations less developed than Great Britain to start with the methods and the technology with which the British had started in the beginning and middle of the eighteenth century, and slowly, step by step — always far below the technological level of the British economy — try to imitate what the British had done.

It would have taken many, many decades for these countries to attain the standard of technological development which Great Britain had reached a hundred years or more before them. But the great event that helped all these countries was foreign investment.

Foreign investment meant that British capitalists invested British capital in other parts of the world. They first invested it in those European countries which, from the point of view of Great Britain, were short of capital and backward in their development. It is a well-known fact that the railroads of most European countries, and also of the United States, were built with the aid of British capital. You know that the same happened in this country, in Argentina.

The gas companies in all the cities of Europe were also British. In the mid 1870s, a British author and poet criticized his countrymen. He said: "The British have lost their old vigor and they have no longer any new ideas. They are no longer an important or leading nation in the world." To which Herbert Spencer, the great sociologist, answered: "Look at the European continent. All European capitals have light because a British gas company provides them with gas." This was, of course, in what seems to us the "remote" age of gas lighting. Further answering this British critic, Herbert Spencer added: "You say that the Germans are far ahead of Great Britain. But look at Germany. Even Berlin, the capital of the German Reich, the capital of *Geist*, would be in the dark if a British gas company had not invaded the country and lighted the streets."

In the same way, British capital developed the railroads and many branches of industry in the United States. And, of course, as long as a country imports capital its balance of trade is what the noneconomists call "unfavorable." That means that it has an excess of imports over exports. The reason for the "favorable balance of trade" of Great Britain was that the British factories sent many types of equipment to the United States, and this equipment was not paid for by anything other than shares of American corporations. This period in the history of the United States lasted, by and large, until the 1890s.

But when the United States, with the aid of British capital — and later with the aid of its own procapitalistic policies — developed its own economic system in an unprecedented way, the Americans began to buy back the capital stocks they had once sold to foreigners. Then the United States had a surplus of exports over imports. The difference was paid by the importation — by the repatriation, as one called it — of American common stock.

This period lasted until the First World War. What happened later is another story. It is the story of the American subsidies for the belligerent countries in between and after two world wars: the loans, the investments the United States made in Europe, in addition to lend-lease, foreign aid, the Marshall Plan, food that was sent overseas, and other subsidies. I emphasize this because people sometimes believe that it is shameful or degrading to have foreign capital working in their country. You have to realize that, in all countries except England, foreign capital investment played a considerable part in the development of modern industries.

If I say that foreign investment was the greatest historical event of the nineteenth century, you must think of all those things that would not have come into being if there had not been any foreign investment. All the railroads, the harbors, the factories and mines in Asia, and the Suez Canal and many other things in the Western hemisphere, would not have been constructed had there been no foreign investment.

Foreign investment is made in the expectation that it will not be expropriated. Nobody would invest anything if he knew in advance that somebody would expropriate his investments. At the time when these foreign investments were made in the nineteenth century, and at the beginning of the twentieth century, there was no question of expropriation. From the beginning, some countries showed a certain hostility toward foreign capital, but for the most part they realized very well that they derived an enormous advantage from these foreign investments.

In some cases, these foreign investments were not made directly to foreign capitalists, but indirectly by loans to the foreign government. Then it was the government that used the money for investments. Such was, for instance, the case in Russia. For purely political reasons, the French invested in Russia, in the two decades preceding the First World War, about twenty billion gold francs, lending them chiefly to the Russian government. All the great enterprises of the Russian government — for instance, the railroad that connects Russia from the Ural Mountains, through the ice and snow of Siberia, to the Pacific — were built mostly with foreign capital lent to the Russian government. You will realize that the French did not assume that one day there would be a communist Russian government that would simply declare it would not pay the debts incurred by its predecessor, the tsarist government.

Starting with the First World War, there began a period of worldwide open warfare against foreign investments. Since there is no remedy to prevent a government from expropriating invested capital, there is practically no legal protection for foreign investments in the world today. The capitalists did not foresee this. If the capitalists of the capital exporting countries had realized it, all foreign investments would have come to an end forty or fifty years ago. But the capitalists did not believe that any country would be so unethical as to renege on a debt, to expropriate and confiscate foreign capital. With these acts, a new chapter began in the economic history of the world.

With the end of the great period in the nineteenth century when foreign capital helped to develop, in all parts of the world, modern methods of transportation, manufacturing, mining, and agriculture, there came a new era in which the governments and the political parties considered the foreign investor as an *exploiter* who should be expelled from the country.

In this anti-capitalist attitude the Russians were not the only sinners. Remember, for example, the expropriation of the American oil fields in Mexico, and all the things that have happened in *this* country (Argentina) which I have no need to discuss.

The situation in the world today, created by the system of expropriation of foreign capital, consists either of direct expropriation or of indirect expropriation through foreign exchange control or tax discrimination. This is mainly a problem of developing nations.

Take, for instance, the biggest of these nations: India. Under the British system, British capital — predominately British capital, but also capital of other European countries — was invested in India. And the British exported to India something else which also has to be mentioned in this connection; they exported into India modern methods of fighting contagious diseases. The result was a tremendous increase in the Indian population and a corresponding increase in the country's troubles. Facing such a worsening situation, India turned to expropriation as a means of dealing with its problems. But it was not always direct expropriation; the government harassed foreign capitalists, hampering them in their investments in such a way that these foreign investors were forced to sell out.

India could, of course, accumulate capital by another method: the *domestic* accumulation of capital. However, India is as hostile to the domestic accumulation of capital as it is to foreign capitalists. The Indian government says it wants to industrialize India, but what it really has in mind is to have *socialist* enterprises.

A few years ago the famous statesman Jawaharlal Nehru published a collection of his speeches. The book was published with the intention of making foreign investment in India more attractive. The Indian government is not opposed to foreign investment *before* it is invested. The hostility begins only when it is *already* invested. In this book — I am quoting literally from the book — Mr. Nehru said: "Of course, we want to socialize. But we are not opposed to private enterprise. We want to encourage in every way private enterprise. We want to promise the entrepreneurs who invest in our country, that we will not expropriate them nor socialize them for ten years, perhaps even for a longer time." And he thought this was an invitation to come to India!

The problem — as you know — is domestic capital accumulation. In all countries today there are very heavy taxes on corporations. In fact, there is double taxation on corporations. First, the profits of corporations are taxed very heavily, and the dividends which corporations pay to their shareholders are taxed again. And this is done in a progressive way.

Progressive taxation of income and profits means that precisely those parts of the income which people would have saved and invested are taxed away. Take the example of the United States. A few years ago, there was an "excess-profit" tax, which meant that out of one dollar earned, a corporation retained only eighteen cents. When these eighteen cents were paid out to the shareholders, those who had a great number of shares had to pay another sixty or eighty or even greater percent of it in taxes. Out of the dollar of profit they retained about seven cents, and ninety-three cents went to the government. Of this ninety-three percent, the greater part would have been saved and invested. Instead, the government used it for current expenditure. This is the policy of the United States.

I think I have made it clear that the policy of the United States is not an example to be imitated by other countries. This policy of the United States is worse than bad — it is *insane*. The only thing I would add is that a rich country can afford more bad policies than a poor country. In the United States, in spite of all these methods of taxation, there is still some additional accumulation of capital and investment every year, and therefore there is still a trend toward an improvement of the standard of living.

But in many other countries the problem is very critical. There is no — or not sufficient — domestic saving, and capital investment from abroad is seriously reduced by the fact that these countries are openly hostile to foreign investment. How can they talk about industrialization, about the necessity to develop new plants, to improve conditions, to raise the standard of living, to have higher wage rates, better means of transportation, if they are doing things that will have precisely the opposite effect? What their policies actually accomplish is to prevent or to slow down the accumulation of domestic capital and to put obstacles in the way of foreign capital.

The end result is certainly very bad. Such a situation must bring about a loss of confidence, and there is now more and more distrust of foreign investment in the world. Even if the countries concerned were to change their policies immediately and were to make all possible promises, it is very doubtful that they could once more inspire foreign capitalists to invest.

There are, of course, some methods to avoid this consequence. One could establish some international statutes, not only agreements, that would withdraw the foreign investments from national jurisdiction. This is something the United Nations could do. But the United Nations is simply a meeting place for useless discussions. Realizing the enormous importance of foreign investment, realizing that foreign investment alone can bring about an improvement in political and economical world conditions, one could try to do something from the point of view of international legislation.

This is a technical legal problem, which I only mention, because the situation is not hopeless. If the world really wanted to make it possible for the developing countries to raise their standard of living to the level of the American way of life, then it could be done. It is only necessary to realize *how* it could be done.

What is lacking in order to make the developing countries as prosperous as the United States is only one thing: *capital* — and, of course, the freedom to employ it under the discipline of the market and not the discipline of the government. These nations must accumulate domestic capital, and they must make it possible for foreign capital to come into their countries.

For the development of domestic saving it is necessary to mention again that domestic saving by the masses of the population presupposes a stable monetary unit. This implies the absence of *any* kind of inflation.

A great part of the capital at work in American enterprises is owned by the workers themselves and by other people with modest means. Billions and billions of saving deposits, of bonds, and of insurance policies are operating in these enterprises. On the American money market today it is no longer the banks, it is the insurance companies that are the greatest money lenders. And the money of the insurance company is — not legally, but economically — the property of the insured. And practically everybody in the United States is insured in one way or another.

The prerequisite for more economic equality in the world is industrialization. And this is possible only through increased capital investment, increased capital accumulation. You may be astonished that I have not mentioned a measure which is considered a prime method to industrialize a country. I mean protectionism. But tariffs and foreign exchange controls are exactly the means to *prevent* the importation of capital and industrialization into the country. The only way to increase industrialization is to have more capital. Protectionism can only divert investments from one branch of business to another branch.

Protectionism, in itself, does not add anything to the capital of a country. To start a new factory one needs capital. To improve an already existing factory one needs capital, and not a tariff.

I do not want to discuss the whole problem of free trade or protectionism. I hope that most of your textbooks on economics represent it in a proper way. Protection does not change the economic situation in a country for the better. And what *certainly* does not change it for the better is labor unionism. If conditions are unsatisfactory, if wages are low, if the wage earner in a country looks to the United States and reads about what is going on there, if he sees in the movies how the home of an average American is equipped with all modern comforts, he may be envious. He is perfectly right in saying: "We ought to have the same thing." But the only way to obtain it is through an increase in capital.

Labor unions use violence against entrepreneurs and against people they call strikebreakers. Despite their power and their violence, however, unions cannot raise wages continually for all wage earners. Equally ineffective are government decrees fixing minimum wage rates. What the unions *do* bring about (if they succeed in raising wage rates) is permanent, lasting unemployment.

But unions cannot industrialize the country, they cannot raise the standard of living of the workers. And this is the decisive point: One must realize that all the policies of a country that wants to improve its standard of living must be directed toward an increase in the capital invested per capital. This per capita investment of capital is still increasing in the United States, in spite of all of the bad policies there. And the same is true in Canada and in some of the West European countries. But it is unfortunately decreasing in countries like India.

We read every day in the newspapers that the population of the world is becoming greater, by perhaps 45 million people — or even more — per year. And how will this end? What will the results and the consequences be? Remember what I said about Great Britain. In 1750 the British people believed that six million constituted a tremendous overpopulation of the British Isles and that they were headed for famines and plagues. But on the eve of the last world war, in 1939, fifty million people were living in the British Isles, and the standard of living was incomparably higher than it had been in 1750. This was the effect of what is called industrialization — a rather inadequate term.

Britain's progress was brought about by increasing the per capita investment of capital. As I said before, there is only one way a nation can achieve prosperity: if you increase capital, you increase the marginal productivity of labor, and the effect will be that real wages will rise.

In a world without migration barriers, there would be a tendency all over the world toward an equalization of wage rates. If there were no migration barriers today, probably twenty million people would try to reach the United States every year, in order to get higher wages. The inflow would reduce wages in the United States, and raise them in other countries.

I do not have time to deal with this problem of migration barriers. But I do want to say that there is another method toward the equalization of wage rates all over the world. This other method, which operates in the absence of the freedom to migrate, is the *migration of capital*. Capitalists have the tendency to move towards those countries in which there is plenty of labor available and in which labor is reasonable. And by the fact that they bring capital into these countries, they bring about a trend toward higher wage rates. This has worked in the past, and it will work in the future, in the same way.

When British capital was first invested in, let us say, Austria or Bolivia, wage rates there were much, much lower than they were in Great Britain. But this additional investment brought about a trend toward higher wage rates in those countries. And such a tendency prevailed all over the world. It is a very well-known fact that as soon as, for instance, the United Fruit Company moved into Guatemala, the result was a general tendency toward higher wage rates, beginning with the wages which United Fruit Company paid, which then made it necessary for other employers to pay higher wages also. Therefore, there is no reason at all to be pessimistic in regard to the future of "undeveloped" countries.

I fully agree with the Communists and the labor unions, when they say: "What is needed is to raise the standard of living." A short time ago, in a book published in the United States, a professor said: "We now have enough of everything, why should people in the world still work so hard? We have everything already." I do not doubt that this professor has everything. But there are other people in other countries, also many people in the United States, who want and should have a better standard of living.

Outside of the United States — in Latin America, and still more in Asia and Africa — everyone wishes to see conditions improved in his own country. A higher standard of living also brings about a higher standard of culture and civilization.

So I fully agree with the ultimate goal of raising the standard of living everywhere. But I disagree about the measures to be adopted in attaining this goal. What measures will attain this end? Not protection, not government interference, not socialism, and certainly not the violence of the labor unions (euphemistically called collective bargaining, which, in fact, is bargaining *at the point of a gun*).

To attain the end, as I see it, there is only one way! It is a slow method. Some people may say, it is too slow. But there are no short cuts to an earthly paradise. It takes time, and one has to work. But it does not take as much time as people believe, and finally an equalization will come.

Around 1840, in the western part of Germany — in Swabia and Würtemberg, which was one of the most industrialized areas in the world — it was said: "We can never attain the level of the British. The English have a head start and they will forever be ahead of us." Thirty years later the British said: "This German competition, we cannot stand it; we have to do something against it." At that time, of course, the German standard was rapidly rising and was, even then, approaching the British standard. And today the German income per capita is not behind that of Great Britain at all.

In the center of Europe, there is a small country, Switzerland, which nature has endowed very poorly. It has no coal mines, no minerals, and no natural resources. But its people, over the centuries, have continually pursued a capitalistic policy. They have developed the highest standard of living in continental Europe, and their country ranks as one of the world's great centers of civilization. I do not see why a country such as Argentina — which is much larger than Switzerland both in population and in size — should not attain the same high standard of living after some years of good policies. But — as I pointed out — the policies must be good. ❯

HUMAN ACTION[2]

9. Entrepreneurial Profits and Losses in a Progressing Economy

In the imaginary construction of a stationary economy the total sum of all entrepreneurs' profits equals the total sum of all entrepreneurs' losses. What one entrepreneur profits is in the total economic system counterbalanced by another entrepreneur's loss. The surplus which all the consumers together expend for the acquisition of a certain commodity is counterbalanced by the reduction in their expenditure for the acquisition of other commodities.[3]

It is different in a progressing economy.

We call a progressing economy an economy in which the per capita quota of capital invested is increasing. In using this term we do not imply value judgments. We adopt neither the "materialistic" view that such a progression is good nor the "idealistic" view that it is bad or at least irrelevant from a "higher point of view." Of course, it is a well-known fact that the immense majority of people consider the consequences of progress in this sense as the most desirable state of affairs and yearn for conditions which can be realized only in a progressing economy.

---

[2][Ludwig von Mises, *Human Action* (1949; Auburn, Ala.: Mises Institute, 1998), chap. 15: "The Market," pp. 292–96.]

[3]If we were to apply the faulty concept of a "national income" as used in popular speech, we would have to say that no part of national income goes into profits.

In the stationary economy the entrepreneurs, in the pursuit of their specific functions, cannot achieve anything other than to withdraw factors of production, provided that they are still convertible, from one line of business in order to employ them in another line, or to direct the restoration of the equivalent of capital goods used up in the course of production processes toward the expansion of certain branches of industry at the expense of other branches. In the progressing economy the range of entrepreneurial activities includes, moreover, the determination of the employment of the additional capital goods accumulated by new savings. The injection of these additional capital goods is bound to increase the total sum of the income produced, i.e., of that supply of consumers' goods which can be consumed without diminishing the capital equipment used in its production thereby without impairing the output of future production. The increase of income is effected either by an expansion of production without altering the technological methods of production or by an improvement in technological methods which would not have been feasible under the previous conditions of a less ample supply of capital goods.

It is out of this additional wealth that the surplus of the total sum of entrepreneurial profits over the total sum of entrepreneurial losses flows. But it can be easily demonstrated that this surplus can never exhaust the total increase in wealth brought about by economic progress. The laws of the market divide this additional wealth between the entrepreneurs and the suppliers of labor and those of certain material factors of production in such a way that the lion's share goes to the nonentrepreneurial groups.

First of all we must realize that entrepreneurial profits are not a lasting phenomenon but only temporary. There prevails an inherent tendency for profits and losses to disappear. The market is always moving toward the emergence of the final prices and the final state of rest. If new changes in the data were not to interrupt this movement and not to create the need for a new adjustment of production to the altered conditions, the prices of all complementary factors of production would — due allowance being made for time preference — finally equal the price of the product, and nothing would be left for profits or losses. In the long run every increase in productivity benefits exclusively the workers and some groups of the owners of land and of capital goods.

In the groups of the owners of capital goods there are benefited:

1. Those whose saving has increased the quantity of capital goods available. They own this additional wealth, the outcome of their restraint in consuming.

2. The owners of those capital goods already previously existing which, thanks to the improvement in technological methods of production, are now better utilized than before. Such gains are, of course, temporary only. They are bound to disappear as they cause a tendency toward an intensified production of the capital goods concerned.

On the other hand, the increase in the quantity of capital goods available lowers the marginal productivity of capital; it thus brings about a fall in the prices of the capital goods and thereby hurts the interests of all those capitalists who did not share at all or not sufficiently in the process of saving and the accumulation of the additional supply of capital goods.

In the group of the landowners all those are benefited for whom the new state of affairs results in a higher productivity of their farms, forests, fisheries, mines, and so on. On the other hand, all those are hurt whose property may become submarginal on account of the higher return yielded by the land owned by those benefited.

In the group of labor all derive a lasting gain from the increase in the marginal productivity of labor. But, on the other hand, in the short run some may suffer disadvantages. These are people who were specialized in the performance of work which becomes obsolete as a result of technological improvement and are fitted only for jobs in which — in spite of the general rise in wage rates — they earn less than before.

All these changes in the prices of the factors of production begin immediately with the initiation of the entrepreneurial actions designed to adjust the processes of production to the new state of affairs. In dealing with this problem as with the other problems of changes in the market data, we must guard ourselves against the popular fallacy of drawing a sharp line between short-run and long-run effects. What happens in the short run is precisely the first stages of the chain of successive transformations which tend to bring about the long-run effects. The long-run effect is in our case the disappearance of entrepreneurial profits and losses. The short-run effects are the preliminary stages of this process of elimination which finally, if not interrupted by a further change in the data, would result in the emergence of the evenly rotating economy.

It is necessary to comprehend that the very appearance of an excess in the total amount of entrepreneurial profits over the total amount of entrepreneurial losses depends upon the fact that this process of the elimination of entrepreneurial profit and loss begins at the same time as the entrepreneurs begin to adjust the complex of production activities to the changed data. There is never in the whole sequence of events an instant in which the advantages derived from the increase in the amount of capital available and from technical improvements benefit the entrepreneurs only. If the wealth and the income of the other strata were to remain unaffected, these people could buy the additional products only by restricting their purchases of other products accordingly. Then the profits of one group of entrepreneurs would exactly equal the losses incurred by other groups.

What happens is this: The entrepreneurs embarking upon the utilization of the newly accumulated capital goods and the improved technological methods of production are in need of complementary factors of production. Their demand for these factors is a new additional demand which must raise their prices. Only as far as this rise in prices and wage rates occurs, are the consumers in a position to buy the new products without curtailing the purchase of other goods. Only so far can a surplus of the total sum of all entrepreneurial profits over all entrepreneurial losses come into existence.

The vehicle of economic progress is the accumulation of additional capital goods by means of saving and improvement in technological methods of production the execution of which is almost always conditioned by the availability of such new capital. The agents of progress are the promoting entrepreneurs intent upon profiting by means of adjusting the conduct of affairs to the best possible satisfaction of the consumers. In the performance of their projects for the realization of progress they are bound to share the benefits derived from progress with the workers and also with a part of the capitalists and landowners and to increase the portion allotted to these people step by step until their own share melts away entirely.

From this it becomes evident that it is absurd to speak of a "rate of profit" or a "normal rate of profit" or an "average rate of profit." Profit is not related to or dependent on the amount of capital employed by the entrepreneur. Capital does not "beget" profit. Profit and loss are entirely determined by the success or failure of the entrepreneur to adjust production to the demand of the consumers. There is nothing "normal" in profits and there can never be an "equilibrium" with regard to them. Profit and loss are, on the contrary, always a phenomenon of a deviation from "normalcy," of changes unforeseen by the majority, and of a "disequilibrium." They have no place in an imaginary world of normalcy and equilibrium. In a changing economy there prevails always an inherent tendency for profits and losses to disappear. It is only the emergence of new changes which revives them again. Under stationary conditions the "average rate" of profits and losses is zero. An excess of the total amount of profits over that of losses is a proof of the fact that there is economic progress and an improvement in the standard of living of all strata of the population. The greater this excess is, the greater is the increment in general prosperity.

Many people are utterly unfit to deal with the phenomenon of entrepreneurial profit without indulging in envious resentment. In their eyes the source of profit is exploitation of the wage earners and the consumers, i.e., an unfair reduction in wage rates and a no less unfair increase in the prices of the products. By rights there should not be any profits at all.

Economics is indifferent with regard to such arbitrary value judgments. It is not interested in the problem of whether profits are to be approved or condemned from the point of view of an alleged natural law and of an alleged eternal and immutable code of morality about which personal intuition or divine revelation are supposed to convey precise information. Economics merely establishes the fact that entrepreneurial profits and losses are essential phenomena of the market economy. There cannot be a market economy without them. It is certainly possible for the police to confiscate all profits. But such a policy would by necessity convert the market economy into a senseless chaos. Man has, there is no doubt, the power to destroy many things, and he has made in the course of history ample use of this faculty. He could destroy the market economy too.

If those self-styled moralists were not blinded by their envy, they would not deal with profit without dealing simultaneously with its corollary, loss. They would not pass over in silence the fact that the preliminary conditions of economic improvement are an achievement of those whose saving accumulates the additional capital goods and of the inventors, and that the utilization of these conditions for the realization of economic improvement is effected by the entrepreneurs. The rest of the people do not contribute to progress, but they are benefited by the horn of plenty which other people's activities pour upon them. ▶

CHAPTER 18

The Importance of Liberty

LIBERTY AND PROPERTY[1]

I

A t the end of the eighteenth century there prevailed two notions of liberty, each of them very different from what we have in mind today referring to liberty and freedom.

The first of these conceptions was purely academic and without any application to the conduct of political affairs. It was an idea derived from the books of the ancient authors, the study of which was then the sum and substance of higher education. In the eyes of these Greek and Roman writers, freedom was not something that had to be granted to all men. It was a privilege of the minority, to be withheld from the majority. What the Greeks called democracy was, in the light of present-day terminology, not what Lincoln called government by the people, but oligarchy, the sovereignty of full-right citizens in a community in which the masses were meteques or slaves. Even this rather limited freedom after the fourth century before Christ was not dealt with by the philosophers, historians, and orators as a practical constitutional institution. As they saw it, it was a

---

[1] [Ludwig von Mises, *Liberty and Property* (1958; Auburn, Ala.: Mises Institute, 1988).]

feature of the past irretrievably lost. They bemoaned the passing of this golden age, but they did not know any method of returning to it.

The second notion of liberty was no less oligarchic, although it was not inspired by any literary reminiscences. It was the ambition of the landed aristocracy, and sometimes also of urban patricians, to preserve their privileges against the rising power of royal absolutism. In most parts of continental Europe, the princes remained victorious in these conflicts. Only in England and in the Netherlands did the gentry and the urban patricians succeed in defeating the dynasties. But what they won was not freedom for all, but only freedom for an elite, for a minority of the people.

We must not condemn as hypocrites the men who in those ages praised liberty, while they preserved the legal disabilities of the many, even serfdom and slavery. They were faced with a problem which they did not know how to solve satisfactorily. The traditional system of production was too narrow for a continually rising population. The number of people for whom there was, in a full sense of the term, no room left by the pre-capitalistic methods of agriculture and artisanship was increasing. These supernumeraries were starving paupers. They were a menace to the preservation of the existing order of society and, for a long time, nobody could think of another order, a state of affairs, that would feed all of these poor wretches. There could not be any question of granting them full civil rights, still less of giving them a share of the conduct of affairs of state. The only expedient the rulers knew was to keep them quiet by resorting to force.

II

The pre-capitalistic system of product was restrictive. Its historical basis was military conquest. The victorious kings had given the land to their paladins. These aristocrats were lords in the literal meaning of the word, as they did not depend on the patronage of consumers buying or abstaining from buying on a market. On the other hand, they themselves were the main customers of the processing industries which, under the guild system, were organized on a corporative scheme. This scheme was opposed to innovation. It forbade deviation from the traditional methods of production. The number of people for whom there were jobs even in agriculture or in the arts and crafts was limited. Under these conditions, many a man, to use the words of Malthus, had to discover that "at nature's mighty feast there is no vacant cover for him" and that "she tells him to be gone."[2] But some of these outcasts nevertheless managed to survive, begot children, and made the number of destitute grow hopelessly more and more.

But then came capitalism. It is customary to see the radical innovations that capitalism brought about in the substitution of the mechanical factory for the more primitive and less efficient methods of the artisans' shops. This is a rather superficial view. The characteristic feature of capitalism that distinguishes it from pre-capitalist methods of production was its new principle of marketing. Capitalism is not simply mass production, but mass production to satisfy the needs of the masses. The arts and crafts of the good old days had catered almost exclusively to the wants of the well-to-do. But the factories produced cheap goods for the many. All the early factories turned out was designed to serve the masses, the same strata that worked in the factories. They served them either by supplying them directly or indirectly by exporting and thus providing for them foreign food and raw materials. This principle of marketing was the signature of early capitalism as it is of present-day capitalism. The employees themselves are the customers consuming the much greater part of all goods produced. They are the sovereign customers who are "always right." Their buying or abstention from buying determines what has to be produced, in what quantity, and of what quality. In buying what suits them best they make some enterprises profit and expand and make other enterprises lose money and shrink. Thereby they are continually shifting control of the factors of production into the hands of those businessmen who are most successful in filling their wants. Under capitalism private property of the factors of production is a social function. The entrepreneurs, capitalists, and land owners are mandataries, as it were, of the consumers, and their mandate is revocable. In order to be rich, it is not sufficient to have once saved and accumulated capital. It is necessary to invest it again and again in those lines in which it best fills the wants of the consumers. The market process is a daily repeated plebiscite, and it ejects inevitably from the ranks of profitable people those who do not employ their property according to the orders given by the public. But business, the target of fanatical hatred on the part of all contemporary governments and self-styled intellectuals, acquires and preserves bigness only because it works for the masses. The plants that cater to the luxuries of the few never attain big size.

---

[2][Thomas R. Malthus, *An Essay on the Principle of Population*, 2d ed. (London, 1803), p. 531.]

The shortcoming of nineteenth-century historians and politicians was that they failed to realize that the workers were the main consumers of the products of industry. In their view, the wage earner was a man toiling for the sole benefit of a parasitic leisure class. They labored under the delusion that the factories had impaired the lot of the manual workers. If they had paid any attention to statistics they would easily have discovered the fallaciousness of their opinion. Infant mortality dropped, the average length of life was prolonged, the population multiplied, and the average common man enjoyed amenities of which even the well-to-do of earlier ages did not dream.

However this unprecedented enrichment of the masses were merely a by-product of the Industrial Revolution. Its main achievement was the transfer of economic supremacy from the owners of land to the totality of the population. The common man was no longer a drudge who had to be satisfied with the crumbs that fell from the tables of the rich. The three pariah castes which were characteristic of the pre-capitalistic ages — the slaves, the serfs, and those people whom patristic and scholastic authors as well as British legislation from the sixteenth to the nineteenth centuries referred to as the poor — disappeared. Their scions became, in this new setting of business, not only free workers, but also customers. This radical change was reflected in the emphasis laid by business on markets. What business needs first of all is markets and again markets. This was the watch-word of capitalistic enterprise. Markets, that means patrons, buyers, consumers. There is under capitalism one way to wealth: to serve the consumers better and cheaper than other people do.

Within the shop and factory the owner — or in the corporations, the representative of the shareholders, the president — is the boss. But this mastership is merely apparent and conditional. It is subject to the supremacy of the consumers. The consumer is king, is the real boss, and the manufacturer is done for if he does not outstrip his competitors in best serving consumers.

It was this great economic transformation that changed the face of the world. It very soon transferred political power from the hands of a privileged minority into the hands of the people. Adult franchise followed in the wake of industrial enfranchisement. The common man, to whom the market process had given the power to choose the entrepreneur and capitalists, acquired the analogous power in the field of government. He became a voter.

It has been observed by eminent economists, I think first by the late Frank A. Fetter, that the market is a democracy in which every penny gives a right to vote. It would be more correct to say that representative government by the people is an attempt to arrange constitutional affairs according to the model of the market, but this design can never be fully achieved. In the political field it is always the will of the majority that prevails, and the minorities must yield to it. It serves also minorities, provided they are not so insignificant in number as to become negligible. The garment industry produces clothes not only for normal people, but also for the stout, and the publishing trade publishes not only westerns and detective stories for the crowd, but also books for discriminating readers.

There is a second important difference. In the political sphere, there is no means for an individual or a small group of individuals to disobey the will of the majority. But in the intellectual field private property makes rebellion possible. The rebel has to pay a price for his independence; there are in this universe no prizes that can be won without sacrifices. But if a man is willing to pay the price, he is free to deviate from the ruling orthodoxy or neo-orthodoxy. What would conditions have been in the socialist commonwealth for heretics like Kierkegaard, Schopenauer, Veblen, or Freud? For Monet, Courbet, Walt Whitman, Rilke, or Kafka? In all ages, pioneers of new ways of thinking and acting could work only because private property made contempt of the majority's ways possible. Only a few of these separatists were themselves economically independent enough to defy the government into the opinions of the majority. But they found in the climate of the free economy among the public people prepared to aid and support them. What would Marx have done without his patron, the manufacturer Friedrich Engels?

III

What vitiates entirely the socialists' economic critique of capitalism is their failure to grasp the sovereignty of the consumers in the market economy. They see only hierarchical organization of the various enterprises and plans, and are at a loss to realize that the profit system forces business to serve the consumers. In their dealings with their employers, the unions proceed as if only malice and greed were to prevent what they call management from paying higher wage rates. Their shortsightedness does not see anything beyond the doors of the factory. They and their henchmen talk about the concentration of economic power, and do not realize that economic power is ultimately vested in the hands of the buying public of which the employees themselves form the immense majority. Their inability to comprehend things as they are is reflected in such inappropriate metaphors as industrial kingdom and dukedoms. They are too dull to see the difference between a sovereign king or duke who could be dispossessed only by a more powerful conqueror and a "chocolate king" who forfeits his "kingdom" as soon as the customers prefer to patronize another supplier.

This distortion is at the bottom of all socialist plans. If any of the socialist chiefs had tried to earn his living by selling hot dogs, he would have learned something about the sovereignty of the customers. But they were professional revolutionaries and their only job was to kindle civil war. Lenin's ideal was to build a nation's production effort according to the model of the post office, an outfit that does not depend on the consumers, because its deficits are covered by compulsory collection of taxes. "The whole of society," he said, was to "become one office and one factory."[3] He did not see that the very character of the office and the factory is entirely changed when it is alone in the world and no longer grants to people the opportunity to choose among the products and services of various enterprises. Because his blindness made it impossible for him to see the role the market and the consumers play under capitalism, he could not see the difference between freedom and slavery. Because in his eyes the workers were only workers and not also customers, he believed they were already slaves under capitalism, and that one did not change their status when nationalizing all plants and shops. Socialism substitutes the sovereignty of a dictator, or committee of dictators, for the sovereignty of the consumers. Along with the economic sovereignty of the citizens disappears also their political sovereignty. To the unique production plan that annuls any planning on the part of the consumers corresponds in the constitutional sphere the one party principle that deprives the citizens of any opportunity to plan the course of public affairs. Freedom is indivisible. He who has not the faculty to choose among various brands of canned food or soap, is also deprived of the power to choose between various political parties and programs and to elect the officeholders. He is no longer a man; he becomes a pawn in the hands of the supreme social engineer. Even his freedom to rear progeny will be taken away by eugenics. Of course, the socialist leaders occasionally assure us that dictatorial tyranny is to last only for the period of transition from capitalism and

---

3[V.I.] Lenin, *State and Revolution* (New York: International Publishers, s.d.) p. 84.

representative government to the socialist millennium in which every-body's wants and wishes will be fully satisfied.[4] Once the socialist regime is "sufficiently secure to risk criticism," Miss Joan Robinson, the eminent representative of the British neo-Cambridge school, is kind enough to promise us, "even independent philharmonic societies" will be allowed to exist.[5] Thus the liquidation of all dissenters is the condition that will bring us what the communists call freedom. From this point of view we may also understand what another distinguished Englishman, Mr. J.G. Crowther, had in mind when he praised inquisition as "beneficial to science when it protects a rising class."[6] The meaning of all this is clear. When all people meekly bow to a dictator, there will no longer be any dissenters left for liquidation. Caligula, Torquemada, Robespierre would have agreed with this solution.

The socialists have engineered a semantic revolution in converting the meaning of terms into their opposite. In the vocabulary of their "New-speak," as George Orwell called it, there is a term "the one-party principle." Now etymologically party is derived from the noun part. The brotherless part is no longer different from its antonym, the whole; it is identical with it. A brotherless party is not a party, and the one party principle is in fact a no-party principle. It is a suppression of any kind of opposition. Freedom implies the right to choose between assent and dissent. But in Newspeak it means the duty to assent unconditionally and strict interdiction of dis-sent. This reversal of the traditional connotation of all words of the politi-cal terminology is not merely a peculiarity of the language of the Russian Communists and their Fascist and Nazi disciples. The social order that in abolishing private property deprives the consumers of their autonomy and independence, and thereby subjects every man to the arbitrary discretion of the central planning board, could not win the support of the masses if they were not to camouflage its main character. The socialists would have never duped the voters if they had openly told them that their ultimate end is to cast them into bondage. For exoteric use they were forced to pay lip-service to the traditional appreciation of liberty.

---

[4][Karl] Marx, *Sur Kritik des Sozialdemoskratischen Programms von Gotha*, ed. Kreibich (Reichenberg, 1920), p. 23.

[5]Joan Robinson, *Private Enterprise and Public Control* (published for the Association for Education in Citizenship by the English Universities Press, Ltd., s.d.), pp. 13–14.

[6]J.G. Crowther, *Social Relations of Science* (London, 1941), p. 333.

IV

It was different in the esoteric discussions among the inner circles of the great conspiracy. There the initiated did not dissemble their intentions concerning liberty. Liberty was, in their opinion, certainly a good feature in the past in the frame of bourgeois society because it provided them with the opportunity to embark on their schemes. But once socialism has triumphed, there is no longer any need for free thought and autonomous action on the part of individuals. Any further change can only be a deviation from the perfect state that mankind has attained in reaching the bliss of socialism. Under such conditions, it would be simply lunacy to tolerate dissent.

Liberty, says the Bolshevist, is a bourgeois prejudice. The common man does not have any ideas of his own, he does not write books, does not hatch heresies, and does not invent new methods of production. He just wants to enjoy life. He has no use for the class interests of the intellectuals who make a living as professional dissenters and innovators.

This is certainly the most arrogant disdain of the plain citizen ever devised. There is no need to argue this point. For the question is not whether or not the common man can himself take advantage of the liberty to think, to speak, and to write books. The question is whether or not the sluggish routinist profits from the freedom granted to those who eclipse him in intelligence and will power. The common man may look with indifference and even contempt upon the dealings of better people. But he is delighted to enjoy all the benefits which the endeavors of the innovators put at his disposal. He has no comprehension of what in his eyes is merely inane hair-splitting. But as soon as these thoughts and theories are utilized by enterprising businessmen for satisfying some of his latent wishes, he hurries to acquire the new products. The common man is without doubt the main beneficiary of all the accomplishments of modern science and technology.

It is true, a man of average intellectual abilities has no chance to rise to the rank of a captain of industry. But the sovereignty that the market assigns to him in economic affairs stimulates technologists and promoters to convert to his use all the achievements of scientific research. Only people whose intellectual horizon does not extend beyond the internal organization of the factory and who do not realize what makes the businessmen run, fail to notice this fact.

The admirers of the Soviet system tell us again and again that freedom is not the supreme good. It is "not worth having," if it implies poverty. To sacrifice it in order to attain wealth for the masses, is in their eyes fully justified. But for a few unruly individualists who cannot adjust themselves to the ways of regular fellows, all people in Russia are perfectly happy. We may leave it undecided whether this happiness was also shared by the millions of Ukrainian peasants who died from starvation, by the inmates of the forced labor camps, and by the Marxian leaders who were purged. But we cannot pass over the fact that the standard of living was incomparably higher in the free countries of the West than in the communist East. In giving away liberty as the price to be paid for the acquisition of prosperity, the Russians made a poor bargain. They now have neither the one nor the other.

V

Romantic philosophy labored under the illusion that in the early ages of history the individual was free and that the course of historical evolution deprived him of his primordial liberty. As Jean Jacques Rousseau saw it, nature accorded men freedom and society enslaved him. In fact, primeval man was at the mercy of every fellow who was stronger and therefore could snatch away from him the scarce means of subsistence. There is in nature nothing to which the name of liberty could be given. The concept of freedom always refers to social relations between men. True, society cannot realize the illusory concept of the individual's absolute independence. Within society everyone depends on what other people are prepared to contribute to his well-being in return for his own contribution to their well-being. Society is essentially the mutual exchange of services. As far as individuals have the opportunity to choose, they are free; if they are forced by violence or threat of violence to surrender to the terms of an exchange, no matter how they feel about it, they lack freedom. This slave is unfree precisely because the master assigns him his tasks and determines what he has to receive if he fulfills it.

As regards the social apparatus of repression and coercion, the government, there cannot be any question of freedom. Government is essentially the negation of liberty. It is the recourse to violence or threat of violence in order to make all people obey the orders of the government, whether they like it or not. As far as the government's jurisdiction extends, there is coercion, not freedom. Government is a necessary institution, the means to make the social system of cooperation work smoothly without being disturbed by violent acts on the part of gangsters whether of domestic or of foreign origin. Government is not, as some people like to say, a necessary evil; it is not an evil, but a means, the only means available to make peaceful human coexistence possible. But it is the opposite of liberty. It is beating, imprisoning, hanging. Whatever a government does it is ultimately supported by the actions of armed constables. If the government operates a school or a hospital, the funds required are collected by taxes, i.e., by payments exacted from the citizens.

If we take into account the fact that, as human nature is, there can neither be civilization nor peace without the functioning of the government apparatus of violent action, we may call government the most beneficial human institution. But the fact remains that government is repression not freedom. Freedom is to be found only in the sphere in which government does not interfere. Liberty is always freedom from the government. It is the restriction of the government's interference. It prevails only in the fields in which the citizens have the opportunity to choose the way in which they want to proceed. Civil rights are the statutes that precisely circumscribe the sphere in which the men conducting the affairs of state are permitted to restrict the individuals' freedom to act.

The ultimate end that men aim at by establishing government is to make possible the operation of a definite system of social cooperation under the principle of the division of labor. If the social system which people want to have is socialism (communism, planning) there is no sphere of freedom left. All citizens are in every regard subject to orders of the government. The state is a total state; the regime is totalitarian. The government alone plans and forces everybody to behave according with this unique plan. In the market economy the individuals are free to choose the way in which they want to integrate themselves into the frame of social cooperation. As far as the sphere of market exchange extends, there is spontaneous action on the part of individuals. Under this system that is called laissez-faire, and which Ferdinand Lassalle dubbed as the nightwatchman state, there is freedom because there is a field in which individuals are free to plan for themselves.

The socialists must admit there cannot be any freedom under a socialist system. But they try to obliterate the difference between the servile state and economic freedom by denying that there is any freedom in the mutual exchange of commodities and services on the market. Every market exchange is, in the words of a school of pro-socialist lawyers, "a coercion over other people's liberty." There is, in their eyes, no difference worth mentioning between a man's paying a tax or a fine imposed by a magistrate, or his buying a newspaper or admission to a movie. In each of these cases the man is subject to governing power. He's not free, for, as professor Hale says, a man's freedom means "the absence of any obstacle to his use of material goods."[7] This means: I am not free, because a woman who has knitted a sweater, perhaps as a birthday present for her husband, puts an obstacle to my using it. I myself am restricting all other people's freedom because I object to their using my toothbrush. In doing this I am, according to this doctrine, exercising private governing power, which is analogous to public government power, the powers that the government exercises in imprisoning a man in Sing Sing.

Those expounding this amazing doctrine consistently conclude that liberty is nowhere to be found. They assert that what they call economic pressures do not essentially differ from the pressures the masters practice with regard to their slaves. They reject what they call private governmental power, but they don't object to the restriction of liberty by public government power. They want to concentrate all what they call restrictions of liberty in the hands of the government. They attack the institution of private property and the laws that, as they say, stand "ready to enforce property rights — that is, to deny liberty to anyone to act in a way which violates them."[8]

A generation ago all housewives prepared soup by proceeding in accordance with the recipes that they had got from their mothers or from a cookbook. Today many housewives prefer to buy a canned soup, to warm it and to serve it to their family. But, say our learned doctors, the canning corporation is in a position to restrict the housewife's freedom because, in asking a price for the tin can, it puts an obstacle to her use of it. People who did not enjoy the privilege of being tutored by these eminent teachers, would say that the canned product was turned out by the cannery, and that the corporation in producing it removed the greatest obstacle to a consumer's getting and using a can, viz., its nonexistence. The mere essence of a product cannot gratify anybody without its existence. But they are wrong, say the doctors. The corporation dominates the housewife, it destroys by its excessive concentrated power over her individual freedom, and it is the duty of the government to prevent such a gross offense. Corporations, say,

---

[7]Robert L. Hale, *Freedom Through Law, Public Control of Private Governing Power* (New York: Columbia University, 1952), pp. 4ff.

[8]Ibid., p. 5.

under the auspices of the Ford Foundation, another of this group, Professor Berle, must be subjected to the control of the government.[9]

Why does our housewife buy the canned product rather than cling to the methods of her mother and grandmother? No doubt because she thinks this way of acting is more advantageous for her than the traditional custom. Nobody forced her. There were people — they are called jobbers, promoters, capitalists, speculators, stock exchange gamblers — who had the idea of satisfying a latent wish of millions of housewives by investing in the cannery industry. And there are other equally selfish capitalists who, in many hundreds of other corporations, provide consumers with many hundreds of other things. The better a corporation serves the public, the more customers it gets, the bigger it grows. Go into the home of the average American family and you will see for whom the wheels of the machines are turning.

In a free country nobody is prevented from acquiring riches by serving the consumers better than they are served already. What he needs is only brains and hard work. "Modern civilization, nearly all civilization," said Edwin Cannan, the last in a long line of eminent British economists, "is based on the principle of making things pleasant for those who please the market, and unpleasant for those who fail to do so."[10] All this talk about the concentration of economic power is vain. The bigger a corporation is, the more people it serves, the more does it depend on pleasing the consumers, the many, the masses. Economic power, in the market economy, is in the hands of the consumers.

Capitalistic business is not perseverance in the once attained state of production. It is rather ceaseless innovation, daily repeated attempts to improve the provision of the consumers by new, better and cheaper products. Any actual state of production activities is merely transitory. There prevails incessantly the tendency to supplant what is already achieved by something that serves the consumers better. There is consequently under capitalism a continuous circulation of elites. What characterizes the men whom one calls the captains of industry is the ability to contribute new ideas and to put them to work. However big a corporation must be, it is doomed as soon as it does not succeed in adjusting itself daily anew to the

---

[9]A.A. Berle, Jr., *Economic Power and the Free Society, a Preliminary Discussion of the Corporation* (New York: The Fund for the Republic, 1954).

[10]Edwin Cannan, *An Economist's Protest* (London, 1928), pp. VIff.

best possible methods of serving the consumers. But the politicians and other would-be reformers see only the structure of industry as its exists today. They think that they are clever enough to snatch from business control of the plants as they are today, and to manage them by sticking to already established routines. While the ambitious newcomer, who will be the tycoon of tomorrow, is already preparing plans for things unheard of before, all they have in mind is to conduct affairs along tracks already beaten. There is no record of an industrial innovation contrived and put into practice by bureaucrats. If one does not want to plunge into stagnation, a free hand must be left to those today unknown men who have the ingenuity to lead mankind forward on the way to more and more satisfactory conditions. This is the main problem of a nation's economic organization.

Private property of the material factors of production is not a restriction of the freedom of all other people to choose what suits them best. It is, on the contrary, the means that assigns to the common man, in his capacity as a buyer, supremacy in all economic affairs. It is the means to stimulate a nation's most enterprising men to exert themselves to the best of their abilities in the service of all of the people.

VI

However, one does not exhaustively describe the sweeping changes that capitalism brought about in the conditions of the common man if one merely deals with the supremacy he enjoys on the market as a consumer and in the affairs of state as a voter and with the unprecedented improvement of his standard of living. No less important is the fact that capitalism has made it possible for him to save, to accumulate capital and to invest it. The gulf that in the pre-capitalistic status and caste society separated the owners of property from the penniless poor has been narrowed down. In older ages the journeyman had such a low pay that he could hardly lay by something and, if he nevertheless did so, he could only keep his savings by hoarding and hiding a few coins. Under capitalism his competence makes saving possible, and there are institutions that enable him to invest his funds in business. A not inconsiderable amount of the capital employed in American industries is the counterpart of the savings of employees. In acquiring savings deposits, insurance policies, bonds and also common stock, wage earners and salaried people are themselves earning interest and dividends and thereby, in the terminology of Marxism, are exploiters. The common man is directly interested in the flowering of business not only as a consumer and as an employee, but also as an investor. There prevails a tendency to efface to some extent the once sharp difference between those who own factors of production and those who do not. But, of course, this trend can only develop where the market economy is not sabotaged by allegedly social policies. The welfare state with its methods of easy money, credit expansion and undisguised inflation continually takes bites out of all claims payable in units of the nation's legal tender. The self-styled champions of the common man are still guided by the obsolete idea that a policy that favors the debtors at the expense of the creditors is very beneficial to the majority of the people. Their inability to comprehend the essential characteristics of the market economy manifests itself also in their failure to see the obvious fact that those whom they feign to aid are creditors in their capacity as savers, policy holders, and owners of bonds.

VII

The distinctive principle of Western social philosophy is individualism. It aims at the creation of a sphere in which the individual is free to think, to choose, and to act without being restrained by the interference of the social apparatus of coercion and oppression, the State. All the spiritual and material achievements of Western civilization were the result of the operation of this idea of liberty.

This doctrine and the policies of individualism and of capitalism, its application to economic matters, do not need any apologists or propagandists. The achievements speak for themselves.

The case for capitalism and private property rests, apart from other considerations, also upon the incomparable efficiency of its productive effort. It is this efficiency that makes it possible for capitalistic business to support a rapidly increasing population at a continually improving standard of living. The resulting progressive prosperity of the masses creates a social environment in which the exceptionally gifted individuals are free to give to their fellow-citizens all they are able to give. The social system of private property and limited government is the only system that tends to debarbarize all those who have the innate capacity to acquire personal culture.

It is a gratuitous pastime to belittle the material achievements of capitalism by observing that there are things that are more essential for mankind than bigger and speedier motorcars, and homes equipped with central heating, air conditioning, refrigerators, washing machines, and television sets. There certainly are such higher and nobler pursuits. But they are higher and nobler precisely because they cannot be aspired to by any external effort, but require the individual's personal determination and exertion. Those levelling this reproach against capitalism display a rather crude and materialistic view in assuming that moral and spiritual culture could be built either by the government or by the organization of production activities. All that these external factors can achieve in this regard is to bring about an environment and a competence which offers the individuals the opportunity to work at their own personal perfection and edification. It is not the fault of capitalism that the masses prefer a boxing match to a performance of Sophocles's *Antigone*, jazz music to Beethoven symphonies, and comics to poetry. But it is certain that while pre-capitalistic conditions as they still prevail in the much greater part of the world makes these good things accessible only to a small minority of people, capitalism gives to the many a favorable chance of striving after them.

From whatever angle one may look at capitalism there is no reason to lament the passing of the allegedly good old days. Still less is it justified to long for the totalitarian utopias, whether of the Nazi or of the Soviet type.

We are inaugurating tonight the ninth meeting of the Mont Pelerin Society. It is fitting to remember on this occasion that meetings of this kind in which opinions opposed to those of the majority of our contemporaries and to those of their governments are advanced and are possible only in the climate of liberty and freedom that is the most precious mark of Western civilization. Let us hope that this right to dissent will never disappear. ▶

CHAPTER 19

Economic Method

MONEY, METHOD, AND THE MARKET PROCESS[1]

"SOCIAL SCIENCE AND NATURAL SCIENCE"

I

The foundations of the modern social sciences were laid in the eighteenth century. Up to this time we find history only. Of course, the writings of the historians are full of implications which purport to be valid for all human action irrespective of time and milieu, and even when they do not explicitly set forth such theses they necessarily base their grasp of the facts and their interpretation on assumptions of this type. But no attempt was made to clarify these tacit suppositions by special analysis.

On the other hand the belief prevailed that in the field of human action no other criterion could be used than that of good and bad. If a policy did not attain its end, its failure was ascribed to the moral insufficiency of man or to the weakness of the government. With good men and strong governments everything was considered feasible.

---

[1][Ludwig von Mises, *Money, Method, and the Market Process: Essays by Ludwig von Mises,* ed. Richard Ebeling (1942; Boston: Kluwer, 1990), chap. 1, pp. 3–15.]

Then in the eighteenth century came a radical change. The founders of Political Economy discovered regularity in the operation of the market. They discovered that to every state of the market a certain state of prices corresponded and that a tendency to restore this state made itself manifest whenever anything tried to alter it. This insight opened a new chapter in science. People came to realize with astonishment that human actions were open to investigation from other points of view than that of moral judgment. They were compelled to recognize a regularity which they compared to that with which they were already familiar in the field of the natural sciences.

Since the days of Cantillon, Hume, the Physiocrats and Adam Smith, economic theory has made continuous — although not steady — progress. In the course of this development it has become much more than a theory of market operations within the frame of a society based on private ownership of the means of production. It has for some time been a general theory of human action, of human choice and preference.

II

The elements of social cognition are abstract and not reducible to any concrete images that might be apprehended by the senses. To make them easier to visualize one likes to have recourse to metaphorical language. For some time the biological metaphors were very popular. There were writers who overworked this metaphor to ridiculous extremes. It will suffice to cite the name of Lilienfeld.[2]

Today the mechanistic metaphor is much more in use. The theoretical basis for its application is to be found in the positivist view of social science. Positivism blithely waved aside everything which history and economics taught. History, in its eyes, is simply no science; economics a special kind of metaphysics. In place of both, Positivism postulates a social science which has to be built up by the experimental method as ideally applied in Newtonian physics. Economics has to be experimental, mathematical and quantitative. Its task is to measure, because science is measurement. Every statement must be open to verification by facts.

Every proposition of this positivist epistemology is wrong.

The social sciences in general and economics in particular cannot be based on experience in the sense in which this term is used by the natural sciences.

---

[2]Cf. for instance Paul von Lilienfeld *La Pathologie Sociale* (Paris, 1896).

Social experience is historical experience. Of course every experience is the experience of something passed. But what distinguishes social experience from that which forms the basis of the natural sciences is that it is always the experience of a complexity of phenomena. The experience to which the natural sciences owe all their success is the experience of the experiment. In the experiments the different elements of change are observed in isolation. The control of the conditions of change provides the experimenter with the means of assigning to each effect its sufficient cause. Without regard to the philosophical problem involved he proceeds to amass "facts." These facts are the bricks which the scientist uses in constructing his theories. They constitute the only material at his disposal. His theory must not be in contradiction with these facts. They are the ultimate things.

The social sciences cannot make use of experiments. The experience with which they have to deal is the experience of complex phenomena. They are in the same position as acoustics would be if the only material of the scientist were the hearing of a concerto or the noise of a waterfall. It is nowadays fashionable to style the statistical bureaus laboratories. This is misleading. The material which statistics provides is historical, that means the outcome of a complexity of forces. The social sciences never enjoy the advantage of observing the consequences of a change in one element only, other conditions being equal.

It follows that the social sciences can never use experience to verify their statements. Every fact and every experience with which they have to deal is open to various interpretations. Of course, the experience of a complexity of phenomena can never prove or disprove a statement in the way in which an experiment proves or disproves. We do not have any historical experience whose import is judged identically by all people. There is no doubt that up to now in history only nations which have based their social order on private ownership of the means of production have reached a somewhat high stage of welfare and civilization. Nevertheless, nobody would consider this as an incontestable refutation of socialist theories. In the field of the natural sciences there are also differences of opinion concerning the interpretation of complex facts. But here freedom of explanation is limited by the necessity of not contradicting statements satisfactorily verified by experiments. In the interpretation of social facts no such limits exist. Everything could be asserted about them provided that we are not confined within the bounds of principles of whose logical nature we intend to speak later. Here however we already have to mention that every discussion concerning the meaning of historical experience imperceptibly passes over into a discussion of these principles without any further reference to experience. People may begin by discussing the lesson to be learnt from an import duty or from the Russian Soviet system; they will very quickly be discussing the general theory of interregional trade or the no less pure theory of socialism and capitalism.

The impossibility of experimenting means concomitantly the impossibility of measurement. The physicist has to deal with magnitudes and numerical relations, because he has the right to assume that certain invariable relations between physical properties subsist. The experiment provides him with the numerical value to be assigned to them. In human behavior there are no such constant relations, there is no standard which could be used as a measure and there are no experiments which could establish uniformities of this type.

What the statistician establishes in studying the relations between prices and supply or between supply and demand is of historical importance only. If he determines that a rise of 10 per cent in the supply of potatoes in Atlantis in the years between 1920 and 1930 was followed by a fall in the price of potatoes by 8 percent, he does not say anything about what happened or may happen with a change in the supply of potatoes in another country or at another time. Such measurements as that of elasticity of demand cannot be compared with the physicist's measurement, e.g., specific density or weight of atoms. Of course everybody realizes that the behavior of men concerning potatoes and every other commodity is variable. Different individuals value the same things in a different way, and the valuation changes even with the same individual with changing conditions. We cannot categorize individuals in classes which react in the same way, and we cannot determine the conditions which evoke the same reaction. Under these circumstances we have to realize that the statistical economist is an historian and not an experimenter. For the social sciences, statistics constitutes a method of historical research.

In every science the considerations which result in the formulation of an equation are of a non-mathematical character. The formulation of the equation has a practical importance because the constant relations which it includes are experimentally established and because it is possible to introduce specific known values in the function to determine those unknown. These equations thus lie at the basis of technological designing; they are not only the consummation of the theoretical analysis but also the starting point of practical work. But in economics, where there are no constant relations between magnitudes, the equations are void of practical application. Even if we could dispose of all qualms concerning their formulation we would still have to realize that they are without any practical use.

But the chief objection which must be raised to the mathematical treatment of economic problems comes from another ground: it really does not deal with the actual operations of human actions but with a fictitious concept that the economist builds up for instrumental purposes. This is the concept of static equilibrium.

For the sake of grasping the consequences of change and the nature of profit in a market economy the economist constructs a fictitious system in which there is no change. Today is like yesterday and tomorrow will be like today. There is no uncertainty about the future, and activity therefore does not involve risk. But for the allowance to be made of interest, the sum of the prices of the complementary factors of production exactly equals the price of the product, which means there is no room left for profit. But this fictitious concept is not only unrealizable in actual life; it cannot even be consistently carried to its ultimate conclusions. The individuals in this fictitious world would not act, they would not have to make choices, they would just vegetate. It is true that economics, exactly because it cannot make experiments, is bound to apply this and other fictitious concepts of a similar type. But its use should be restricted to the purposes which it is designed to serve. The purpose of the concept of static equilibrium is the study of the nature of the relations between costs and prices and thereby of profits. Outside of this it is inapplicable, and occupation with it vain.

Now all that mathematics can do in the field of economic studies is to describe static equilibrium. The equations and the indifference curves deal with a fictitious state of things, which never exists anywhere. What they afford is a mathematical expression of the definition of static equilibrium. Because mathematical economists start from the prejudice that economics has to be treated in mathematical terms they consider the study of static equilibrium as the whole of economics. The purely instrumental character of this concept has been overshadowed by this preoccupation.

Of course, mathematics cannot tell us anything about the way by which this static equilibrium could be reached. The mathematical determination of the difference between any actual state and the equilibrium state is not a substitute for the method by which the logical or non-mathematical economists let us conceive the nature of those human actions which necessarily would bring about equilibrium provided that no further change occurs in the data.

Occupation with static equilibrium is a misguided evasion of the study of the main economic problems. The pragmatic value of this equilibrium concept should not be underrated, but it is an instrument for the solution of one problem only. In any case the mathematical elaboration of static equilibrium is mere by-play in economics.

The case is similar with the use of curves. We may represent the price of a commodity as the point of intersection of two curves, the curve of demand and the curve of supply. But we have to realize that we do not know anything about the shape of these curves. We know *a posteriori* the prices, which we assume to be the points of intersection, but we do not know the form of the curve either in advance or for the past. The representation of the curves is therefore nothing more than a didactic means of rendering the theory graphic and hence more easily comprehensible.

The mathematical economist is prone to consider the price either as a measurement of value or as equivalent to the commodity. To this we have to say that prices are not measured in money but that they are the amount of money exchanged for a commodity. The price is not equivalent to the commodity. A purchase takes place only when the buyer values the commodity higher than the price, and the seller values it lower than the price. Nobody has the right to abstract from this fact and to assume an equivalence where there is a difference in valuation. When either one of the parties considers the price as the equivalent of the commodity no transaction takes place. In this sense we may say every transaction is for both parties a "bargain."

III

Physicists consider the objects of their study from without. They have no knowledge of what is going on in the interior, in the "soul," of a falling stone. But they have the opportunity to observe the falling of the stone in experiments and thereby to discover what they call the laws of falling. From the results of such experimental knowledge they build up their theories proceeding from the special to the more general, from the concrete to the more abstract.

Economics deals with human actions, not as it is sometimes said, with commodities, economic quantities or prices. We do not have the power to experiment with human actions. But we have, being human ourselves, a knowledge of what goes on within acting men. We know something about the meaning which acting men attach to their actions. We know why men wish to change the conditions of their lives. We know something about that uneasiness which is the ultimate incentive of the changes which they bring about. A perfectly satisfied man or a man who although unsatisfied did not see any means of improvement would not act at all.

Thus the economist is, as Cairnes says, at the outset of his researches already in possession of the ultimate principles governing the phenomena which form the subject of his study, whereas mankind has no direct knowledge of ultimate physical principles. Herein lies the radical difference between the social sciences (moral sciences, *Geisteswissenschaften*) and the natural sciences. What makes natural science possible is the power to experiment; what makes social science possible is the power to grasp or to comprehend the meaning of human action.

We have to distinguish two quite different kinds of this comprehension of the meaning of action: we conceive and we understand.

We conceive the meaning of an action, that is to say, we take an action to be such. We see in the action the endeavor to reach a goal by the use of means. In conceiving the meaning of an action we consider it as a purposeful endeavor to reach some goal, but we do not regard the quality of the ends proposed and of the means applied. We conceive activity as such, its logical (praxeological) qualities and categories. All that we do in this conceiving is by deductive analysis to bring to light everything which is contained in the first principle of action and to apply it to different kinds of thinkable conditions. This study is the object of the theoretical science of human action (praxeology) and in particular of its hitherto most developed branch, economics (economic theory).

Economics therefore is not based on or derived (abstracted) from experience. It is a deductive system, starting from the insight into the principles of human reason and conduct. As a matter of fact all our experience in the field of human action is based on and conditioned by the circumstance that we have this insight in our mind. Without this a priori knowledge and the theorems derived from it we could not at all realize what is going on in human activity. Our experience of human action and social life is predicated on praxeological and economic theory.

It is important to be aware of the fact that this procedure and method are not peculiar only to scientific investigation but are the mode of ordinary daily apprehension of social facts. These aprioristic principles and the deductions from them are applied not only by the professional economist but by everybody who deals with economic facts or problems. The layman does not proceed in a way significantly different from that of the scientist;

only he sometimes is less critical, less scrupulous in examining every step in the chain of his deductions and therefore sometimes more subject to error. One need only observe any discussion on current economic problems to realize that its course turns very soon towards a consideration of abstract principles without any reference to experience. You cannot, for instance, discuss the Soviet system without falling back on the general principles both of capitalism and socialism. You cannot discuss a wage and hours bill without falling back on the theory of wages, profits, interests and prices, that means the general theory of a market society. The "pure fact" — let us set aside the epistemological question whether there is such a thing — is open to different interpretations. These interpretations require elucidation by theoretical insight.

Economics is not only not derived from experience, it is even impossible to verify its theorems by appeal to experience. Every experience of a complex phenomenon, we must repeat, can be and is explained in different ways. The same facts, the same statistical figures are claimed as confirmations of contradictory theories.

It is instructive to compare the technique of dealing with experience in the social sciences with that in the natural sciences. We have many books on economics which, after having developed a theory, annex chapters in which an attempt is made to verify the theory developed by an appeal to the facts. This is not the way which the natural scientist takes. He starts from facts experimentally established and builds up his theory in using them. If his theory allows a deduction that predicts a state of affairs not yet discovered in experiments he describes what kind of experiment would be crucial for his theory; the theory seems to be verified if the result conforms to the prediction. This is something radically and significantly different from the approach taken by the social sciences.

To confront economic theory with reality we do not have to try to explain in a superficial way facts interpreted differently by other people so that they seem to verify our theory. This dubious procedure is not the way in which reasonable discussion can take place. What we have to do is this: we have to inquire whether the special conditions of action which we have implied in our reasoning correspond to those we find in the segment of reality under consideration. A theory of money (or rather of indirect exchange) is correct or not without reference to the question of whether the actual economic system under examination employs indirect exchange or only barter.

The method applied in these theoretical aprioristic considerations is the method of speculative constructions. The economist — and likewise the layman in his economic reasoning — builds up an image of a non-existent state of things. The material for this construction is drawn from an insight into the conditions of human action. Whether the state of affairs which these speculative constructions depict corresponds or could correspond to reality is irrelevant for their instrumental efficiency. Even unrealizable constructions can render valuable service in giving us the opportunity to conceive what makes them unrealizable and in what respect they differ from reality. The speculative construction of a socialist community is indispensable for economic reasoning notwithstanding the question of whether such a society could or could not be realized.

One of the best known and most frequently applied speculative constructions is that of a state of static equilibrium mentioned above. We are fully aware that this state can never be realized. But we cannot study the implications of changes without considering a changeless world. No modern economist will deny that the application of this speculative concept has rendered invaluable service in elucidating the character of entrepreneur's profits and losses and the relation between costs and prices.

All our economic reasoning operates with these speculative concepts. It is true that the method has its dangers; it easily lends itself to errors. But we have to use it because it is the only method available. Of course, we have to be very careful in using it.

To the obvious question, how a purely logical deduction from aprioristic principles can tell us anything about reality, we have to reply that both human thought and human action stem from the same root in that they are both products of the human mind. Correct results from our aprioristic reasoning are therefore not only logically irrefutable, but at the same time applicable with all their apodictic certainty to reality provided that the assumptions involved are given in reality. The only way to refuse a conclusion of economics is to demonstrate that it contains a logical fallacy. It is another question whether the results obtained apply to reality. This again can be decided only by the demonstration that the assumptions involved have or do not have any counterpart in the reality which we wish to explain.

The relation between historical experience — for every economic experience is historical in the sense that it is the experience of something past — and economic theory is therefore different from that generally assumed. Economic theory is not derived from experience. It is on the contrary the indispensable tool for the grasp of economic history. Economic history can neither prove nor disprove the teachings of economic theory. It is on the contrary economic theory which makes it possible for us to conceive the economic facts of the past.

IV

But to orient ourselves in the world of human actions we need to do more than merely conceive the meaning of human action. Both the acting man and the purely observing historian have not only to conceive the categories of action as economic theory does; they have besides to understand (*verstehen*) the meaning of human choice.

This understanding of the meaning of action is the specific method of historical research. The historian has to establish the facts as far as possible by the use of all the means provided both by the theoretical sciences of human action — praxeology and its hitherto most developed part, economics — and by the natural sciences. But then he has to go farther. He has to study the individual and unique conditions of the case in question. *Individuum est ineffabile*. Individuality is given to the historian, it is exactly that which cannot be exhaustively explained or traced back to other entities. In this sense individuality is irrational. The purpose of specific understanding as applied by the historical disciplines is to grasp the meaning of individuality by a psychological process. It establishes the fact that we face something individual. It fixes the valuations, the aims, the theories, the beliefs and the errors, in a word, the total philosophy of the acting individuals and the way in which they envisaged the conditions under which they had to act. It puts us into the milieu of the action. Of course this specific understanding cannot be separated from the philosophy of the interpreter. That degree of scientific objectivity which can be reached in the natural sciences and in the aprioristic sciences of logic and praxeology can never be attained by the moral or historical sciences (*Geisteswissenschaften*) in the field of the specific understanding. You can understand in different ways. History can be written from different points of view. The historians may agree in everything that can be established in a rational way and nevertheless widely disagree in their interpretations. History therefore has always to be rewritten. New philosophies demand a new representation of the past.

The specific understanding of the historical sciences is not an act of pure rationality. It is the recognition that reason has exhausted all its resources and that we can do nothing more than to try as well as we may to give an explanation of something irrational which is resistant to exhaustive and unique description. These are the tasks which the understanding has to fulfill. It is, notwithstanding, a logical tool and should be used as such. It should never be abused for the purpose of smuggling into the historical work obscuranticism, mysticism and similar elements. It is not a free charter for nonsense.

It is necessary to emphasize this point because it sometimes happens that the abuses of a certain type of historicism are justified by an appeal to a wrongly interpreted "understanding." The reasoning of logic, praxeology and of the natural sciences can under no circumstances be invalidated by the understanding. However strong the evidence supplied by the historical sources may be, and however understandable a fact may be from the point of view of theories contemporaneous with it, if it does not fit into our rationale, we cannot accept it. The existence of witches and the practice of witchcraft are abundantly attested by legal proceedings; yet we will not accept it. Judgments of many tribunals are on record asserting that people have depreciated a country's currency by upsetting the balance of payments; yet we will not believe that such actions have such effects.

It is not the task of history to reproduce the past. An attempt to do so would be vain and would require a duplication not humanly possible. History is a representation of the past in terms of concepts. The specific concepts of historical research are type concepts. These types of the historical method can be built up only by the use of the specific understanding and they are meaningful only in the frame of the understanding to which they owe their existence. Therefore not every type-concept which is logically valid can be considered as useful for the purpose of understanding. A classification is valid in a logical sense if all the elements united in one class are characterized by a common feature. Classes do not exist in actuality, they are always a product of the mind which in observing things discovers likenesses and differences. It is another question whether a classification which is logically valid and based on sound considerations can be used for the explanation of given data. There is for instance no doubt that a type or class "Fascism" which includes not only Italian Fascism but also German Nazism, the Spanish system of General Franco, the Hungarian system of Admiral Horthy and some other systems can be constructed in a logically valid way and that it can be contrasted to a type called "Bolshevism," which includes the Russian Bolshevism and the system of Bela Kun in Hungary and of the short Soviet episode of Munich. But whether this classification and the inference from it which sees the world of the last twenty years divided into the two parties, Fascists and Bolsheviks, is the right way to understand present-day political conditions is open to question. You can understand this period of history in a quite different way by using other types. You may distinguish Democracy and Totalitarianism, and then let the type Democracy include the Western Capitalist system and the type Totalitarianism include both Bolshevism and what the other classification terms Fascism. Whether you apply the first or the second typification depends on the whole mode in which you see things. The understanding decides upon the classification to be used, and not the classification upon the understanding.

The type-concepts of the historical or moral sciences (*Geisteswissenschaften*) are not statistical averages. Most of the features used for classification are not subject to numerical determination, and this alone renders it impossible to construct them as statistical averages. These type-concepts (in German one uses the term *Ideal-Typus* in order to distinguish them from the type-concepts of other sciences, especially of the biological ones) ought not to be confused with the praxeological concepts used for the conceiving of the categories of human action. For instance: the concept "entrepreneur" is used in economic theory to signify a specific function, that is the provision for an uncertain future. In this respect everybody has to some extent to be considered as an entrepreneur. Of course, it is not the task of this classification in economic theory to distinguish men, but to distinguish functions and to explain sources of profit or loss. Entrepreneur in this sense is the personification of the function which results in profit or loss. In economic history and in dealing with current economic problems the term "entrepreneur" signifies a class of men who are engaged in business but who may in many other respects differ so much that the general term entrepreneur seems to be meaningless and is used only with a special qualification, for instance big (medium-sized, small) business, "Wall Street," armaments business, German business, etc. The type entrepreneur as used in history and politics can never have the conceptual exactitude which the praxeological concept entrepreneur has. You never meet in life men who are nothing else than the personification of one function only.[3]

---

[3]For the sake of completeness we have to remark that there is a third use of the term entrepreneur in law which has to be carefully distinguished from the two mentioned above.

V

The preceding remarks justify the conclusion that there is a radical difference between the methods of the social sciences and those of the natural sciences. The social sciences owe their progress to the use of their particular methods and have to go further along the lines which the special character of their object require. They do not have to adopt the methods of the natural sciences.

It is a fallacy to recommend to the social sciences the use of mathematics and to believe that they could in this way be made more "exact." The application of mathematics does not render physics more exact or more certain. Let us quote Einstein's remark: "As far as mathematical propositions refer to reality they are not certain and as far as they are certain they do not refer to reality." It is different with praxeological propositions. These refer with all their exactitude and certainty to the reality of human action. The explanation of this phenomenon lies in the fact that both — the science of human action and human action itself — have a common root, i.e., human reason. It would be a mistake to assume that the quantitative approach could render them more exact. Every numerical expression is inexact because of the inherent limitations of human powers of measurement. For the rest we have to refer to what has been said above on the purely historical character of quantitative expressions in the field of the social sciences.

The reformers who wish to improve the social sciences by adopting the methods of the natural sciences sometimes try to justify their efforts by pointing to the backward state of the former. Nobody will deny that the social sciences and especially economics are far from being perfect. Every economist knows how much remains to be done. But two considerations must be kept in mind. First, the present unsatisfactory state of social and economic conditions has nothing to do with an alleged inadequacy in economic theory. If people do not use the teachings of economics as a guide for their policies they cannot blame the discipline for their own failure. Second, if it may some day be necessary to reform economic theory radically this change will not take its direction along the lines suggested by the present critics. The objections of these are thoroughly refuted forever. ▶

CHAPTER 20

Appreciations

ECONOMIC FREEDOM AND INTERVENTIONISM[1]

"MAN, ECONOMY, AND STATE"

Most of what goes today under the label of the social sciences is poorly disguised apologetics for the policies of governments. What the philosopher George Santayana (1863–1952) once said about a teacher of philosophy of the, then Royal Prussian, University of Berlin, that it seemed to this man "that a professor's business was to trudge along a governmental towpath with a legal cargo," is today everywhere true for the majority of those appointed to teach economics. As these doctors see it, all the evils that plague mankind are caused by the acquisitiveness of greedy exploiters, speculators and monopolists, who are supreme in the conduct of affairs in the market economy. The foremost task of good government is to curb these scoundrels by suppressing their "economic freedom" and subjecting all affairs to the decisions of the central authority. Full government control of everybody's activities — whether called

---

[1] ["*Man, Economy, and State: A New Treatise on Economics*," in *Economic Freedom and Interventionism: An Anthology of Articles and Essays*, ed. Bettina Bien Greaves (1962; Indianapolis, Ind.: Liberty Fund, 1990), chap. 36.]

planning, socialism, communism, or any other name — is praised as the panacea.

To make these ideas plausible one had to proscribe as orthodox, classical, neoclassical, and reactionary all that economics had brought forward before the emergence of the New Deal, the Fair Deal, and the New Frontier. Any acquaintance with pre-Keynesian economics is considered as rather unsuitable and unseemly for an up-to-date economist. It could easily raise in his mind some critical thoughts. It could encourage him to reflect, instead of meekly endorsing the empty slogans of governments and powerful pressure groups. There is, in fact, in the writings and teaching of those who nowadays call themselves "economists," no longer any comprehension of the operation of the economic system as such. Their books and articles do not describe, analyze, or explain the economic phenomena. They do not pay attention to the interdependence and mutuality of the various individuals' and groups' activities. In their view, there exist different economic spheres that have to be treated by and large as isolated domains. They dissolve economics into a number of special fields, such as economics of labor, agriculture, insurance, foreign trade, domestic trade, and so on. These books and articles deal with the height of wage rates, for example, as if it were possible to treat this subject independently of the problems of commodity prices, interest, profit and loss, and all the other issues of economics. They assemble, without any idea for what purpose they are doing it, a vast array of statistical and other historical data about the recent past, which they choose to style the "present." They entirely fail to comprehend the interconnectedness and mutual determination of the actions of the various individuals whose behavior results in the emergence of the market economy.

The economic writings of the last decades provide a pitiful story of progressing deterioration and degradation. Even a comparison of the recent publications of many older authors with their previous writings, shows an advancing decline. The few, very few, good contributions that came out in our age were smeared as old-fashioned and reactionary by the government economists, boycotted by the universities, the academic magazines and the newspapers, and ignored by the public.

Let us hope that the fate of Murray N. Rothbard's book *Man, Economy and State* (Princeton: D. Van Nostrand, 1962) will be different. Dr. Rothbard is already well known as the author of several excellent monographs. Now, as the result of many years of sagacious and discerning meditation, he joins the ranks of eminent economists by publishing a voluminous work, a systematic treatise on economics.

The main virtue of this book is that it is a comprehensive and methodical analysis of all activities commonly called economic. It looks upon these activities as human action, i.e., as conscious striving after chosen ends by resorting to appropriate means. This cognition exposes the fateful efforts of the mathematical treatment of economic problems. The mathematical economist attempts to ignore the difference between physical phenomena, on the one hand, the emergence and consummation of which man is unable to see the operation of any final causes and which can be studied scientifically only because there prevails a perceptible regularity in their concatenation and succession, and praxeological phenomena, on the other hand, that lack such a regularity but are conceivable to the human mind as the outcomes of purposeful aiming at definite ends chosen. Mathematical equations, says Rothbard, are appropriate and useful where there are constant quantitative relations among unmotivated variables; they are inappropriate in the field of conscious behavior. In a few brilliant lines he demolishes the main device of mathematical economists, viz., the fallacious idea of substituting the concepts of mutual determination and equilibrium for the allegedly outdated concept of cause and effect. And he shows that the concepts of equilibrium and the evenly rotating economy do not refer to reality; although indispensable for any economic inquiry, they are merely auxiliary mental tools to aid us in the analysis of real action.

The equations of physics describe a process through time, while those of economics do not describe a process at all, but merely the final equilibrium point, a hypothetical situation that is outside of time and will never be reached in reality. Furthermore, they cannot say anything about the path by which the economy moves in the direction of the final equilibrium position. As there are no constant relations between any of the elements which the science of action studies, there is no measurement possible and all numerical data available have merely an historical character; they belong to economic history and not to economics as such. The positivist slogan, "science is measurement," in no way refers to the sciences of human action; the claims of "econometrics" are vain.

In every chapter of his treatise, Dr. Rothbard, adopting the best of the teachings of his predecessors, and adding to them highly important observations, not only develops the correct theory but is no less anxious to refute all objections ever raised against these doctrines. He exposes the fallacies and contradictions of the popular interpretation of economic affairs. Thus, for instance, in dealing with the problem of unemployment he points out: in the whole modern and Keynesian discussion of this subject the missing link is precisely the wage rate. It is meaningless to talk of unemployment or employment without reference to a wage rate. Whatever supply of labor service is brought to market can be sold, but only if wages are set at whatever rate will clear the market. If a man wishes to be employed, he will be, provided the wage rate is adjusted according to what Rothbard calls his discounted marginal value product, i.e., the present height of the value which the consumers — at the time of the final sale of the product — will ascribe to his contribution to its production. Whenever the job-seeker insists on a higher wage, he will remain unemployed. If people refuse to be employed except at places, in occupations, or at wage rates they would like, then they are likely to be choosing unemployment for substantial periods. The full import of this state of affairs becomes manifest if one gives attention to the fact that, under present conditions, those offering their services on the labor market themselves represent the immense majority of the consumers whose buying or abstention from buying ultimately determines the height of wage rates.

Less successful than his investigations in the fields of general praxeology and economics are the author's occasional observations concerning the philosophy of law and some problems of the penal code. But disagreement with his opinions concerning these matters cannot prevent me from qualifying Rothbard's work as an epochal contribution to the general science of human action, praxeology, and its practically most important and up-to-now best elaborated part, economics. Henceforth all essential studies in these branches of knowledge will have to take full account of the theories and criticisms expounded by Dr. Rothbard.

The publication of a standard book on economics raises again an important question, viz., for whom are essays of this consequence written: only for specialists, the students of economics, or for all of the people?

To answer this question we have to keep in mind that the citizens in their capacity as voters are called upon to determine ultimately all issues of economic policies. The fact that the masses are ignorant of physics and do not know anything substantial about electricity does not obstruct the endeavors of experts who utilize the teachings of science for the satisfaction of the wants of the consumers. From various points of view one may deplore the intellectual insufficiency and indolence of the multitude. But their ignorance regarding the achievements of the natural sciences does not endanger our spiritual and material welfare.

It is quite different in the field of economics. The fact that the majority of our contemporaries, the masses of semi-barbarians led by self-styled intellectuals, entirely ignore everything that economics has brought forward, is the main political problem of our age. There is no use in deceiving ourselves. American public opinion rejects the market economy, the capitalistic free enterprise system that provided the nation with the highest standard of living ever attained. Full government control of all activities of the individual is virtually the goal of both national parties. The individual is to be deprived of his moral, political and economic responsibility and autonomy and to be converted into a pawn in the schemes of a supreme authority aiming at a "national" purpose. His "affluence" is to be cut down for the benefit of what is called the "public sector," i.e., the machine operated by the party in power. Hosts of authors, writers, and professors are busy denouncing alleged shortcomings of capitalism and exalting the virtues of "planning." Full of a quasi-religious ardor, the immense majority is advocating measures that step by step lead to the methods of administration practiced in Moscow and in Peking.

If we want to avoid the destruction of Western civilization and the relapse into primitive wretchedness, we must change the mentality of our fellow citizens. We must make them realize what they owe to the much vilified "economic freedom," the system of free enterprise and capitalism. The intellectuals and those who call themselves educated must use their superior cognitive faculties and power of reasoning for the refutation of erroneous ideas about social, political, and economic problems and for the dissemination of a correct grasp of the operation of the market economy. They must start by familiarizing themselves with all the issues involved in order to teach those who are blinded by ignorance and emotions. They must learn in order to acquire the ability to enlighten the misguided many.

It is a fateful error on the part of our most valuable contemporaries to believe that economics can be left to specialists in the same way in which various fields of technology can be safely left to those who have chosen to make any one of them their vocation. The issues of society's economic organization are every citizen's business. To master them to the best of one's ability is the duty of everyone.

Now such a book as *Man, Economy, and State* offers to every intelligent man an opportunity to obtain reliable information concerning the great controversies and conflicts of our age. It is certainly not easy reading and asks for the utmost exertion of one's attention. But there are no shortcuts to wisdom. ▶

"The Economist Eugen v. Böhm-Bawerk: on the Occasion of the Tenth Anniversary of His Death"[2]

Eugen v. Böhm-Bawerk will remain unforgotten for all those who have known him. The students, who enjoyed the fortune of attending his seminars, will never lose what the acquaintance with such a strong mind has given them. For the politicians, who have met him as a statesman, the integrity of his ethos and his altruistic commitment to duty will continue to be exemplary. And no citizen of this country shall forget the minister of finance, the last Austrian minister of finance, who, in spite of all obstacles, earnestly aimed at balancing the public budget and preventing the upcoming financial catastrophe. But even when the lives of all those, who had known him personally, have come to an end, his scientific *oeuvre* shall live on and bear fruit.

In his scientific work Böhm-Bawerk focused from the outset on the central problem of theoretical economics, the interest problem. At the age of twenty-five, in the spring of 1876, he gave a lecture on the interest on capital in the Knies seminar in Heidelberg, which already contained the main features of what would later become his famous agio theory of interest. Before he could however publish his work, there were difficult preliminary questions to answer. It was to these questions that he dedicated his work. Always keeping the ultimate object in mind, he published *Rechte und Verhältnisse vom Standpunkte der volkswirtschaftlichen Güterlehre* in 1881, *Die Geschichte und Kritik der Kapitalzinstheorien in 1884, Grundzüge der Theorie des wirtschaftlichen Güterwertes* in 1886, and finally his *Positive Theorie des Kapitals* in 1889. His work was thereby brought to completion. As Senior Legal Secretary and Head of Division in the ministry of finance, as k. u. k. minister of finance and President of the Senate of the Higher

---

2[A transcript of the German language original under the title "Der Economist Eugen v. Böhm-Bawerk — Zu seinem 10. Todestage" was found in one of Bettina Bien Greaves's books at the Mises Institute. The text was originally published in the *Neue Freie Presse* (New Free Press), a Viennese newspaper which was founded by Adolf Werthner, Max Friedländer, and Michael Etienne. It existed from 1864 until 1938. Böhm-Bawerk's last publication *Unsere passive Handelsbilanz* (Our passive balance of trade), from which Mises quotes, was also published in this newspaper, and has, to our knowledge, never been translated into English. Translated from German by Karl-Friedrich Israel.]

Administrative Court, he had very little leisure in the following years to perform any scientific work. Only since 1904 when he retired from office for the third and last time could he devote himself again undisturbed to his research. A series of excellent works is the fruit of the tireless effort during the last decade that he was allowed to live. He died on August 27 in 1914, when the Austrian armies were about to fight the first battles of the Great War in Poland and Eastern Galicia.

Böhm-Bawerk's scientific work has quickly found the recognition it richly deserves. His *magnum opus* [*The Positive Theory of Capital*] was translated into English by William Smart as early as 1890; shortly afterward a French edition followed. In England, the United States, France, Italy, the Netherlands, Sweden, and Denmark his doctrine became the starting point for further in-depth analyses and studies. Sure enough, in Germany an understanding of Böhm's achievements was long missing. The prevailing doctrine at the universities ignored him. It took decades until the accomplishments of the "Austrian school" were recognized in the Reich. Today, however, it is considered a grave mischief that only Böhm-Bawerk's *magnum opus*, which is already in its fourth German language edition, is easily accessible. His shorter writings, which are indispensable for any friend of economic enquiry, are rather difficult to access. It is therefore a thankworthy enterprise to republish them in a collected edition. A student of Böhm-Bawerk, well known for several scientific works, has addressed himself to this task.[3] The well-endowed volume, which is graced with a felicitous portrait of Böhm, contains the above mentioned work *Rechte und Verhältnisse*, along with a tract on general theory and methodology, essays on the theory of value, and finally an essay that has been published on January 6, 8, and 9, 1924 in the *Neue Freie Presse*, entitled *Unsere passive Handelsbilanz*. It starts with a short biographical introduction by the editor, Dr. Franz X. Weiss. The essays on capital and interest, which are not contained in this collection, shall be republished in a separate volume.

To praise the tremendous value of the theoretical works collected in this volume would be like bringing owls to Athens. For the experts and numerous intellectuals who are concerned with economic questions, this would hardly constitute anything new. Let us however quote some sentences from the above mentioned essay on the passive balance of trade, merely to emphasize the sharpness with which Böhm has early on pointed

---

[3]*Gesammelte Schriften von Eugen von Böhm-Bawerk*, edited by Franz X. Weiss and published by Hölder-Pichler-Tempsky A.G., Vienna and Leipzig, 1924.

to the fundamental problem underlying our state finances. It reads: "thrift is never popular. … If parliaments have historically been the guardians of — thrift, they now have turned much rather into its sworn enemies. Nowadays, the political and national parties — maybe not exclusively in our own country, but certainly also here tend to develop a certain covetousness, almost considered to be dutiful, for all kinds of benefits for their own electorate at the expense of the general public. And when the political situation is relatively convenient, that is to say, if it is relatively inconvenient for the government, one's ends can be achieved through political pressure." Our population suffers from economical megalomania. This is among other things shown by the "investments from the public purse." One is often mistaken when using the famous slogan of "indirect productivity" of public spending, even if at times the indirect advantages of public enterprises, which are unprofitable by themselves, may exceed the amount that has to be paid from public funds for their passive operations. The "blind eulogists of frivolous investment policies" will feel the mistakes of their approach "only when, like these days, the capital stock has been exhausted by the public sector over many years to a degree that capital is lacking for the most important and vital private businesses in all spheres, only when many enterprises begin to stumble, many projects have to remain undone, and all suffer severely from the increased rate of interest."

These were the last words that Böhm-Bawerk has addressed to Austria's financial authorities. Today they will be valued more highly than at the time when they were first published in this newspaper. ▶

Bibliography

Works Cited

Chamberlain, John. *My Years with Ludwig von Mises. The Freeman,* February, 27, no. 2, 1977.

Hülsmann, Jörg Guido. *Mises: The Last Knight of Liberalism.* Auburn, Ala.: Mises Institute, 2007.

Kirzner, Israel M. *Ludwig von Mises: The Man and His Economics.* Wilmington, Del.: ISI Books, 2001.

Lu, A., 2013. *States Reform Remedial College Education.* Available at: http://www.pewstates.org/projects/stateline/headlines/states-reform-college-remedial-education-85899492704 [Accessed 7 January 2014].

Mises, Ludwig von. *The Anti-Capitalistic Mentality.* New York, N.Y.: D. Van Nostrand Company, 1956.

——. *Economic Calculation in the Socialist Commonwealth.* Auburn, Ala.: Mises Institute, [1920] 1990.

——. *Economic Policy: Thoughts for Tomorrow and Today.* Washington, D.C.: Regnery Gateway, 1979.

——. *Epistemological Problems of Economics.* 3d ed. Auburn, Ala.: Mises Institute, [1933] 2003.

——. *Human Action*. Auburn, Ala.: Mises Institute, [1949] 1998.

——. *Interventionism: An Economic Analysis*. Irvington-on-Hudson, N.Y.: The Foundation for Economic Education, 1998.

——. *Liberty and Property*. Auburn, Ala.: Mises Institute [1958] 1991.

——. "The Main Issues in Present-Day Monetary Controversies." In *Selected Writings of Ludwig von Mises: The Political Economy of International Reform and Reconstruction*. Ed. Richard M. Ebeling. Indianapolis, Ind.: Liberty Fund, 2000.

——. *Memoirs*. Auburn, Ala.: Mises Institute, 2009.

——. "Monetary Stabilization and Cyclical Policy". In *The Causes of the Economic Crisis and Other Essays Before and After the Great Depression*. Ed. Percy L. Greaves, Jr. Auburn, Ala.: Mises Institute, [1929] 2006.

——. *Money, Method, and the Market Process*. Ed. Richard M. Ebeling. Norwell, Mass.: Kluwer Academic Press, 1990.

——. "The Non-Neutrality of Money." In *Money, Method, and the Market Process*. Ed. Richard M. Ebeling. Norwell, Mass.: Kluwer Academic Press, [1938] 1990.

——. *Planning for Freedom and Sixteen Other Essays and Addresses*. South Holland, Ill.: Libertarian Press, 1980.

——. "The Position of Money among Economic Goods." In *Money, Method, and the Market Process*. Ed. Richard M. Ebeling. Norwell, Mass.: Kluwer Academic Press, [1932] 1990.

——. "Profit and Loss." In: *Planning for Freedom and Sixteen Other Essays and Addresses*. 4th ed. South Holland, Ill.: Libertarian Press, [1952] 1980.

——. "Senior's Lectures on Monetary Problems." In *Money, Method, and the Market Process*. Ed. Richard M. Ebeling. Norwell, Mass.: Kluwer Academic Press, [1933] 1990.

——. *Socialism*. Indianapolis, Ind.: Liberty Classics, [1922] 1980.

——. *Theory and History*. Auburn, Ala.: Mises Institute, [1957] 1985.

——— . *The Theory of Money and Credit.* Irvington-on-Hudson, N.Y.: The Foundation for Economic Education, [1952] 1971.

——— . *The Ultimate Foundation of Economic Science.* 2d ed. Kansas City, Mo.: Sheed Andrews and McMeel, [1962] 1978.

Mises, Margit von. *My Years with Ludwig von Mises.* New Rochelle, N.Y.: Arlington Press, 1976.

Rothbard, Murray N. 1971. "Ludwig von Mises and the Paradigm for our Age." *Modern Age* (Fall).

——— . *The Essential von Mises.* Auburn, Ala.: Mises Institute. 2009.

Index

THE MISES INSTITUTE

The Mises Institute, founded in 1982, is a teaching and research center for the study of Austrian economics, libertarian and classical liberal political theory, and peaceful international relations. In support of the school of thought represented by Ludwig von Mises, Murray N. Rothbard, Henry Hazlitt, and F.A. Hayek, we publish books and journals, sponsor student and professional conferences, and provide online education. Mises.org is a vast resource of free material for anyone in the world interested in these ideas. The Mises Institute is funded entirely by voluntary contributions. We do not accept government funding and never will.

Printed in Poland
by Amazon Fulfillment
Poland Sp. z o.o., Wrocław

30709661R00177